THE ONLY WAY TO...
LEARN
ASTROLOGY
VOLUME III

HOROSCOPE
ANALYSIS

Also published by ASTRO COMPUTING SERVICES

The American Atlas
The American Book of Tables
The American Ephemeris for the 20th Century [Midnight]
The American Ephemeris for the 20th Century [Noon]
The American Ephemeris for the 21st Century
The American Ephemeris 1901 to 1930
The American Ephemeris 1931 to 1980 & Book of Tables
The American Ephemeris 1941 to 1950
The American Ephemeris 1951 to 1960
The American Ephemeris 1961 to 1970
The American Ephemeris 1971 to 1980
The American Ephemeris 1981 to 1990
The American Ephemeris 1991 to 2000
The American Sidereal Ephemeris 1976 to 2000
The American Heliocentric Ephemeris 1901 to 2000
Basic Astrology: A Guide for Teachers and Students (Negus)
Basic Astrology: A Workbook for Students (Negus)
Cosmic Combinations (Negus)
Interpreting the Eclipses (Jansky)
The American Book of Charts (Rodden)
The Gauquelin Book of American Charts (Gauquelin)
Astrological Insights Into Personality (Lundsted)
The Fortunes of Astrology (Granite)
Planetary Planting (Riotte)
Planting by the Moon (Best & Kollerstrom)
The Only Way to...Learn Astrology, Vol. I
    Basic Principles (March & McEvers)
The Only Way to...Learn Astrology, Vol. II
    Math & Interpretation Techniques (March & McEvers)
The Lively Circle (Koval)
The Psychology of the Planets (F. Gauquelin)

THE ONLY WAY TO...
LEARN ASTROLOGY
VOLUME III

HOROSCOPE ANALYSIS

BY MARION D. MARCH & JOAN McEVERS

International Standard Book Number 0-917086-43-0
Printed in the United States of America

Published by ACS Publications
P.O. Box 16430
San Diego, CA 92116

Also distributed by Para Research, Inc.
Whistlestop Mall
Rockport, MA 01966

First Edition, September, 1982
Second Printing, December, 1982

We dedicate this book to our children Mikki Andina, Nick March, Woody, Brent, Daren and Bridget McEvers, who knowingly or unknowingly taught us much of what we needed to learn.

Contents

Part II

Part III

All chart sources are indicated and classified according to Lois Rodden's
system:
A   = ACCURATE DATA
B   = BIOGRAPHIES or AUTOBIOGRAPHIES
C   = CAUTION, no source of origin
DD = DIRTY DATA, more than one time/date/place

INDEX OF HOROSCOPES IN VOLUMES I AND II

Numbers represent volume (Roman numeral), and page.

INDEX OF HOROSCOPES IN VOLUME III

All chart sources are indicated and classified according to Lois Rodden's system:

A = ACCURATE DATA
B = BIOGRAPHIES or AUTOBIOGRAPHIES
C = CAUTION, no source or origin
DD = DIRTY DATA, more than one time/date/place

Data for Horoscopes in Volume III

DATA FOR CHARTS OF PART I OF *The Only Way... Vol. III*

BAILEY, Pearl [A]
March 29, 1918 — 7:00 AM EST
Newport News, VA, 76W25 36N59.
Source: McEvers says "from her to mutual friend."

BALDWIN, Faith [A]
Oct. 1, 1893 — 8:00 AM EST
New Rochelle, NY, 73W47 40N55.
Source: *Church of Light* from B. Holmes "from her."

BROWNING, Elizabeth Barrett [B]
March 6, 1806 — 7:00 PM LMT
Carlton Hall, England, 1W34 54N56.
Source: Biography *A Life* by D. Hambate.

BROWNING, Robert [C]
May 7, 1812 — 10:00 PM LMT
London, England, 0W06 51N31.
Source: *Church of Light* from Ruth Oliver.

BUCK, Pearl [C]
June 26, 1892 — 12:30 PM EST
Hillsboro, WV, 80W13 38N08.
Source: Ebertin as from L. Bonnet.

CALDWELL, Erskine [DD]
Dec. 17, 1903 — 8:55 PM CST
Coweta County, GA, 84W48 33N23.
Source: Rodden *The American Book of Charts.*

CLAVELL, James [A]
Oct. 10, 1924—9:50 AM Zone 10
Sidney, Australia, 151E10 33S55.
Source: Wagner states "from him" acc. to *Mercury Hour.*

COHEN, Mickey [C]
Sept. 4, 1913 — 6:44 AM EST
New York, NY, 73W58 40N45.
Source: Rodden *The American Book of Charts.*

DIETRICH, Marlene [A]
Dec. 27, 1901 — 10:08 PM CET
Berlin, Germany, 13E24 52N30.
Source: Birth records found in Berlin and photographed.

EDDY, Mary Baker [C]
July 16, 1821 — 5:38 PM LMT
Bow, NH, 71W19 44N21.
Source: Rodden *Profiles of Women.*

EINSTEIN, Albert [A]
March 14, 1879 — 11:30 AM LMT
Ulm, Germany, 10E00 48N30.
Source: Ebertin from copy of birth certificate.

FELLINI, Federico [A]
Jan. 20, 1920 — 9:00 PM CET
Rimini, Italy, 12E35 44N03.
Source: Lockart quotes Messina in *Horoscope* 1965.

FITZGERALD, F. Scott [B]
Sept. 24, 1896 — 3:30 PM LMT
St. Paul, MN, 93W06 44N57.
Source: Biography *"Exiles from Paradise".*

FRIEDAN, Betty [C]

Feb. 4, 1921 — 4:00 AM CST
Peoria, IL, 89W36 40N42.
Source: Jansky states from birth certificate.

GANDHI, Indira [C]

Nov. 19, 1917 — 11:40 PM Zone 5.5
Allahabad, India, 81E58 25N30.
Source: Barbara Watters, (conf. by info.
from India).

GERSHWIN, George [C]

Sept. 26, 1898 — 11:09 AM EST
Brooklyn, NY, 73W50 40N38.
Source: *Church of Light*.

GROFE, Ferde [C]

March 27, 1892 — 4:00 AM EST
New York, NY, 73W57 40N45.
Source: Rodden *American Book of Charts*.

HAYES, Helen [C]

October 10, 1900 — 3:25 AM EST
Washington, DC, 77W02 38N54.
Source: Rodden *Profiles of Women*.

HEFNER, Hugh [A]

April 9, 1926 — 4:20 PM CST
Chicago, IL, 41N52 87W39.
Source: *Gauquelin Book of American
Charts*

JOHN PAUL, II (Pope)

May 18, 1920 — 7:30 AM CET
Wadowice, Poland, 19E55 50N07.
Source: Letter that he was born at time of
total Sun Eclipse acc. to *Mercury Hour* Jan.
1980.

KISSINGER, Henry [A]

May 27, 1923 — 5:30 AM CET
Furth, Germany, 11E00 49N28.
Source: Astrological Association of London
"birth certificate."

KOUFAX, Sandy [A]

December 30, 1935 — 11:30 AM EST
Brooklyn, NY, 40N42 74W00
Source: Ruth Hale Oliver

KUBLER-ROSS, Elisabeth [A]

July 8, 1926 — 10:45 PM CET
Zurich, Switzerland, 8E32 47N23.
Source: Letter from her seen by Rodden as
of Sept. 24, 1980.

MacDONALD, John D. [A]

July 24, 1916 — 8:05 PM EST
Sharon, PA, 80W31 41N14.
Source: *Contemporary Sidereal Horoscopes*.

MATTHIAS, Bob [A]

Nov. 17, 1930 — 7:47 AM PST
Tulare, CA, 119W21 36N13.
Source: *Contemporary Sidereal Horoscopes*.

MEAD, Margaret [C]

Dec. 16, 1901 — 9:30 AM EST
Philadelphia, PA, 75W10 39N57.
Source: Rodden *Profiles of Women*.

MITCHELL, John [A]

Sept. 5, 1913 — 3:30 AM CST
Detroit, MI, 83W03 42N20.
Source: *Contemporary Sidereal Horoscopes*.

MONDALE, W. (Fritz) [A]

Jan. 5, 1928 — 10:30 AM CST
Ceylon, MN, 94W38 43N32.
Source: *Contemporary Sidereal Horoscopes.*

MONROE, Marilyn [A]

June 1, 1926 — 9:30 AM PST
Los Angeles, CA, 118W15 34N03.
Source: Photograph of birth certificate in
biography.

POLANSKI, Roman [C]

Aug. 18, 1933 — 2:47 PM CET
Krakow, Poland, 19E58 50N04.
Source: Rodden *American Book of Charts.*

PORTER, Sylvia [A]

June 18, 1913 — 3:50 PM EST
New York, NY, 73W57 40N45.
Source: Jansky states "from birth
certificate."

REMARQUE, Erich Maria [A]

June 22, 1898 — 8:15 PM CET
Osnabruck, Germany, 8E03 52N17.
Source: Sabian Symbols (conf. by his sister).

RODGERS, Richard [B]

June 28, 1902 — 2:30 AM EST
Hammels Station, NY, 73W52 40N43.
Source: Biography *Richard Rodgers* by D.
Ewen.

ROOSEVELT, Eleanor [DD]

Oct. 11, 1884 — 11:00 AM EST
New York, NY, 73W57 40N45.
Source: *Family Bible* acc. to Rodden, other
times also cited.

RUDOLPH, Wilma [B]

June 23, 1940 — 5:00 AM CST
Bethel Springs, TN, 88W36 35N14.
Source: Drew.

VIVEKANANDA, Swami [A]

Jan. 12, 1863 — 6:33 AM LMT
Calcutta, India, 88E20 22N30.
Source: "Birth certificate" acc. to F.C. Dutt
in Calcutta.

DATA FOR CHARTS OF PART II OF *The Only Way . . .* Vol. III

DIANA, Princess of Wales [A] July 1, 1961 — 7:45 PM BDT
Sandringham, England, 0E30 52N50
Source: "Mother" conf. by Buckingham Palace
acc. to Charles Harvey.

HEMINGWAY, Ernest [A] July 21, 1899 — 8:00 AM CST
Oak Park, IL, 87W47 41N53
Source: *Mother's Diary* acc. to biographer
Carlos Baker.

PATTON, George [A] Nov. 11, 1885 — 6:38 PM PST
San Marino, CA, 118W06 34N07
Source: *Family Bible* acc. to biography *Patton*
by Ladislas Farago.

STREISAND, Barbra [C] April 24, 1942 — 5:04 AM EWT
Brooklyn, NY, 73W56 40N38
Source: *Church of Light* quotes *Predictions* of
1967.

DATA FOR CHARTS OF PART III OF *The Only Way . . .* Vol. III

Chart #1 June 10, 1924 — 8:30 AM PST
Los Angeles, CA, 118W15 34N03.

Chart #2 March 26, 1943 — 7:45 AM CDT
Milwaukee, WI, 87W55 43N02.

Chart #3 Aug. 2, 1920 — 10:40 AM EST
Boston, MA, 71W04 42N22.

Chart #4 Sept. 4, 1944 — 7:55 AM PWT
Los Angeles, CA, 118W15 34N03.

Chart #5 April 18, 1946 — 5:18 PM PST
Glendale, CA, 118W15 34N08.

Chart #6 July 26, 1948 — 12:01 PM CST
Chicago, IL, 87W39 41N52.

Chart #7 April 5, 1924 — 7:05 AM CST
Detroit, MI, 83W03 42N20.

Chart #8 March 6, 1951 — 2:48 AM PST
Los Angeles, CA, 118W15 34N03.

Chart #9 October 28, 1953 — 0:14 AM PDT
Los Angeles, CA, 118W15 34N03.

Chart #10 June 24, 1937 — 1:20 PM PST
Los Angeles, CA, 118W15 34N03.

Chart #11 April 9, 1940 — 6:19 PM EST
York, PA, 76W44 39N58.

Chart #12 August 22, 1942 — 8:15 AM EDT
Wilmington, NC, 77W55 34N14.

Chart #13 April 14, 1947 — 3:00 AM CST
Harvey, ND, 99W56 47N47.

ASNER, Ed [A] Nov. 15, 1929 — 6:00 AM CST
Kansas City, MO, 94W35 39N06.
Source: Penfield quotes baby book.

GREY, Joel [A] April 11, 1932 — 9:52 PM EST
Cleveland, OH, 81W42 41N30
Source: *Gauquelin Book of American Charts.*

IVES, Burl [B] June 14, 1909 — 6:00 AM CST
Hunt, IL, 88W01 39N00
Source: Autobiography *Wayfaring Stranger.*

MIDLER, Bette [A] December 1, 1945 — 2:19 PM Zone 10.5
Honolulu, HI 157W52 21N19
Source: *Contemporary Sidereal Horoscopes.*

PECK, Gregory [A] April 5, 1916 — 8:00 AM PST
La Jolla, CA, 117W16 32N51
Source: AFA from birth certificate.

POITIER, Sidney [A] February 20, 1927 — 9:00 PM EST
Miami, FL, 80W11 25N47
Source: From him on the Dick Cavett show.

QUEEN ELIZABETH II [DD] April 21, 1926 — 2:40 AM BDT
London, England, 0W06 51N31
Source: Fagan in *American Astrology* states
"recorded." Gallo has 2:22 AM BDT.

REDFORD, Robert [A] Aug. 18, 1936 — 8:02 PM PST
Santa Monica, CA, 118W29 34N01
Source: Rodden *American Book of Charts.*

REYNOLDS, Burt [A] February 11, 1936 — 12:10 PM EST
Lansing, MI, 84W33 42N44
Source: Rodden *American Book of Charts.*

SPACEK, Sissy [A] December 25, 1949 — 12:02 AM CST
Tyler, TX, 95W18 32N21
Source: From her to Lois Rodden.

WALTERS, Barbara [C] September 25, 1931 — 6:50 AM EST
Boston, MA, 71W04 42N22
Source: Lois Rodden says birth certificate, but
cannot trace source.

Preface

It has taken five years to finally finish this long promised book on chart interpretation. We hope the wait was worth it.

Since this book follows the March/McEvers teaching method, it slowly and systematically leads you into a deeper knowledge and understanding of astrology. In Volume I you learned the basics — the signs of the zodiac, planets, houses, aspects and some keywords and key phrases that helped you interrelate the different principles involved.

In Volume II we taught you the mathematics of erecting a horoscope and some refinements to sharpen your interpretive ability and teach you further insights into chart delineation.

In this third volume (of a series of five or six projected books) we again offer you three distinct parts:

Part I   Provides the last necessary tool for chart interpretation, namely HOUSE RULERS. Where is the ruler of the 1st house and what does it mean? Where is the ruler of the 2nd house and so on through the houses and the 144 possible positions. To illustrate and make the learning more interesting, we have included 36 charts of famous people.

Part II   Provides you with the in-depth delineation of four famous people: General George Patton, author Ernest Hemingway, Princess Diana of Wales and entertainer Barbra Streisand. Each horoscope is based on different interpretation techniques to give you choices and options in perfecting your own skills.

Part III Provides methods of finding specific areas of interest in a chart, such as: What kind of partner am I looking for? What are my vocational aptitudes? What or where are my physical, weaknesses?

The approach of this book is on a more advanced level than the two beginning volumes which were strictly basic astrology. We assume that by now you can take our keywords and phrases and turn them around to suit your own vocabulary; that when you look at a horoscope and see certain planetary positions, some words come to your mind without looking at our books.

But even if you are still dependent on us and our words, don't despair — take time to delineate the four charts in this volume, go back to Volumes I and II of *The Only Way To . . . Learn Astrology* to see why we chose certain phrases and not others. We explain the methods used in the introduction to Part II. By the time you finish this book, you will be ready for the next step.

That step will be the transition into intermediate astrology, which involves updating or progressing the horoscope and using transits, comparing your chart with that of another person and erecting a composite chart of the two, relocating the horoscope to somewhere other then your birthplace, and the mundane approach to astrology. In the distant future lies the advanced March/McEvers outline which includes solar and lunar returns, horary, vocational and esoteric astrology.

As stressed throughout our teaching, we reemphasize that you will only learn astrology if you spend time applying the learning. Look at the charts we use in Part II of this book and see how close your delineation comes to ours. There are many more charts in Part I of this book; look at them and interpret the ones that appeal to you. Since all of them are famous people, you can get biographical material on most of them in any public library to check your interpretation for accuracy. In other words, WORK with this book, don't just glance at it or read it like a novel.

We hope you enjoy yourself while you are learning.

Joan and Marion

Introduction
House Rulers

When reading a horoscope house rulers may not be the most important area of delineation. Most astrologers feel that the planet itself, the aspects it makes, and the sign and house it is located in are more important. Some astrologers don't use any rulership, neither planetary nor house, but we feel that both play a part in the art of delineating. For instance, if your Sun is in Gemini, and Mercury (the ruler of Gemini) is in Taurus, you will express your individuality quite differently than if the ruler Mercury were in Cancer.

By now we are sure you have learned to blend the planet, the sign, the house and the ruler's sign and house, as we have constantly stressed in Volumes I and II of *The Only Way to . . . Learn Astrology*. But what about house rulers? Why do we need one more overtone or blending? Assume you have Gemini on the cusp of the 2nd house and the ruler Mercury is in the 5th house. Is your sense of values or your earning ability the same as when Mercury is found in the 7th house? We don't think so. Furthermore, if a house has no planets placed in it (after all, there are twelve houses and only ten planets), through which planetary energy does it express itself if not the ruler? In chart interpretation everything has to be taken into account, and house rulership is just one more area that must be understood.

In the old days house rulership was mainly used for horary astrology, and as that branch of astrology became separated from the more humanistic or psychological chart interpretation widely used today, few books bothered with this topic. In fact the last book we could find that went into any detail on the subject was Llewellyn George's *A to Z Horoscope Maker* with the many dire and absolute statements still fashionable in those days. We hope to remedy this neglect by giving you a brief run down of the possibilities or opportunities offered by the different positions of house rulers.

Technically, the ruler of each house is the OWNER of the house it rules (we have translated and modernized the rather antiquated expression "Lord of a house") therefore this ruler will describe the house better than any planet placed in that house. If you have Gemini on the 2nd house cusp, Mercury "owns" the entire 2nd house, and though the Moon or Jupiter may be placed in the 2nd house, Mercury as the "owner" runs the house and sets the rules and regulations, while the Moon or Jupiter may be considered guests, visiting in a house which is not really theirs.

As you read the subsequent interpretations, you need to keep many factors in mind and blend the different areas involved, as we have taught you in Volumes I and II. For example: Author Ernest Hemingway (see chart on page 140) has the ruler of his 10th house in the 12th. He should have been a prison warden. After all, the 10th house shows his career and the 12th represents confinement and institutions! But Hemingway has Gemini on the 10th house cusp, and the ruler Mercury is in Leo. Gemini is the sign of communication, so his career may involve some form of communicating and with the ruler in the 12th something he can do by himself, privately, alone; but since the ruler is in Leo, his career needs to be one in which he can shine, rather than the usual "behind the scenes" interpretation of the 12th house. What better way to shine than through his books. You also need to keep in mind that Hemingway's Mercury exactly sextiles Neptune, planet of imagination, which would confirm a more imaginative career than being a male nurse or a prison warden.

We are giving you a thorough description of all twelve houses, written so that you can understand the underlying principle involved in each house. Once you comprehend the real meaning of the houses, you will have no trouble delineating the purpose each ruler fulfills. We are using many examples in our description of the rulers in the different houses, and hope that you will look up the charts offered in this book and in our previous books, Volumes I and II of *The Only Way To . . . Learn Astrology*, in order to practice and hone your skills. The method of learning has not changed. Start by using our key words and key phrases; as you progress and really understand these, you will find yourself using your own words. After practicing with the charts offered here, you will know how to blend all the factors involved and not even have to look at our text.

Lesson 1
First House Rulers

This house is a very special one and to understand the strength of its ruler, also called the CHART RULER, you need to understand the principle involved. The first house, as its name implies, is the beginning — the beginning of you as a person in this world, as a body with form and shape. The cusp of the 1st house, called the ASCENDANT, can be calculated only if your exact birthtime is known. The sign and degree will show the eastern horizon at the moment of birth or, symbolically, the moment the day was born. All the other planets in the chart are expressed through the sign on the Ascendant, so you can see how important it is to thoroughly understand this house.

The 1st house is considered angular, meaning it is active, dynamic and initiating. It is the first of the houses of life, and as such it represents the physical aspect of the personal houses, the body. (Of the other houses of life, the 5th is considered the soul and the 9th the mind or spirit). Since this is the house where your physical body emerges, it describes your appearance and your outer personality. It is also descriptive of the way you wish to appear, the face you want to show the world, and the way you have decided to package or market yourself.

Aries is the natural sign of the 1st house, and Mars is its natural ruler; so regardless of what sign is on the Ascendant, the feeling of "I" and "me" is an innate feeling of this house. In the beginning the newborn can only think of the self and the primal needs of the self to survive. This basic feeling will be carried by the ruler and toned up or down depending on the sign and house involved. Hand in hand with this basic egocentric orientation goes the marvelous feeling of newness, exploration and enthusiasm which is always an automatic part of anything that is first. Where the ruler of the Ascendant is placed by house is where you really want to be.

Ruler of the 1st in the 1st: Since the 1st house has to do with appearance, bearing, attitudes and primarily the self, the person who has the Ascendant ruler in this house is very self motivated, self-interested and at times somewhat egotistical, depending of course, on the aspects to this planet. Your appearance is important and you pay attention to grooming, how you dress and how you look. Your own wishes and ideas are paramount, and very often this comes across as a "me first" attitude. You usually create your own conditions, good or bad, and if the energy is properly handled you live a long life in pleasant living conditions. You may have a relatively happy childhood and good relationships with your family. If on the other hand you do not handle the aspects well, you will have to overcome some behavioral problems before you can achieve happiness and contentment.

Two formidable sportsmen come to mind as examples. Jean Claude Killy with Leo rising and the Sun in the 1st house shows the dedication and self-interest that drove him to his unique achievements in the skiing world. With the Sun square Mars and Uranus, he demonstrated the positive use of these challenging aspects to gain his ego needs — to "be first." (His chart is in Volume II of *The Only Way To . . . Learn Astrology*.) Babe Ruth, the great home run hitter, had Cancer rising and the Moon in the 1st house trine the Midheaven, Mercury, Venus and Saturn; these flowing aspects can readily account for his tremendous public popularity. It was easy for him to use his physical ability, and he certainly embodied the nonchalant personality often associated with trines.

Ruler of the 1st in the 2nd: You are the person who establishes your own value system, picking and choosing what avenues are right for you and often disregarding convention and what is expected, especially if the ruler happens to be Mars or Uranus. You may be strongly financially motivated, and much time and work may be given to earning a living. Money and what it stands for will be important, and often this is the placement of a person who earns his living in some monetary field. If the ruler is well aspected, the financial flow is smooth, the value system is orderly and well motivated and the earning ability is strong. If there are difficult aspects to this planet, there may be financial struggles, a lack of proper values and a wasting of your innate talent.

Larry Flynt, publisher of *Hustler* magazine, has Cancer rising and the Moon in Leo in the 2nd house, so he feels a sense of self worth and importance by having the public (Moon) accept his values. Since his Moon sextiles Mercury, he is able to do this by communicating through his publications rather intensely with Pluto also in Leo in the 2nd house.

Ruler of the 1st in the 3rd: Communication of ideas — your ideas — is very important. You have definite views about everything and expressing them becomes your primary interest. Travel is something you really enjoy and it may be involved with your career. You are frequently caught up in the affairs of your brothers and sisters, possibly being in business with them, or if they are younger than you are, you may have responsibility for them. If the energies are not properly used, there may be some delay or challenge concerning your education, but you have a need to learn and are often a dedicated reader. Usually gifted with a sense of humor, you are able to poke fun at yourself and this ability enables you to take a lighthearted approach to life.

Puppeteer and ventriloquist Shari Lewis has Libra rising and Venus in the 3rd house in Capricorn; she has been able to communicate her ideas in a most artistic and yet realistic way, creating personalities and almost an alter ego through her puppets. Venus trine Neptune enhances her creativity and imagination. Daredevil Evel Kneivel has Aquarius rising and Uranus in the 3rd house (motorized vehicles.) He certainly communicates with the public in an unusual way (Aquarius). Uranus squares the Moon (public) and Jupiter which enables him to do his thing in a larger-than-life style.

Ruler of the 1st in the 4th: Your home and family are the focal point of your life and there may be a very strong attachment to one of your parents, probably your mother. This can be a loving and rewarding relationship if the planet has supportive aspects; but if the energy is not properly used, you may have a great deal to learn about familial relationships. Often the parent indicated is strong, supportive and dominant and you may follow in his or her footsteps. Your home represents security to you and even if you do not own property (which would be surprising),you make wherever you happen to be your home with all the little things that you need to make it livable.

Marlene Dietrich, the perennial glamour girl, is known for her ability to turn wherever she is staying into a very comfortable home. She is not above getting down on her hands and knees to scrub the floor of a hotel room. With neat and orderly Virgo on the Ascendant and the ruler Mercury in Capricorn in the 4th, this is easy to understand. (See her chart on next page.) Another example is Christian Science founder Mary Baker Eddy, whose strong root system (Jupiter in Aries in the 4th) was expressed as religion through her Sagittarian Ascendant. (See her chart on page 81.)

Ruler of the 1st in the 5th: Artists Paul Cezanne and Vincent Van Gogh (see his chart in Volume II) both have this creative placement. Fun loving, generous and dramatic, drawn to both the arts and music, you are quite open and theatrical and may be caught up in social whirl. On another level you can be adventurous, sports loving and daring, taking a chance on life and love. Children will probably play an important part in your life. If you don't have any of your own, other people's children will be attracted to you and

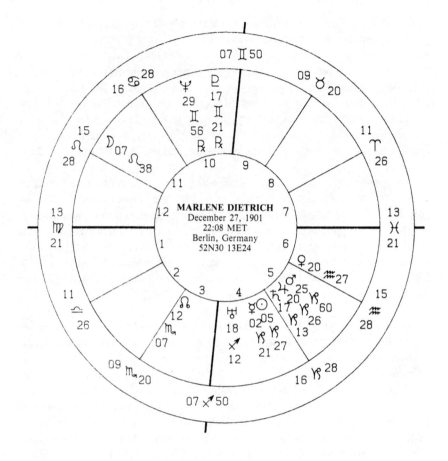

you to them. A born romantic, love and all its attendant trappings appeal to you and depending on the aspects, your love life will proceed smoothly or with great ups and downs. In other words, you are in love with love. Zany Carole Lombard, movie comedienne of the thirties, had Pisces rising and Neptune in the 5th house. Her sense of humor and love of life were well chronicled in the movie magazines. Even though Neptune squared her Sun and Uranus, she was capable of handling the energy generated in a positive, creative way.

Ruler of the 1st in the 6th: Work is the name of your game and if the planet is well aspected, you do it willingly and graciously. You may be concerned with diet, health and hygiene, and are either incredibly neat and well organized or dreadfully messy. Surprisingly, many sports-oriented people have this placement. Among them are baseball players Jackie Robinson, Larry Sherry and Eddie Mathews, jockey Billy Hartack and Olympic champion swimmer Mark Spitz. Perhaps it is the method and organization associated with sports that attracts them. You are a creature of habit and as long as others respect this, you are easy to get along with.

When there are challenging aspects to your ruler, you may have to deal with health problems related to the planet and the sign, but it you use the energies for work instead, you won't have time to be sick. Sigmund Freud (see his chart in Volume II), the founder of psychoanalysis, had Scorpio rising and Pluto in the 6th house and he demonstrated his ability for organization by cataloging all our phobias and developing treatments for them. He was a perfectionist in his work, but since Pluto inconjuncts Mars, the co-ruler of the Ascendant, he was rather untidy about his person.

Ruler of the 1st in the 7th: You're a people person who needs the appreciation and approbation of others to feel complete. If the energies are not used properly, you can be very competitive, argumentative, and even hard to get along with. But when you integrate this planet into the chart in a positive way, you are a good salesperson, mediator and public relations type. You like people and are genuinely liked in return. It is rare that anyone ever sees you alone. You want and need a partner and if other things in your chart support it, this is a good indication of an early marriage. You feel incomplete without a partner. With difficult aspects you may be afraid of constant upsets and may prefer to stay single.

Joan Sutherland (see chart in Volume II) is an example of the positive use of Taurus rising with Venus in the 7th house to give pleasure to the public. Venus conjunct the Sun gives charm and appeal as well as a remarkable voice, and its opposition to Mars provides the energy for her to use that voice to express herself. Her husband, conductor Richard Bonynge, is her marital and business partner, guiding her career and conducting every one of her operas and concerts.

Ruler of the 1st in the 8th: Your interest centers on all 8th house matters, and depending on what planet rules the Ascendant, you could be good at math or making money. Sex or the occult could appeal to you. In our clientele we find many doctors with this placement. You often have great charisma and sex appeal and you may excel at money management, accounting, banking or bookkeeping. You could show the reticence, probity and incisiveness of a Scorpio regardless of what sign your Sun or Ascendant is in. Deep and reserved, you have a caustic wit if other aspects in your chart support this. Certainly the serious side of life attracts you.

We have three very apt illustrations of this placement. John F. Kennedy with Libra rising and Venus in Taurus in the 8th is the prime example of charisma, sex appeal and the sense of responsibility. Sports announcer Howard Cosell with Leo on the Ascendant and the Sun in Aries in the 8th house certainly demonstrates the intensity of this position. Howard never does anything without coming on full bore. Humorist Ogden Nash, with Cancer rising and the Moon in Aquarius in the 8th, shows the unique wit and humor associated with this position. (All of these charts may be found in Volume II.)

Ruler of the 1st in the 9th: A dreamer of possible dreams, that's you, especially when the energy is handled in a positive way. A born philosopher and romantic, you see life as happy, hopeful and optimistic. The 9th is the house of aspiration and that is your keyword. You feel that you can achieve whatever you aspire to, and only very difficult aspects will keep you from your lofty aims. Travel and legal matters may play a large part in your life and the outcome must be judged from the planet in question, its sign and aspects.

Roman Polanski, (see his chart on page 71) the Polish movie director who has Sagittarius rising and Jupiter, the ruler, in the 9th house, has gained his greatest fame in a country far from his place of birth, and he has had the legal hassles indicated by Jupiter inconjunct to Uranus. He also has demonstrated the ability to achieve his aspirations as a successful movie director, helped by Jupiter's sextiles to the Moon and Pluto. Swami Vivekananda, with Saturn in Libra in the 9th ruling his Ascendant, brought his message to far away America and Europe. (See his chart on next page.)

Ruler of the 1st in the 10th: Rarely will you take a back seat. If politics isn't your game, then acting, entertaining or being in charge somehow surely is. You like to be noticed and feel an inherent need for recognition. This driving need could cause some scandal if the planet is poorly aspected. You usually are a take-charge person, and once you learn to handle yourself well, others will look to you for all the answers. With this placement, a parent may be very important in your life.

Film director Vittorio de Sica has a Virgo Ascendant and Mercury in Cancer in the 10th house, and he certainly is a take-charge person with a strong sense of responsibility since Mercury opposes Saturn in his 4th house of foundations. Singer Linda Ronstadt (see chart in Volume II) uses her Jupiter, ruler of the Ascendant in the 10th house, to be in the limelight and attract attention by her performing. Her Jupiter trine Uranus in the 6th house affords her the opportunity to draw attention to herself in an acceptable, working way.

Ruler of the 1st in the 11th: You can be quite venturesome, even daring, and if your ruler has challenging aspects, you could take pleasure in some very risky field. You may even be the victim of circumstances that lead you into rather perilous areas. An example is Lord Louis Mountbatten, who was killed by Irish terrorists. His Moon, ruler of his Cancer Ascendant, conjuncts Pluto and opposes Uranus. The need here is to learn good judgment

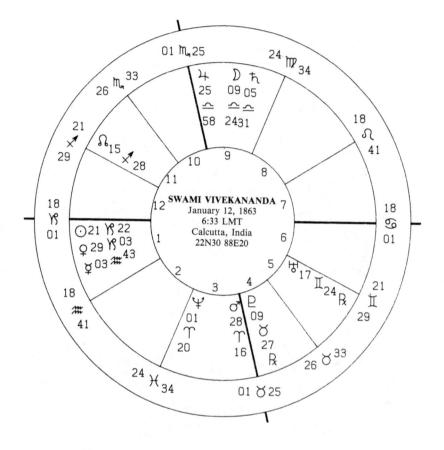

SWAMI VIVEKANANDA
January 12, 1863
6:33 LMT
Calcutta, India
22N30 88E20

in your dealings with others because what other people think may be important to you. Friends are significant to your self understanding; it is wise to
choose them carefully.

Often this is the placement of the true humanitarian who serves in some
large organizational capacity to help others and lead the way. Pope John
Paul the II is a good example of this last statement. He has Cancer rising
and the Moon in Taurus in the 11th house exactly conjunct his Sun, so he
is genuinely concerned with the welfare of the people of his church. He
presents a nurturing and caring attitude toward all the people of the world.
(His chart is on next page.)

Ruler of the 1st in the 12th: Somewhat withdrawn and shy as a youngster,
as you mature you learn to rely on your own inner strength. Many times
this placement leads to a career in show business or to one as a writer, detective, ambassador or public relations expert, since you are able to manipulate

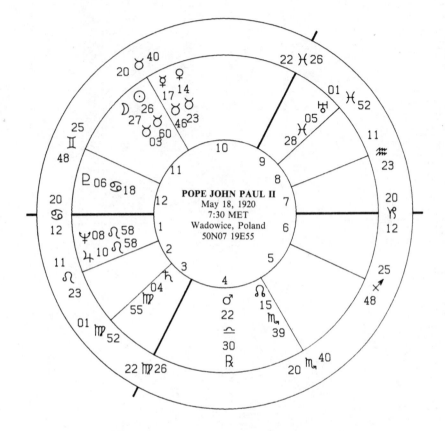

POPE JOHN PAUL II
May 18, 1920
7:30 MET
Wadowice, Poland
50N07 19E55

so well from behind the scenes. You're not exactly a shrinking violet, but you know when to keep your own counsel and so give the impression of great wisdom. You are not afraid to be alone and in fact, you enjoy your own company. With difficult aspects, you must be careful, not to withdraw from the world and forget to come back.

Former Secretary of State Henry Kissinger has Gemini on the Ascendant and Mercury in Gemini in the 12th house, and he is well known for his diplomacy and ability to smooth negotiations between two opposing factors. (His chart is on page 92.) Although he is quite loquacious, he definitely knows when to keep his own counsel, because Mercury trines Saturn. Author Theodore Dreiser, whose Ascendant ruler Venus squares Saturn from the 12th house, suffered a nervous breakdown before he was able to achieve writing success.

Lesson 2
Second House Rulers

In the flat chart the 2nd house is Taurus and its natural ruler is Venus. If the 1st house is "I," my body, then the 2nd house is "mine," that which belongs to me, my possessions, encompassing the key phrase "I have" which is always used for Taurus. It also incorporates the sense of value of its natural ruler, Venus, and will describe your attitude toward your belongings as well as what you value in the more abstract terms of your personality, such as your self worth.

The 2nd house is succedent and a house of substance and represents some of the tangible aspects of your life. Its earthy approach shows the way you can earn money. Its Venusian or creative approach shows your inner and outer talents and resources. Astrologer Isabel Hickey used to call it the house of freedom, because if you make good use of your resources, you will be free to be who you are.

Ruler of the 2nd in the 1st: Your sense of values is most personal, and is formed more by your life experiences than by your upbringing. You will be able to earn a living by your own efforts with ease or difficulty determined by the aspects the ruler makes. If that ruler is not very challenged, you establish your self worth at a rather early age; if it is challenged the outside world may force values and self evaluations upon you early in life. This was the case with child star Shirley Temple whose 1st house Saturn rules her 2nd house. squares Mars and the Midheaven and inconjuncts Pluto.

Former Attorney General John Mitchell (see his chart below) has Virgo on the cusp of the 2nd and the ruler Mercury in Virgo in the 1st house. He chose his career fairly early in life and earned a good living much of the time. Mercury trines Jupiter, enabling him to expand and make big money; it sextiles Pluto, adding the opportunity of involvement with large groups of people and power of concentration.

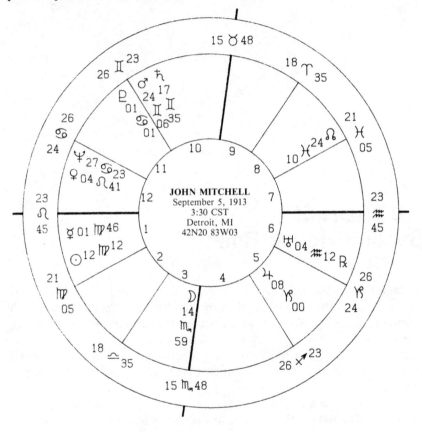

Ruler of the 2nd in the 2nd: Much of your security is found in relying on your own talents and resources. The sooner you realize that material possessions are no solution to any problems you may encounter, the easier it will be for you to establish a healthy sense of values. You are able to earn money through your own industry and may do so much of your life. Your feet are planted solidly on the ground, and regardless how scattered or idealistic you may be in other areas of your life, when it comes to money you know your way around. Olympic gold medal skier Jean-Claude Killy (see chart in Volume II) has Virgo on the cusp and Mercury in the 2nd; he knew when to switch from being an amateur to professional and how to successfully enter the commercial world.

Nutritionist Adelle Davis had Capricorn on the cusp of the 2nd house and the ruler Saturn in the 2nd in Aquarius. The Capricorn seriousness and ambition to succeed, blended with the Aquarian need to be different, helped Davis pick a rather unique field and develop many controversial ideas, especially in her approach to vitamins. The 2nd house becomes doubly important in her chart, since Venus (what you like to do), Mercury (reasoning ability) and the Sun (need to shine) are all placed in this house. Saturn has a close trine to her 6th house (nutrition) Moon, and Pluto conjuncts Mercury, giving her tremendous strength of purpose.

Ruler of the 2nd in the 3rd: You need to communicate your values in some way, shape or form. Your income may be derived from a job or career which involves communication, the written or spoken word, the arts, politics or acting. Relatives, especially brothers or sisters if you have any, can be helpful to your money earning capability. Travel or commuting may be required in order for you to earn a living. An example is conductor Zubin Mehta, (Aries on the 2nd, ruler Mars in the 3rd), who communicates through music. He also conducts in many countries and zips all over the world with the same ease most of us commute from home to work.

Author Hermann Hesse has Capricorn on the 2nd house and the ruler Saturn is in the 3rd in Pisces. He earned his living through his writings; his sense of values was formed by his spiritual and rather mystical approach to religion, life and death. Saturn is involved in a T-square to a 1st house Jupiter and 7th house Mercury, confirming his need for self-expression and adding a desire for one-to-one relations. A trine to Venus in the 8th and a sextile to Pluto in the 5th confirms his creative urges, occult leanings and also his ability to make a good living, despite occasional challenges and setbacks brought on by his use of the squares. (Both Mehta's and Hesse's charts can be found in Volume II).

Ruler of the 2nd in the 4th: You may derive your income from working out of your home. Many leaders such as Indira Gandhi (whose chart is on page 37) and Charles de Gaulle have this placement, since they usually live and work in a governmental residence or palace. You may also be involved in real estate ventures or be an interior decorator, to cite two possibilities. Your values will have been molded through your parental home and one or both of your parents may exert a strong influence over you much of your life. To own your own home will be very important and will help you to establish your own identity.

Former President Gerald Ford has Gemini on the 2nd house cusp, and the ruler Mercury is placed in his 4th house in Leo. He presided over the United States from his home, the White House. With the ruler Mercury square

Mars and the Ascendant, he had enough energy at his disposal, but did not always use it to properly analyze a situation. Saturn and Pluto in his 2nd house show his intense need to prove himself to family and country.

Ruler of the 2nd in the 5th: Of course a lot of actors and writers have the ruler of the 2nd in the 5th and earn their living through their creative endeavors. Romance is an important part of your value system and if Venus is involved, social pleasures will play a large role in your estimation of your self worth. Writer Scott Fitzgerald, for example, had Pisces on the 2nd house and Neptune in Gemini in the 5th. He not only valued a very social life but used his imagination to write about it. (See his chart below.) As a parent you may find your own worth through a child by either forcing your values on your offspring or by gaining a sense of who you are through the achievements of a son or daughter (like a stage mother). If the rest of the chart confirms, you may earn money through speculation; or investing could be one way to derive your income.

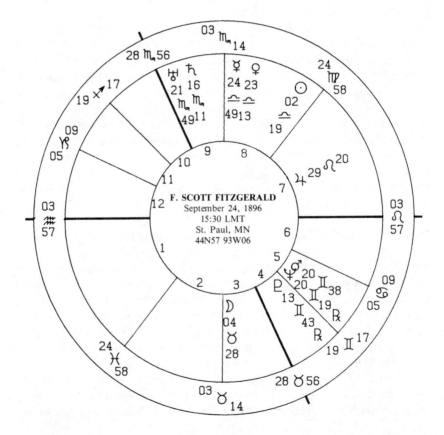

F. SCOTT FITZGERALD
September 24, 1896
15:30 LMT
St. Paul, MN
44N57 93W06

Actor Burt Reynolds has Cancer on his 2nd house and the Moon is in Libra in the 5th. He earns his living through his creative efforts as an actor. The Moon closely trines his Ascendant, Mercury and Midheaven, promising success and giving easy access to money if he makes good use of these aspects and learns to work with the Moon's inconjunct to Saturn by accepting himself, and finding his need for emotional security in areas other than just the material aspects of the 2nd house.

Ruler of the 2nd in the 6th: You will probably earn your living through your work which may not necessarily be your final career. One of our clients, for example, sells real estate and earns her living this way. She is a writer, but is realistic enough to know that with the uncertainty of her book sales she had better have another source of income in order to eat and pay the rent.

Many of your values may depend on some sort of service you wish to render and you could earn money through the health, hygiene or nutrition fields. Since many politicians feel they are rendering a service to their nation or constituents, you will find quite a few senators and congressmen with this placement. Former President Nixon has Venus in Pisces in the 6th ruling his Libra 2nd house. Illinois Senator Charles Percy has Gemini on the 2nd house cusp and Mercury in Libra in the 6th.

Senator Eugene McCarthy, for example, has Pisces on the 2nd house and Neptune in Cancer in the 6th. His need to serve the public (Cancer) was so strong that he ran in a hopeless presidential race to give the people an alternative between George McGovern and Richard Nixon. Neptune trines his Midheaven and Mercury (in the 2nd), making a grand trine, enabling him to earn a good living, and also making his values very idealistic and patriotic. Some of you who have the ruler of the 2nd in the 6th may spend a lot of money on your pet who may be one of the things you value.

Ruler of the 2nd in the 7th: Your money earning capacity may be enhanced or hindered by a partner. The public could play an important role in your earning ability, therefore sales can be a good field for you. Your self worth is very dependent upon your relationship with a mate, and Elizabeth Taylor with seven husbands to her credit, serves as a good example. The cusp of her 2nd house is Libra and the ruler Venus is in Aries, confirming the interpretation. (See her chart on page 69.)

As you learn to establish a one-to-one relationship or understand other people's needs, you will better understand your own security needs and find your own values and priorities. The way you earn your livelihood may involve legal affairs, such as contracts and agreements.

The "Sleeping Prophet" Edgar Cayce had Virgo on his 2nd house and Mercury in Pisces in his 7th in a tight conjunction with the North Node, Saturn and Venus. Cayce's value system was established through his relations with the public; his own self worth and self understanding were enhanced through his partners (both his wife and the doctor who first helped him find his special talent and then became his partner for many years.) When you consider the stellium in Pisces which includes his Sun, you can understand that this would be expressed in a psychic and spiritual way rather than in the practical or material manner often associated with the 2nd house.

Ruler of the 2nd in the 8th: Your income may be derived from such sources as banking, brokerage, insurance or politics — all areas where you handle other people's resources or where you need the support of others in order to achieve your security aims. Sex can also be one of the commodities you use in order to make a living, as does Farrah Fawcett (Leo on the 2nd, ruler Sun in Aquarius in the 8th — her chart is in Volume II) or sex may become an important factor in achieving your security or coming to grips with your values.

You may inherit money, especially if the planet is Venus or Jupiter, but if the ruler has many challenging aspects, an inheritance may be denied. You may find that your sense of values changes as you utilize your 8th house ruler for transformation rather than material gain. Your own resources become clearer and your priorities different as you gain understanding of life versus death, and the value of standing on your own two feet versus letting a partner take care of you.

Bette Midler has Taurus on the 2nd house and the ruler Venus in Scorpio in the 8th. Much of her income is derived by selling herself and her songs through sexual innuendos and rather openly Scorpionic overtones. She knows how to take good material advantage of her talents and resources, not only because of earthy Taurus on the cusp, but also because Venus makes an exact trine to Saturn, adding discipline.

Ruler of the 2nd in the 9th: Philosophy, religion, ideas and ideals are very involved with your values. Higher education may be a necessity if you wish to take full advantage of your talents and resources. You may earn your living through such fields as publishing, teaching in a university, working in a library or spreading religion as did faith healer Kathryn Kuhlman. Her 9th house Pluto ruling her 2nd house helped her reach large masses of people and she not only made many converts but earned a good living doing it.

Long distance travel can play an important role in the way you earn your money or it may change your values. Foreign trade could also be one of the areas through which you increase your income. Your self worth can be helped through your partner's kin or hindered if the aspects to the ruler are very difficult and tension producing.

German writer Thomas Mann had Libra on his 2nd house cusp and Venus in Taurus in the 9th house. He made a very good living through his books, which were not only his artistic (Venus/Taurus/Libra) expression, but also portrayed his philosophical attitude toward life and death. The intensity found in his works can be seen by the conjunction of Venus and Pluto in the 9th house. Venus in the 9th also shows that Mann had to leave his native Germany and travel to distant America to find the freedom to continue his writings.

Ruler of the 2nd in the 10th: Success in a career, finding your own identity and meeting your ego needs are most important in order for you to establish your value system. Without some sense of achievement you will easily flounder and doubt your own worth. Your earnings may be aided by the efforts of one of your parents, often the father as with Princess Caroline of Monaco. You may earn your living in some government capacity and your income may come through your career or profession; the status you achieve will determine your feeling of being free or not.

Former Vice President Walter (Fritz) Mondale is a good example of having earned his living by working for the government. He has Aries on his 2nd house and Mars in Sagittarius in the 10th house, closely conjunct the Midheaven. He put a lot of effort into achieving his high position and in fact, is talking of running for president in 1984, a rather typical expression of the drive and energy manifested by Mars. Mondale's value system is also influenced by his Sagittarian Mars and Pisces Ascendant which make him quite idealistic and philosophical. (See his chart on page 54.)

Ruler of the 2nd in the 11th: Your values are often closely linked with those of friends and with your success or failure in social situations. The amount of love you receive can make a difference in the self worth you feel. Your income may derive through the influence of friends and acquaintances or from a business that you establish yourself. Until you formulate your hopes and wishes, it will be difficult to come to grips with your inner resources or determine their use.

Lenny Bruce (whose chart can be found in Volume II) with Capricorn on the 2nd is a case in point. If Neptune or the Moon is the planet ruling your 2nd house, it is especially important that you build your value system on a sound basis. Actor Gregory Peck has Gemini on the cusp of the 2nd and Mercury in Aries in the 11th. Since Jupiter and his Sun are also in Aries in the 11th, his need to express in an Aries way is very strong. Mercury rules Peck's 2nd house as well as his Ascendant, and he earns a living through his own resources, his own personality. Mercury's trine to Mars and sextile to Venus gives him charm and his deep, distinctive voice.

Ruler of the 2nd in the 12th: You may earn your livelihood by acting behind the scenes or in a private setting. Your income could be derived from an institution like a hospital, so you may be a nurse or doctor. Your values are formed by truly looking deep within your own subconscious or by spending much time alone. You may find your self worth after going through some sort of psychoanalysis or self-analysis. You need to understand your inner strengths and weaknesses in order to find your real values. Some seclusion or time for yourself can be most helpful in this pursuit. T.E. Lawrence, better known as "Lawrence of Arabia," serves as a good example of someone who needed to experience loneliness and separation from his usual surroundings to discover his true self. He had Virgo on the 2nd house cusp and Mercury in Leo in the 12th. (See chart in Volume II.)

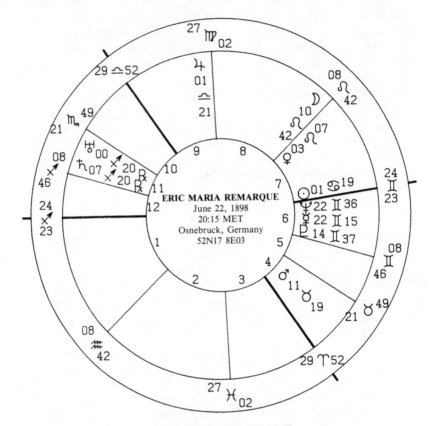

REMARQUE'S CHART

Author Erich Maria Remarque has Capricorn on the 2nd and Saturn in the 12th. Though he was a very outgoing and friendly person (Sagittarius Ascendant), he earned his living by writing; he wrote in total solitude, locked away from everyone, even his wife, for weeks at a time. Money and the luxuries it could buy were important to Remarque (ruler Saturn trine Venus and the Moon). Saturn's conjunction to Uranus explains his need to do and say unique and often unacceptable things such as his anti-war message in *All Quiet on the Western Front* and his overly exuberant life and love style. His need to prove himself to women is confirmed by Saturn's inconjunct to Mars. (See his chart above.)

Lesson 3
Third House Rulers

Because the 3rd house is naturally ruled by Mercury and its natural sign is Gemini, it is considered the house of communication, the area where you need to express your ideas and thoughts orally or in writing. Whereas the 1st house is "me" or "my body" and the 2nd house is "mine" or "what belongs to me," the 3rd house moves you a step further into the "here" or immediate environment. As a house of relationships it encompasses our close relatives, especially sisters and brothers (if there are any), and it describes how we relate to them as well as to our immediate neighborhood. In later years the restlessness of Gemini also manifests as short trips and local transportation of many kinds, such as cars, trains, busses and bicycles. The 3rd house is cadent and indicates the adaptability of your mind (Mercury) to learning and to new ideas, which in its practical form illustrates your early schooling and elementary education.

Ruler of the 3rd in the 1st: You are the person who **must** express your opinions, attitudes and ideas. If the planet ruling the cusp of the 3rd house is the Sun, Mercury or the Moon and it is well integrated into the chart, you are never at a loss for words, much like popular television host Merv Griffin whose Sun is in Cancer in his 1st house ruling his 3rd. His folksy appeal comes across well to his guests and he can disarmingly get them to discuss almost anything. Barbra Streisand, who sings so well and is known for her sharp tongue as well as her wit, has Gemini on the 3rd house and Mercury in the 1st in Taurus conjunct her Sun and square the Moon. (See her chart on page 188.)

If the ruler is Uranus, you will voice your ideas and opinions in a way uniquely your own. Sometimes this placement can be gossipy and chattery, especially if the ruler squares a planet in the 3rd house. Often your dialogue refers to local politics, siblings or acquaintances and you are rarely stumped for a way to express yourself. On another level, you could be a person who is fond of travel or work that you can do with your hands. Above all, you need and create the opportunity to talk about yourself.

Ruler of the 3rd in the 2nd: You may find it necessary to verbalize your value system and you are usually quite adamant about your theories and beliefs. There is often a need to talk about money and possessions, not in a bragging sense, but as an authority. You can be quite practical and this placement may give a pleasant voice and the ability to project it like singers Bobby Darin and David Bowie with Mercury and Jupiter respectively ruling the 3rd, placed in the 2nd.

Actor Clint Eastwood (see his chart in Volume II) has Capricorn on the 3rd house cusp and Saturn in Capricorn in his 2nd house. He earns his living, and it is a good one, by communicating his values through the medium of motion pictures. Since Saturn is retrograde and dignified, he comes across as taciturn, almost forbidding at times. Saturn squares Uranus in the 5th house, giving a charismatic personality and a creative means of self-expression. Saturn's opposition to Venus in the 8th house shows his apparent sexuality on screen but may bring personal problems in love relationships.

Ruler of the 3rd in the 3rd: Many prominent writers have this placement and it surely gives a facility with words, either written or spoken. You need to express your ideas and are quite assertive in your opinions and beliefs; depending on aspects to the planet, you may have to learn to control a tendency to be too outspoken or opinionated. Usually you have a good sense of direction and are very attuned to the here and now.

If the ruler is Mars or Uranus, your early home life could have been chaotic with many changes of residence and school. Among the many writers who have this are Lewis Carroll (Uranus), Truman Capote (Mercury) and Erskine Caldwell (Venus). Caldwell with Libra on the 3rd house cusp and Venus in Scorpio square Saturn and Mars, received very little formal schooling, but with the intensity of Scorpio, he developed his own style and made a big hit with *Tobacco Road* and his ensuing novels. (See his chart on next page.)

Ruler of the 3rd in the 4th: This frequently indicates a sibling who acted in lieu of your parent or vice versa — you became a parental figure to a brother or sister. You are most comfortable in your home environment and have a need for a certain amount of privacy. This gives good lines of communication with a parent if the planet is well aspected, but if not, it may indicate a lack of understanding with one or both parents. Many real estate sales people have this placement, and they find it very easy to talk about land and property and have a genuine interest in matching their client with the right home.

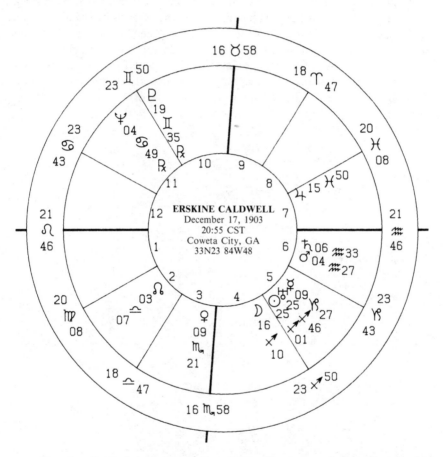

People who feel a need to work at home like writers James Clavell with Aquarius on the 3rd and Uranus in the 4th, as well as Stephen King with Mercury ruling his 3rd in the 4th, are good examples. Both of Clavell's voluminous tomes *Shogun* and *Taipan* tell stories of a person who finds a home in a foreign country. Uranus in his 4th would indicate that he would write about a "home" different than his own and Uranus square to Jupiter may help explain the voluminosity of his writing. (See his chart on next page.)

Ruler of the 3rd in the 5th: You can be the most romantically expressive of all people if you use the ruler well. If not, you may have to curb a tendency to exaggeration and a need to draw attention to yourself by some outlandish behavior like explorer Richard Byrd.

You can be very creative like singer/songwriter Peggy Lee, who has Cancer on the 3rd house cusp and the Moon in Virgo in the 5th trine Venus. Not only does she sing beautifully, but she writes almost all of her own material, including "Fever" and "Is That All There Is?," two of her big hits. Ballerina Margot Fonteyn has Taurus on the cusp of the 3rd and Venus in Cancer in her 5th house. Anyone who has ever seen her perform has been impressed with her grace and romantic interpretation of the ballet. There is often an interest in sports of some kind, especially if the planet involved is Mars or Uranus. Of course, teaching — particularly to children — could well be your forte if other things in the chart confirm this.

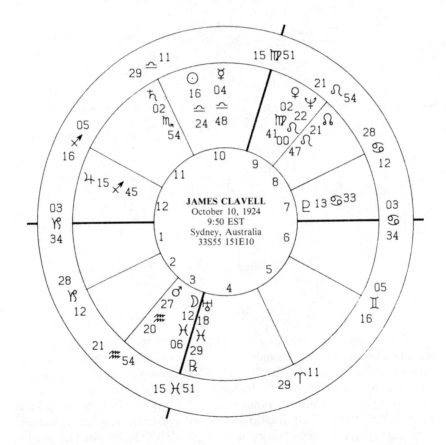

Ruler of the 3rd in the 6th: If you aren't careful you can bore others with your talk about your job, diet or habits. Your work is important to you, and if it embodies communication of some kind, you are usually very happy. Sometimes this placement indicates the opportunity to work with or for a sister or brother. For example, Dianne Lennon of the singing Lennon sisters has Capricorn on the cusp of the 3rd house and Saturn in the 6th and she certainly worked with her siblings. Your work may involve automobiles like Jackie Stewart, the famous race car driver who has Jupiter in Aries in his 6th ruling his 3rd. Since Jupiter opposes his Ascendant, a racing accident almost kept Stewart out of racing competition altogether. The trine to Pluto provided the impetus for him to keep trying and eventually helped to bring him to prominence in his field.

A job that requires travel, such as mail delivery or route sales, could appeal to you because it allows you to be mobile. With very challenging aspects or misuse of the energies, your health could be affected, or you may dabble at some work here or some service there, never getting the satisfaction you need.

Ruler of the 3rd in the 7th: If the planet has demanding aspects, you must take care not to let others influence your opinions unduly. Usually you find it easy to converse with people, to exchange ideas and opinions with them. This is good for politics because with flowing aspects you can be a very persuasive speaker like Joseph McCarthy, Gerald Ford or Benito Mussolini.

You feel the need for a partner who provides intellectual stimulation; one with whom you can discuss and argue ideas, concepts and theories. Your relaxed demeanor in public frequently affords you the opportunity to deal with other people. Television host Mike Douglas has Pisces on the 3rd cusp and Neptune in the 7th house conjunct his Leo Sun. He has a knack for bringing out the best in his guests and his strong stellium in the 7th house more than compensates for his lack of planets in air signs. (See his chart in Volume II.)

Ruler of the 3rd in the 8th: With challenging aspects this may indicate the premature loss of a sibling, as in the case of Ted Kennedy who has Neptune ruling the 3rd in the 8th house in Virgo, opposing the Sun and Mercury and inconjunct Venus. (See his chart in Volume II.) You are usually curious about matters of life and death and very often you engage in research of a very profound kind as did scientist Louis Pasteur whose Jupiter rules the 3rd house in the 8th, trines energetic Mars in Capricorn and sextiles probing Pluto in Pisces.

You may have an interest in occult matters; if not, you can tell a dirty joke in the best locker room tradition. Your daily dialogue may be rather terse since you dislike idle chatter and prefer a meaningful or deep discussion especially if Mercury, Saturn or Pluto are involved. At times you may enjoy a challenging game such as chess or backgammon instead of indulging in what you consider boring chatter.

Ruler of the 3rd in the 9th: Your imagination knows no bounds and your mind is open to new ideas and impressions; you are often able to give your dreams practical expression. Again, this is an indication of an ability to write, especially fantasy like fairy tale teller Hans Christian Andersen, who had Aquarius on the cusp of the 3rd and inventive and imaginative Uranus in the 9th house. With Uranus conjunct Saturn, he was educated by generous, older patrons and then given the opportunity to express his fantasies through stories like "The Snow Queen" and "The Ugly Duckling."

Travel intrigues you as does philosophy and religion and you are quite at ease in discussing these things. Study of foreign languages will more than likely be easy for you. There may be a separation from a close relative, particularly because it is hard for you to remain tied down to one area for any great length of time. Religion probably played an important part in your early education. Improper application of your energy may cause inertia and deny the fulfillment of your ideas and dreams.

Ruler of the 3rd in the 10th: As is true of those whose ruler of the 3rd is in the 1st, you have a great need to be heard and to voice your thoughts and ideas; but you may feel most comfortable doing it from the stage as did John Barrymore or Enrico Caruso, both of whom had Leo on the 3rd house cusp and the Sun in the 10th house. This need for self-expression becomes a projection of your ego and usually catapults you into some sort of limelight. You come to public attention through what you say or write more often than because of what you do.

If the ruling planet has challenging aspects, notoriety may be what you seek, like gangster Mickey Cohen whose Pluto, ruler of the 3rd was in his 10th house in Cancer. (See his chart on next page.) You may have a lot to say but freeze when you have to say it in public. With Jupiter or Sagittarius involved, you are the super salesman of the zodiac.

Adolf Hitler, with Capricorn intercepted in the 3rd house and the ruler Saturn elevated in the 10th, is a perfect example of the persuasiveness connected with this placement. His spellbinding speeches convinced many of the people in Germany that his ideas were valid and acceptable; but Saturn squared Venus and Mars and his inability to properly use those squares contributed to his later undoing. (See his chart in Volume II.)

Ruler of the 3rd in the 11th: You may use your communicating ability to benefit mankind in some way like Carol MacEvoy who has Scorpio on the 3rd house cusp and Pluto in the 11th. She does sign language interpretation for the deaf on television. Or you may use your eloquence to sway your political constituents or excite a whole nation with a bogus communication from Mars like rotund actor Orson Welles who has the Sun that rules his 3rd house in the 11th in Taurus. (See his chart in Volume II.)

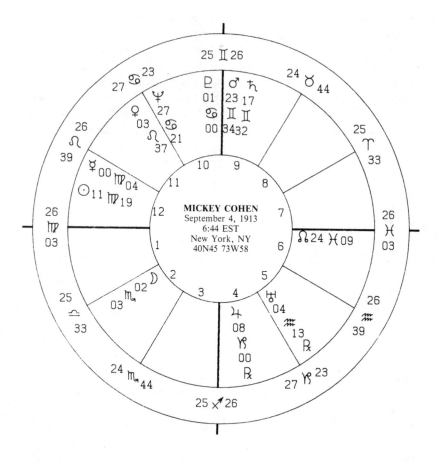

25 ♊ 26

27 ♋ 23

24 ♉ 44

♇ 01   ♂ ♄ 23 17
♋ 00   ♊ ♊ 34 32

♆ 27 ♋
♀ 03 ♋
♌ 37 21

26 ♌ 39

☿ 00 ♍ 04
☉ 11 ♍ 19

10   9

8

25 ♈ 33

12   **MICKEY COHEN**
September 4, 1913
6:44 EST
New York, NY
40N45 73W58   7

26 ♍ 03

1

6   ☋ 24 ♓ 09

26 ♓ 03

☽ 02
♏ 03   2   3   4   5

♅ 04
♒ 13 ℞

26 ♒ 39

25 ♎ 33

♃ 08 ♑ 00 ℞

24 ♏ 44

27 ♑ 23

25 ♐ 26

Often you do your best communicating when you are part of a group. If the aspects to the ruler are difficult, you should always look before you leap, as you could be quite accident prone, especially if the ruling planet is Mars or Uranus. With flowing aspects, friends will play an important part in your routine and often neighbors may provide close friendship. You could be the world's greatest letter writer, staying in communication with friends and acquaintances this way for a lifetime.

Ruler of the 3rd in the 12th: This seems to be a good placement for those with a sense of the ridiculous. Funny man Jim Backus, the voice of Mr. Magoo, has Mercury in the 12th house ruling his 3rd, and comedian Shelley Berman has Taurus on the 3rd cusp and Venus in the 12th. Backus' Mercury trines Neptune, the planet of clowns and comedians, and this can readily account for his success as a voice behind the scenes. He has also been very successful as Mr. Howell on the long running television (Neptune ruled) show *Gilligan's Island*. When you have this placement you are able to see life's funny side, yet you may experience tragedy, perhaps involving a sibling, especially if you have problems integrating the planet and its aspects.

You are able to communicate from behind the scenes as the partner of a successful mate, the "grey eminence" or the ghost writer. Acting and directing may afford a means of self-expression; so does choreography. With flowing aspects, tact and diplomacy come easily to you. Three of our clients with this placement are involved in hospital work connected with 3rd house matters. Two are respiratory therapists, and one works in speech therapy.

Lesson 4
Fourth House Rulers

This is the beginning and the end — the roots, inherited traits and psychological basis. In fact some astrologers, including Robert Hand, feel the 4th should be the beginning of the chart rather than the traditionally used 1st house. You can make a good case for that theory, but we prefer to think that the protective and nurturing Cancer, the natural 4th house sign, as well as the instinctive Moon, representing the mother and being the natural ruler of the 4th, describe the gestation of the native, the true beginning of what later emerges as the "body" in the 1st house. The 4th is a house of endings and it shows a form of transmutation, as do all the houses related to the water signs. The 4th shows the closing years of life as well as the end of the physical body. The 8th is usually considered to be the liberation of your soul; the 12th represents your philosophical death.

In its practical application the 4th house indicates your private life, the type of home you will establish for yourself as well as your parental background, and one of your parents, usually the one you consider mothering or nurturing. It also describes property, such as houses and real estate.

Ruler of the 4th in the 1st: One of your parents may have a deep impact or influence upon you or you may inherit real estate through your family. Regardless of what you do in life, your familial background will be important, and with flowing aspects to the ruler, it will sustain you through difficult or easy times. President Carter has Cancer on the 4th house cusp and his Moon in Scorpio in the 1st, well exemplifying how love of country and his own heritage became such a strong part of his personality that it led to his wish to become president. He was able to do so because the Moon is involved in a grand trine with Uranus and Pluto.

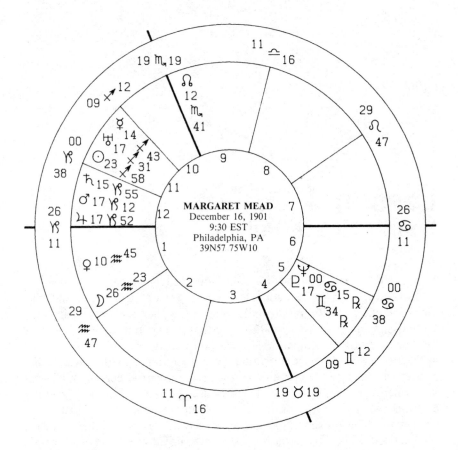

Anthropologist Margaret Mead serves as another example. She has Taurus on the 4th and the ruler, Venus, is in the 1st house in Aquarius. The Moon is also there but not conjunct. Since both the Moon and Venus represent the female principle in astrology and usually the mother, we can see that her mother had a great influence on her and played a large role in making Dr. Mead as independent as she was. Her mother was a suffragette and Dr. Mead remembers handing out tracts on women's rights when she was 10 years old. Venus, ruler of the 4th and also of the 9th, trines Pluto in Gemini; Dr.Mead traveled most of her life and spoke seven of the languages of the people of the Pacific whom she was studying. (See her chart above.)

Ruler of the 4th in the 2nd: People with this placement can develop a very diverse set of values, but obviously the planet and the aspects it makes will determine the results. We have many clients with this position who are extremely money conscious, and they have strong Saturn influences, with either Capricorn on the 4th or Saturn in difficult aspect to the ruler of the 4th. This placement may also signify that you earn your income by working in the home or by dealing in commodities like real estate, agriculture, geology and related fields.

Queen Elizabeth II of England certainly proves the point of heritage and family being the dominant factors in establishing her values and helping her find her own resources. She has Taurus on the 4th and Venus in Pisces in the 2nd. Venus trines Pluto, enabling her to earn a very good living by working out of her homes — Windsor Castle and Buckingham Palace, to name two. Venus, however, inconjuncts the Moon, showing early childhood problems with her mother which she needed to work out. Since the Moon also represents the public and is in the "public" 7th house, she may be expected to make many adjustments throughout her life between her own values and likes, and her public role or what she thinks the public expects of her.

Ruler of the 4th in the 3rd: The manner in which you communicate will greatly depend on your background and how you feel about yourself. Probably your childhood home was one where people did a lot of exchanging of ideas. Relatives, especially brothers and sisters, may have played a very important role in the parental home; whether this was to your liking or disturbed you will depend on the aspects made by the ruler.

In Ted Kennedy's case (see his chart in Volume II), his brothers and sisters most certainly played a very important role in his development and roots. Venus in Aries in the 3rd rules his 4th house Taurus cusp and inconjuncts his Moon; he had to adjust to not being the only one loved by his mother, since he was one of 9 children. Venus is the finger of a yod involving not only the Moon, but also Neptune and the Midheaven and Kennedy used his background and family name to become senator and a presidential candidate. The magnetism and charisma surrounding him, the so-called Camelot syndrome, is really a Kennedy or familial trait. Kennedy's father played a big part in his life, and he used him as a role model in many ways, including womanizing, as shown by Venus conjunct Uranus and many other factors.

In many cases when the ruler of the 4th is in the 3rd, you are raised by a relative or a relative lives with you and becomes an integral part of your family.

Ruler of the 4th in the 4th: Your own home will always play an important part in your life. Even if it is only a hotel room, you will fix it up with your own personal touches; and wherever your home may be, you'll come back to it to recharge your batteries time and time again. Depending on the planet involved, your attitude toward the home and your childhood background will vary. If Saturn is involved, it may indicate a rather difficult childhood with many responsibilities or a very disciplinarian parent who played a dominant role in your youth. Mars shows a very active household, or the parents may have fought a lot. Most people who have this placement feel the need to own some property, preferably their own home or homes. Former President Richard Nixon has Jupiter ruling his 4th in the 4th; typical of Jupiter's expansiveness, he enjoyed large homes, whenever possible with a view.

Jawaharlal Nehru,former Prime Minister of India, had Libra on the 4th house cusp and Venus was placed in the 4th. This is a rather common placement for patriots or leaders who rule, because they truly believe in what they can do for their country, and with very challenging aspects, what their country can do for them. Typical of the Libra need to balance, Nehru tried to find the right approach at a difficult time, India's fight for independence and the assassination of Gandhi. (For Nehru's chart see Volume II.)

One of the parents usually plays an important role in your life and if the ruler has flowing aspects, you may be quite successful in your place of birth. This placement also can signify your enjoyment of antiques, especially if the Cancer/Capricorn axis or the Moon and Saturn are involved.

Ruler of the 4th in the 5th: Love and romance are an integral part of your private life, and if Uranus is the ruling planet, it may not always be the mate who is romanced. Children will play an important role in the home you fashion for yourself; and if you have no children of your own, you may invite other people's to bring life into your house. If Saturn is the ruling planet, the children could be more of a responsibility than the fun you had visualized. Speculating is one of the pleasurable things you do in life, but you'll do it privately or as part of your regular business, like financial wizard and adviser Bernard Baruch who had Pisces on the 4th house and Neptune in Aries in the 5th.

Your home will be part and parcel of your relaxation and leisure time. You may have a sauna or hot tub and maybe some gym equipment, and probably a stationary bike will be part of your furniture, especially if Mars is prominently involved. Former glamour queen Marlene Dietrich (see chart on page 8) has Sagittarius on the 4th house, and Jupiter is in Capricorn in the 5th. She has many hobbies which she brings into her home. Sex and men was one of them, but she also loves to cook and since Jupiter is flanked by Saturn and Mars, all in Capricorn, she does more than just everyday type of cooking; it becomes a very serious hobby and anyone who comes to her home is fed a gourmet meal rarely equalled.

Ruler of the 4th in the 6th: You are not necessarily a hard worker at your job, but you surely love to work around the house, even if just puttering. You may have been raised with some definite attitudes toward giving service so that you find it hard in later years to accept money for services rendered. In many instances your background is such that you had servants around you as a child and you expect to continue in the same vein in your adult years. The Duke of Windsor, for example, had Gemini on his 4th house and Mercury in his 6th. He was brought up with strict ethics about giving service to the public (Mercury is in Cancer), and he was surrounded by servants all his life.

Nelson Rockefeller also had the ruler of his 4th, Saturn in Aries, in the 6th. But Saturn can rarely be satisfied with the status quo and he had to prove that he not only could serve the people, but be elected to do so. It was not always easy. Saturn is the focal planet of a tremendous T-square involving Mercury, Venus, Neptune and the Sun in Cancer and Uranus in Capricorn, all urging Saturn on to succeed regardless of the obstacles. Rockefeller also had servants all his life, and he worked out of his homes — the governor's mansion in Albany, New York and the vice-president's residence in Washington, D.C. His Saturn trines Jupiter and sextiles the Ascendant, helping him to partial success, but he never made the presidency he hungered for.

Ruler of the 4th in the 7th: A partner, marital or business, may be important to your feeling of security; but if the ruler of the 4th is strongly aspected, the exact contrary may happen and you could be someone who will do everything by and for yourself. You might be a very public person, by choice or heritage, yet always have a tremendous need for privacy and few people will really know what goes on behind the closed doors of your home.

Actor Charles Boyer symbolized romance to millions of movie-goers, yet few of them knew that he was married to one woman all his life, a nearly unheard of achievement in Hollywood, and that he committed suicide when she died after 44 years of marriage. Venus ruled Boyer's 4th and was in the 7th conjunct the Sun.

Composer George Gershwin had Pisces on the 4th and Neptune in Gemini in the 7th, conjunct Pluto. He worked with his brother Ira as a partner most of his short yet very productive life. Neptune and Pluto were in a grand air trine with Jupiter in Libra in the 10th and the Moon in Aquarius in the 3rd. The Sun was also in Libra in the 10th, but out of orb. This is a classic position for success, especially in communicating to the public in some artistic form such as music. But Gershwin needed the partner to get him motivated since Neptune had only a very wide square to Mercury to challenge it into action. Both brothers worked out of the home and lived together much of the time. (See chart on next page.)

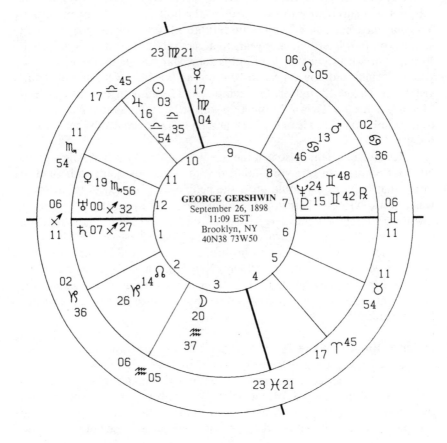

Ruler of the 4th in the 8th: You will probably be a very private person. Regardless of how friendly and outspoken you may appear (depending on the Ascendant), few will know how you really feel or what you really do. Some person's death may have made a great impression on you as a youngster and led you into a deeper approach to life, death and the pursuit of happiness than other people and at an earlier age. There may be a very persuasive quality about you and you may delve into occult realms as you become older. Reverend Jim Jones, who convinced 900 people to follow him into suicide in Guyana, had Aries on his 4th house and the ruler Mars in fiery Leo in the 8th.

In order to really feel secure or live up to what you think your parents expect of you, you may have to go through an extensive transformation. If other factors in the chart confirm this, handling other people's resources or getting support from other people will be a very important part of your root system. Many politicians have this placement.

Evangelist Billy Sunday also had this position. He had Aquarius on the 4th and the ruler Uranus in the 8th. He was an orphan and he became a baseball player; but after falling in love with a very church-involved girl, he went the straight and narrow (his Moon is in the 4th in Pisces) and he became better known than many movie stars with his slogan "Get right with God." Astronaut Buzz Aldrin, who tried to communicate via ESP from outer space, has Virgo on the 4th with Neptune conjunct the IC and the ruler Mercury in Aquarius in the 8th, conjunct the Sun.

Ruler of the 4th in the 9th: Your parents may have given you a solid background where religion and philosophy are concerned. A university or college education may be important to you. Your parents could have been born in a foreign country, or there may have been many foreign or strange cultural influences in your youth. You may live far from your place of birth or be very curious about far away places and may enjoy collecting *objets d'art* from foreign countries. You may even own land or some property in a location rather distant from where you reside.

Desi Arnaz came to the United State from Cuba at age 17. His 4th house Virgo cusp is ruled by Mercury in Aquarius in the 9th, conjunct Uranus and Venus, putting a lot of emphasis on the 9th house, especially since the Sun and Mars are also there. Mercury inconjuncts Saturn, showing the many adjustments he needed to make, not only when the family fled Cuba, but years before, when he was trying to live up to parental (especially his father's) expectations. If the ruler has many tension producing aspects, you can find it very difficult to live up to the high aims inspired by one or both of your parents in your early youth.

Ruler of the 4th in the 10th: Both parents will be most important in your life, since the 4th and 10th represent the parental axis. If you come from a traditional type home where the father was the authoritarian figure, he may have ruled the roost with a rather heavy hand, and if the ruler has many challenging aspects, you may rebel against any form of authority as a result. Angela Davis, beautiful black revolutionary, has Cancer on the 4th and the Moon in Aquarius in the 10th.

Patty Hearst's parents, (see her chart in Volume II) especially her father and the Hearst fortune she will inherit, played a crucial part in her upbringing and her subsequent kidnapping. She has Sagittarius on the cusp of the 4th house and the ruler Jupiter is in Gemini in the 10th in exact square to Mercury in Pisces. Quite often when the ruler of the 4th is in the 10th, your security can be found through one or both of the parents. In Patty's case security may be found through the money she will inherit; however, with Mars in the 4th involved in a T-square, it is questionable how much peace she will ever find within herself.

Both Robert and John Kennedy (chart in Volume II) have this rulership placement and their father was very influential in their lives. We have seen many examples of individuals who prefer staying home to a career in spite of a strong 10th house public influence. They may do some occasional work in order to earn a living, but they really prefer not to be out there in the world competing and facing open criticism. However, in the privacy of their own four walls they are outgoing, well functioning and even assertive.

Ruler of the 4th in the 11th: With this placement you may have grown up in a home where your friends were always welcome and allowed to stay overnight; possibly they even lived with you at times. Your early upbringing could have encouraged you to become quite goal oriented and you may have found your priorities while still living at home. Indira Gandhi, twice elected Prime Minister of India, knew early in life that she wanted to emulate her father Jawaharlal Nehru; she has Scorpio on the 4th house and Pluto is in Cancer in the 11th. (Her chart is on next page.) Sometimes with this position one of the parents is absent through death or divorce and a family friend becomes a substitute parent.

In the home you make for yourself there may be some stepchildren or adopted children and if you do not use the ruler positively, your daily life could become quite hectic. Sally Struthers for example, has Capricorn on her 4th house cusp and the ruler Saturn is in Leo in the 11th house, conjunct Pluto. She is a very active member of a world organization through which one can adopt displaced children; you may have seen her picture in many magazines via which she begged others to join her in this worthwhile venture.

Ruler of the 4th in the 12th: There is a tremendous inner, hidden strength within you that you can call on when needed and which surprises people who do not know you intimately. If your planetary aspects are used positively, you can truly be the Rock of Gibraltar; if these aspects are used negatively, you may dissipate your energies and your insecurities can lead to poor health as one way of escape. Your home will always be very important to you and will serve as a refuge to which you need to withdraw in order to recharge your batteries. You need a corner — regardless of how large or small it may be — that you can call your own and to which you can retreat without being disturbed.

The outside world may think it knows you, but the face you show is not the real you — that person is only known to those who share your home. There may be some secrets surrounding your early background that others are not aware of, some skeleton in the familial closet, or there may be even a drinking or drug problem of a family member which you hope to keep hidden.

Sometimes you wish to hide your entire background, as did Adolf Hitler (see chart in Volume II) whose 4th house Aquarius was ruled by Uranus in Libra in the 12th. Both Venus and Mars inconjuncted the ruler while

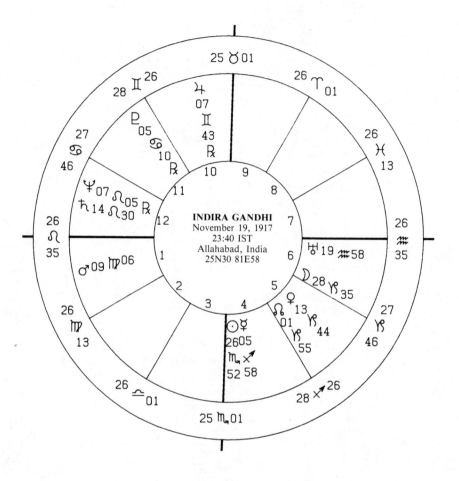

25 ♉ 01

28 ♊ 26
26

26 ♈ 01

27
♋
46

♇ 05
10 ♋
℞

♃ 07
♊ 43 ℞

10   9

11

8

26 ♓ 13

♆ 07 ♌ 05 ℞
♄ 14 ♌ 30

26
♌
35

12

1

INDIRA GANDHI
November 19, 1917
23:40 IST
Allahabad, India
25N30 81E58

7

26
♒
35

♂ 09 ♍ 06

2

3   4

5

6

⛢ 19 ♒ 58

☽ 28 ♑ 35

26
♍
13

☉ ☿
26 05
♏ ⚷
52 58

♀ 13 ♑
☊ 01 ♑
♑ 44
55

27
♑
46

26 ♎ 01

28 ♐ 26

25 ♏ 01

Mercury opposed it. This was not an easy pattern to work with, since the adjustments necessary for a positive feeling about himself or his home life would have to come through some other planet. Uranus had no easy answers for him.

Lesson 5
Fifth House Rulers

This house is still on the personal and subjective side of the horoscope. Me and mine (1st and 2nd) and my neighborhood and my home (3rd and 4th) lead to "my" way of growing, or reaching out just far enough to taste some of the pleasures and joys of what the world has in store for "me." The 5th house is represented by Leo and its natural ruler is the Sun, so here is where you want to shine. It is a house of life which brings with it the energy, enthusiasm and motivating power of fire. The warmth of fire reaches out toward others, which is why this is the house of love given. The love you give here is neither the affection of Venus nor the sexual drive of Mars; it is love from the heart, the Leo principle.

Since each house is always conditioned by what goes before, the succedent 5th house is partly the result of the 4th. Your background and upbringing and the nurturing given you by your parents prepare you for your first giving or creative effort. Whether that creativity is love given, an artistic talent expressed, or the children you create as you mature, it is all part of a joyful step that you take into your own future.

Ruler of the 5th in the 1st: Being creative in some field is the keynote of your life. If the ruler is Venus, the Moon or Sun, you could have a need to totally express your emotional attitudes in a socially acceptable way. Your creativity could be on the inventive level if Uranus or Pluto is involved, literary if the planet is Mercury or Neptune, and musical if it is Saturn. Quite a few sports figures have Aries on the cusp of the 5th house and Mars in the 1st, such as heavy weight champion Max Schmeling and track great Wilma Rudolph. In Wilma's case the energy of Mars, dignified in its own house, helped her to recover from a crippling polio attack at the age of four to go on to win important races in the 1960 Olympics. (See her chart below.)

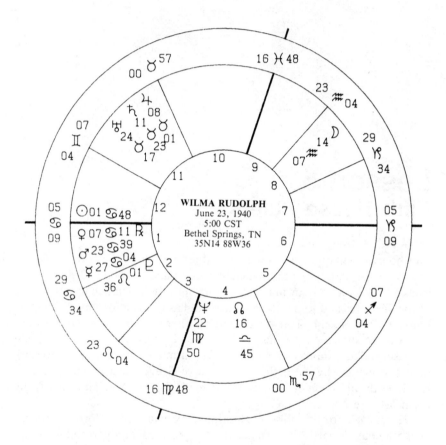

WILMA RUDOLPH
June 23, 1940
5:00 CST
Bethel Springs, TN
35N14 88W36

People with this placement are very close to their children (if they have any) and will make every effort to have good ties with them. Improper use of the energy may cause a bit of indulgence of your offspring; but when the planet is positively integrated into the chart, your relationship with your children can be very rewarding.

Ruler of the 5th in the 2nd: This seems to be the placement of people who make money from their creative endeavors, whether it is composing like Ferde Grofe (whose chart is on page 42), or conducting like Arturo

Toscanini; acting like Marlon Brando and Farrah Fawcett or comedy like Jack Benny. (Charts for the last four people are in Volume II.)

Your value system relates directly to your ability to express your feelings of love, affection and romance. On another level, your income may derive from your investments in real estate or the stock market, and if the ruling planet is well aspected, you may have an uncanny ability for gambling and winning. Children and products related to them may offer an avenue of earning. However, with very challenging aspects it would be wise for you to be cautious in the areas of investing and gambling, especially if the planet involved is Mars, Uranus or Neptune. You would also be wise to avoid overindulging your offspring. There may be a tendency to regard your children as possessions.

Farrah Fawcett has Scorpio on the cusp of the 5th house and Pluto is in the 2nd in Leo, showing very clearly her meteoric rise to fame and recognition and the subsequent earning power. She may feel that what she earns through her 5th house acting is never enough, because Pluto conjuncts Saturn and opposes both Mars and the Sun. Until she learns to handle all this energy in a positive way, it may very well cause problems in her estimation of her self worth.

Ruler of the 5th in the 3rd: You may be daring and adventurous and enjoy fast cars, fast planes and fast living, especially if the planet is Mars, Jupiter or Uranus. On another level creative communication could be your forte and you could be attracted to law, theater or politics. With positive development of energy, this placement may indicate an ability to come across well to children, your own or other people's, and thus you could enjoy teaching. You have an interest in travel, and work in this field is likely if other indications in the chart concur.

Aviator Charles Lindbergh (see chart in Volume II) had Aries on the 5th cusp and Mars in Aquarius in the 3rd, providing him with energy and daring in order to try something unique in aviation annals. With Mars sextile to the Moon and conjunct Venus, his courageous venture had a positive outcome. If Venus or the Sun is the ruler and you are not handling the aspect well, you may be reticent about entering into any love relationship.

Ruler of the 5th in the 4th: The 5th house shows how we express our love. If the ruler is in the 4th house, a love of home and family is usually indicated unless the planet has very challenging aspects. This placement also affords the opportunity to find creative outlets at home, possibly as a writer (Eugene O'Neill) or composer (Frederic Chopin, whose chart is in Volume II.) You may be successful at investing your capital in real estate of some kind; or you may be a person who opens your home to youngsters in need of guidance and nurturing, as does one of our clients who has Cancer on the 5th house cusp and the Moon in Gemini in the 4th conjunct the Sun in Cancer.

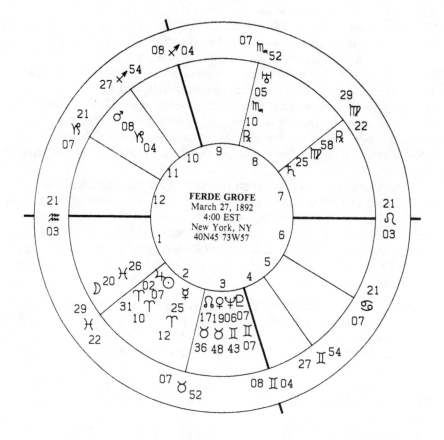

Walt Disney (chart in Volume II) with Capricorn on the 5th cusp and Saturn in Capricorn in the 4th conjunct Jupiter and Mars and square the Moon, is a good example of the use of creative energy invested in a folksy, appealing business that eventually involved people and children (5th house) from all over the world.

Ruler of the 5th in the 5th: Depending on the aspects, of course, you can be a creative genius, especially in the fields of art, composing or performing music. You may find it difficult to settle for one area of expertise if Mercury, Mars, Aries or Gemini are involved. Socially oriented, you like and need approbation; therefore you are often "on stage," whether or not you are actually in the performing arts.

Children will either be very important to you or they won't play any role at all in your life. With challenging aspects you venture any dare and may well be attracted to risky pursuits. This placement often gives an inordinate love of gambling, especially if the energy is not properly integrated into the chart.

Barbra Streisand (her chart is on page 188), with Cancer on the 5th house cusp and the Moon in Leo in the 5th, epitomizes the creativity and performing ability of this position. The conjunction to Pluto indicates the intensity with which she pursues her goals, the square to the Sun and Mercury indicates the obstacles she had to overcome before she achieved monetary success and professional acceptance.

Ruler of the 5th in the 6th: Your field of work may involve children, creative self-expression as with journalist Ernie Pyle (see chart in Volume II), or sports as with boxers Jack Dempsey and Sugar Ray Robinson, baseball great Henry Aaron, basketball star Jerry Lucas and jockey Billy Hartack. You may be the person who loves work so much that you become a workaholic. If the ruler is not well integrated, the reverse side of the coin is your enjoyment of playing; if this is carried to extremes, you do not like to work at all.

A client in our files has Virgo on the 5th house cusp with Mercury in Libra in the 6th house opposing the Moon and square to Saturn. This woman is such a dedicated teacher that she spends her weekends preparing things to make learning more stimulating for her students. Henry Mancini (see Volume II for his chart), the prominent conductor composer, has artistic Taurus on the cusp of the 5th and Venus in communicative Gemini in the 6th, so you can understand his ability to work at creating the beautiful sound of "Moon River."

Ruler of the 5th in the 7th: This promises either great accord or horrendous discord with your partner or the public. Many prominent actors and actresses, people who need to have the spotlight focused on them, have this placement. You seem to wield a lot of influence over other people, but you are most vulnerable because you feel such a strong need to have these people as an approving audience. You seek a partner whom you view as romantic and fun loving, but until you integrate the planetary energy properly, you may be fickle and demanding in partnership and even in your dealings with the general public.

Marilyn Monroe had Sagittarius on the 5th house cusp and the ruler Jupiter in Aquarius in the 7th house, very challengingly aspected. It squared Saturn, opposed Neptune and conjuncted the Moon. She had many lessons to learn about romantic partnership, as demonstrated by three failed marriages; but she also projected an image of romantic appeal, due perhaps in part to Jupiter sextile Venus. (Her chart is on page 111.) Sometimes this signifies the rather old-fashioned attitude of someone who can enjoy love and romance only with a fiance or marriage partner.

Ruler of the 5th in the 8th: This can be a powerhouse placement for financial success. You seem to have an innate understanding of how money and its usage functions. When there are flowing aspects, you do well with investments and the management of finances, even being a fortunate gambler and speculator. You are fun loving and somewhat daring in your approach to life and death matters. If there are challenging aspects, you may have to face financial or sexual hang-ups and may even need psychiatric therapy at some time in your life. There could be the premature loss of a child if other factors in the chart support it.

Convicted murderer Richard Speck has Aquarius on the 5th cusp, indicating an unconventional approach in his romantic inclinations. Uranus is in sensual Taurus in his 8th house, conjunct limiting Saturn and opposition to Mercury. This stressful combination caused him to feel inadequate both sexually and romantically, and probably contributed to the mental imbalance that precipitated his murdering of seven nurses.

Ruler of the 5th in the 9th: Travel for pleasure to far away places marks this placement, as well as the ability to be creative in literature and related fields. With the ruler of the house of children in the house of teaching, obviously you can make learning fun and therefore, you are an excellent teacher when you use the planetary energy in a positive way. Again, this seems to indicate an ability for sports, especially the kind that require you to travel, probably due to the underlying Jupiterian influence.

Golfer Cary Middlecoff has Cancer on the 5th and the Moon in Sagittarius in the 9th house and he travels the pro golf circuit. Bob Mathias, the Olympics decathlon champ and congressional representative from Bakersfield, California, has Aries on the 5th and Mars in Leo in the 9th trine Uranus and the Ascendant. The grand fire trine indicates enthusiasm and the need for achievement and with the ruler of the 5th in the 9th, both sports and politics provide an avenue for him. He also runs a most successful boy's camp in the High Sierras. (See his chart on next page.)

Ruler of the 5th in the 10th: With proper use of the planetary energies, this placement marks you as the person who achieves recognition for your creative, artistic, musical or acting ability. You strongly feel the need to be in the spotlight and to be noticed for your talent in whatever field it lies. The list of prominent people with this placement is endless. In art we have Pablo Picasso with Jupiter, the ruler of his 5th in Taurus in the 10th; Vincent Van Gogh has Scorpio on the 5th and Pluto in the 10th conjunct Uranus and Mercury. Universal genius Albert Schweitzer has Aquarius on the 5th and Uranus in Leo involved in a grand cross. (See these charts in Volume II.) Dancer Mitzi Gaynor has Neptune in the 10th ruling Pisces on the 5th house cusp.

Sometimes you may have a son or daughter who becomes famous in his or her own right as does actress Ann Sothern who has Capricorn on the 5th and Saturn well aspected in the 10th. Her daughter Tish Sterling is also an accomplished actress. With difficult aspects your many fickle romances may attract unwelcome attention or there may be a long struggle before you achieve success and recognition.

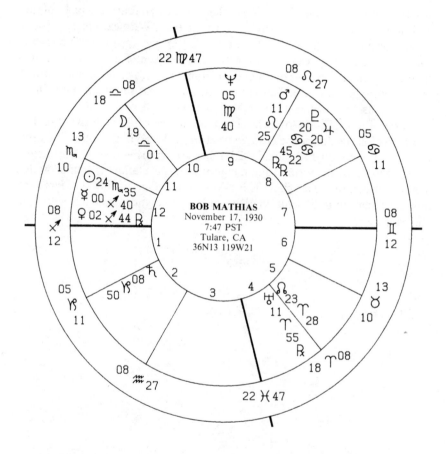

Ruler of the 5th in the 11th: You are very loving and generous to your friends who are legion. Politics and related fields are your bailiwick. You function well as host or hostess, since entertaining comes naturally to you and you are comfortable in almost any social situation. Unless you are using the energy very negatively, you are good friends with your children and their intimates.

Sometimes this placement indicates the dilettante who parties life away, flitting from one social soiree to another like heiress Barbara Hutton (her chart is in Volume II) who had Cancer on the 5th and the Moon in Capricorn in the 11th house conjunct Uranus and opposed to Neptune. Her lack of perspective caused her to feel that she could never be liked for herself alone and her emotional insecurity and loneliness caused her to fail at matrimony seven times. If there are difficult aspects to the ruler, you may choose to be a loner.

Ruler of the 5th in the 12th:　Your pleasure is often found through solitude and deep research into things relating to the past. With extremely difficult aspects or improper handling of the planetary energy, you could experience sorrow through your relationships with your children. There is the possibility of confinement because of an overwhelming need to gamble, not just with money but with your life. This can be the placement for creative writing if the planet is Mercury, Saturn or Neptune.

Poet Emily Dickinson who lived an uneventful, reclusive life had Capricorn on the 5th house cusp and Saturn in Virgo in the 12th. She drew from her deepest inner resources (12th house) to write her poetry, which combined spare lyricism (Saturn) and metaphysical speculation with unorthodox meter and diction. (Her chart is in Volume II.) One of our students with this placement in a difficult chart has a Down's Syndrome child who is in an institution.

Lesson 6
Sixth House Rulers

Cadent, one of the houses of substance, represented by Virgo and in the flat chart ruled by Mercury, the 6th house traditionally is the house of work, health and service. It is still a personal "me"-oriented house. It represents "my" attitude toward giving service. Will I give it willingly or consider it a chore? Will I analyze and dissect it or enjoy it? Will it guide me into my future career (the 10th is the next house of substance) or will it at least support my home needs which it should, being the 2nd house (income) from the 5th (creativity). If the needs are frustrated, if the 5th house does not permit "me" to express, health problems may ensue.

There are a few controversial issues involved here which we would like to discuss. First the HEALTH: Most astrologers are not doctors, and unless schooled in medicine or some related field, we would strongly urge you to stay away from medical, and even nutritional advice, except for the most basic astrological principles. (Aries represents the head, Pisces the feet, etc.) Second, the word SERVICE: We have found that this does not necessarily mean the self-sacrificing or self-effacing act often understood as the word "service" — that is more a 12th house type of giving. In the 6th house, service seems to apply to work done for free or for pay.

The 6th house also shows your habit patterns, routine matters, employees or servants, food, diet and pets.

Ruler of the 6th in the 1st: The kind of work you do must give you personal satisfaction; just doing it for money is not enough for you. Work, in fact, is a way of fulfillment, and you are likely to participate in volunteer activity, if your financial situation permits, just as long as you feel you are making a contribution. Even with the most difficult aspects to the ruler, which many astrologers feel leads to ill health (6th house health/1st house the person's body), we have found that if the same energies are productively used, there is little time or inclination left for sickness.

Many public servants, as politicians like to be called, have this placement. We have two students who have Virgo on the cusp of the 6th and Mercury in Taurus in the 1st. One owns a restaurant (she also has the Sun in Taurus); the other (her Sun is in Aries) works as a waitress, but probably not for long.

Sports reporter Howard Cosell has Saturn in Virgo in the 1st house. It rules his 6th and is in difficult opposition to Venus and Uranus, and it is also part of a yod to his Aries Sun. These kinds of aspects are often misused and could lead to delicate health and a high tension nervous system; yet positively integrated into the chart, as in Cosell's case, they result in a hardworking individual who can outlast many a competitor. (His chart can be found in Volume II.)

Ruler of the 6th in the 2nd: You need to earn money for the work or service you perform, especially if Saturn or Jupiter are the rulers in question. Joe Namath for example, has Jupiter in Cancer in the 2nd ruling his 6th house, and he admittedly seeks to receive as much money for his talents as the market will bear. (See his chart in Volume II.) Much of your work will be tied up with your innate sense of values, and the more pronounced your value system is, the more you will have to express it through the type of work you do. An example is consumer advocate Ralph Nader, who has Gemini on the 6th and Mercury in Pisces in the 2nd, conjunct Mars, with the Sun also in Pisces in the 2nd. Nader has often been compared to "David challenging Goliath" and viewed as an anomaly in a country of profits and pleasures. His values were imbued with Pisces idealism from early childhood and the close conjunction to Mars gives him the guts and impetus to take on the giant corporations.

Many people with this placement work in the field of diet or make a living through nursing, public health agencies and related areas.

Ruler of the 6th in the 3rd: More often than not your work is connected with the media or with some realm of communication. Writers Philip Roth and Scott Fitzgerald, publisher Bennett Cerf and movie makers Vittorio de Sica and Walt Disney all serve as examples of people who used different forms of communication through work. (See Disney chart in Volume II.)

Brothers and sisters may assist you or you could work with a sibling. Billy Carter has Gemini on the 6th house and Mercury in Aries in the 3rd.

He and his brother Jimmy owned a peanut farm together. That some sibling problems could develop can be seen by Mercury inconjunct Neptune, ruler of the 3rd house. Billy had to learn to adjust to his brother's becoming president of the United States and to the resulting shift of management of the peanut farm which was put into a blind trust.

We have a client who is a bus driver and his greatest ambition is to drive a taxi which he wants to own. Commuting and transportation are 3rd house affairs. Jupiter which rules his 6th house is in the 3rd in a partile trine to Saturn. We think that he may realize his dream.

Children who have the ruler of the 6th in the 3rd well aspected often are early talkers. If the ruler is not well integrated or has very challenging aspects, you may become slovenly in your habits or have a hard time establishing a good routine. If you are in a position of authority, you love to communicate with your employees and probably keep in touch by sending them all kinds of memos.

Ruler of the 6th in the 4th: Some people with this placement just love to putter in the home, never resting until every window sparkles, every weed is pulled and every leak sealed. Should the ruler have tension-producing aspects, you dislike being Mr. or Mrs. Fixit and will do anything to avoid those chores, preferring to pay someone else to do them for you. In fact, we have quite a few students who have the ruler of the 6th in the 4th and who so dislike housework that they went to work in order to be able to afford a cleaning lady to do the "dumb routine cleaning" for them.

You may be involved in some work that you can perform from your home. This may involve writing as with Anne Morrow Lindbergh and Ernest Hemingway (see his chart on page 140), keeping books for small companies or working in real estate. We have found that this position frequently leads to having pets in the home or working with animals, especially if the ruler is well integrated in the chart. One of our students has Aries on the 6th and Mars is in the 4th, part of a grand water trine; she works with the dolphins at Sea World, a marine amusement park. You may be pushed into work by one of your parents, such as actress Judy Garland (see chart in Volume I), whose mother was instrumental in putting her on the stage when she was a little girl. Garland's Jupiter in Libra ruling her 6th, is in the 4th conjunct Saturn and the North Node.

Ruler of the 6th in the 5th: If you have this position, you really love to work and always know how to find some occupation that you find pleasurable, especially if the ruler is well integrated into the chart; if it is not, or if the ruler is Jupiter or Venus, you may find any excuse not to work and spend your life dabbling at this and that. In certain instances you may work very hard at a hobby or do some kind of volunteer work that you really enjoy.

Many people who work in a creative endeavor have the ruler of the 6th in the 5th. One of our clients is a goldsmith. She learned this trade as a young woman and was going to make it her career, but she married, had children and somehow never got back into the work market — yet she has been designing and making jewelry for herself and her friends all these years. She has Pisces on the 6th and the ruler Neptune in Leo in the 5th house.

Zsa Zsa Gabor (see chart in Volume II) has Aquarius on the 6th house and the ruler Uranus is in Aquarius in the 5th. She used love and romance in a most creative and unique way as part of her work, appearing on television talk shows to discuss her marriages and amorous adventures. Since in her case the ruler of the 5th, Saturn, is in the 10th, she also used love and romance for her career and multiple changes of status — a double confirmation in this case.

Ruler of the 6th in the 6th: You should be the workaholic of the zodiac, yet we have found that in order to be a hard worker you need squares and oppositions to the ruler to get you going. You need a challenge or Saturn as the ruling planet so you will stick it out. With trines and sextiles to the planet, this position seems to produce a lot of part-time or on and off workers.

If there are too many tension producing aspects or the energy is not positively used, you may fall into poor habit patterns, be unreliable, become a loner or give in to sickness. Marlon Brando has Taurus on the 6th house cusp; the ruler Venus in Taurus in the 6th has only two aspects, an opposition to the Ascendant and an inconjunct to Saturn. He is known to be a loner and his habit pattern is not the best. Errol Flynn's Moon in Cancer rules his 6th house, it squares Saturn, inconjuncts the Ascendant, and makes no other aspects. He led a rather decadent life and died relatively young as a result of his overindulgence. (Both men's charts can be found in Volume II.)

A well-integrated ruler often results in the typical pet lover. Three clients come to mind who have this placement; one owns a pet shop, one works for a veterinarian and one raises purebred German shepherds. You may be very diet conscious and if Jupiter or Venus are involved, love all types of fad foods. If Neptune or Pisces are prominent, you should be careful, since you could have allergic reactions to different drugs.

Ruler of the 6th in the 7th: This position seems to manifest in two ways: You love to work in a very public way as does daredevil Evel Kneivel or work only has meaning when you do it with a partner, such as former first lady Rosalynn Carter or singer Joan Sutherland. (The two ladies' charts are in Volume II.) The latter is the more commonly found manifestation. Some vice presidents have this placement and some well known often married men also fall into this category. Hermann Hesse (see chart in Volume II) and Charles Chaplin (Mars in Taurus in the 7th ruling Aries on the cusp of the 6th) are two examples.

You could work in the legal field handling contracts and agreements or you may specialize as a divorce lawyer. Since the 7th house indicates your attitude toward marriage, you could feel that marriage means hard work and run away from it, if you have not learned to handle the ruler intelligently.

We have found that many of our clients and students who have the ruler of the 6th in the 7th prefer to stay on an equal footing with their mates or live-in partners, working and sharing household chores and expenses.

Ruler of the 6th in the 8th: If the ruler is well integrated in the chart, it will be easy for you to get support for much of the work you do and whatever service you decide to render. If Pluto or Scorpio are involved, you may be engaged in some kind of research. Sex could play an important role in the type of work you do or the manner in which you execute it. Hedy Lamarr was a symbol of sex and of rather overt sensuality, manifested by the movie *Ecstasy* which brought her to fame. She has Jupiter in Aquarius in the 8th, conjunct Uranus in the 1st and square Mercury in the 5th. Here the 6th house of work is involved with the 8th house of sex and the 5th house of romance, love, pleasure and entertainment.

Woolworth heiress Barbara Hutton didn't have to work at all; her daddy and his money supported her throughout life. She had Leo on the cusp of the 6th and the Sun in the 8th trine Neptune. She could never find her proper role in life, neither through work nor service; unfortunately an unfulfilled 6th house can take its toll in health, which it did with Hutton. (Her chart is in Volume II.)

Your work may involve handling other people's money, as did financier Bernard Baruch and as do several of our clients who work in banks or stock brokerage houses and have this placement in their charts.

Ruler of the 6th in the 9th: Not too surprising is the fact that many of our globe-trotting students and clients have this placement. One young lady is married to a navy officer and she has never lived in one place longer than two years. She's a map maker — world maps of course! Another one deals in real estate exchanges for vacations; in exchange for your home, you can rent a similar one any place in the world. She has Capricorn on the 6th and Saturn in Aries in the 9th. She makes excellent money at it, by the way.

Scientist Albert Einstein (see his chart on next page) who used his insight, higher mind, idealism and intuition in his work, had Jupiter, ruler of his 6th in the 9th in Aquarius involved in a T-square with Pluto and Uranus. He was a professor at two different universities, which is fitting work for a person whose 6th house ruler is in the 9th.

The less positive application of this placement is exemplified by a client who has Virgo on his 6th house cusp and the ruler Mercury is in Gemini in the 9th house, conjunct the Sun and both are involved in a T-square with Neptune in Virgo and the Moon in Pisces. He gets car-, train-, sea- and air-

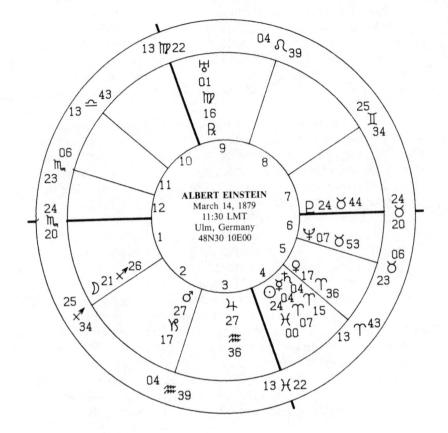

sick, and when he gets to his destination, he catches every bug and invariably returns from a trip with a sore throat, cough or flu. In his own insecurity he feels best when at home, happy in his routine despite the strong 9th house or Gemini restlessness. Unfortunately for him, his work requires that he travel.

Ruler of the 6th in the 10th: The classic interpretation, especially when positively used, is that your work is also your career and that it will bring you the ego satisfaction you are looking for. Your habits and your daily routine will be well organized and you pride yourself on how much you can achieve in any given twelve-hour period. If Saturn or Mars is involved, your timing may also be exquisite, giving you great physical or athletic prowess such as boxer Muhammad Ali with Capricorn on the 6th and Saturn in Taurus in the 10th (see his chart in Volume I); or fastball pitcher, Sandy Koufax (his chart is below) who has Leo on the 6th and the Sun in Capricorn in the 10th.

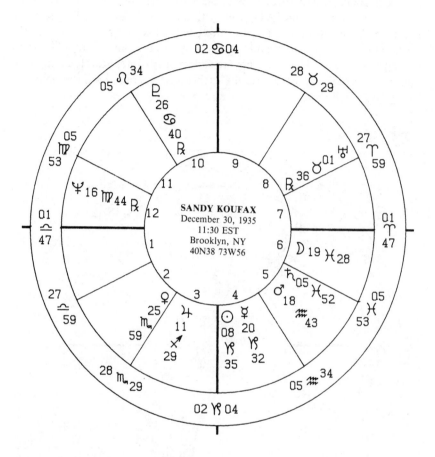

With very challenging aspects you may feel pressured by one of your parents to work harder than you really want to, or to perform some service for which you would just as soon be paid. Even someone with a well-integrated chart may feel very duty bound with this placement, as does Queen Beatrix of Holland (her chart is in Volume II), whose Mercury in Capricorn in the 10th rules her 6th house.

This position is often indicative of leadership potential. At the very least you are ambitious and want to succeed, to better your workmanship, to climb to the top of the ladder. You seem to pay attention to gossip and care what others think or say about you. At times this will produce the contrary effect — you will work very hard at being very different and doing your own thing.

Ruler of the 6th in the 11th: With the ruler of the house of work located in the house of friends, it is logical that you will form friendships and meet people to socialize with through your place of work. But you may also work for friends or they could be helpful in finding work for you. Former Vice President Walter Mondale (see his chart below) is said to owe his start in the Senate to his old friend and mentor Hubert Humphrey. Mondale's Sun in Capricorn in the 11th rules his 6th house cusp. Interestingly enough, in mundane or political astrology, the 11th house is considered the house of Congress.

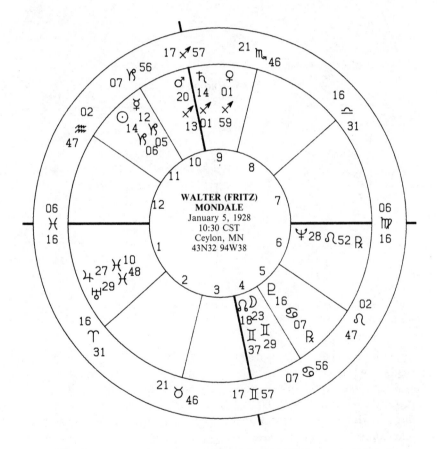

If the ruler of the 6th has many difficult aspects, you may decide you need few or no friends at all and be the loner instead. In our experience we have found that many of the loners pick "man's best friend," a dog or two or three, to replace the human companionship. On the other hand you may be very active in group activities and if Mercury, Jupiter or Venus are involved, you could be the typical community leader, dedicated to keeping your neighborhood clean and safe. If the 6th or 11th house is connected to the 5th, you could be a youth group leader, work with the PTA, or as a crossing guard.

Ruler of the 6th in the 12th: We have found one most interesting factor among the many friends, clients and students whose charts we have studied with this placement. They are all hard working, and when they take on more than they should, which they are in the habit of doing, they get sick instead of learning to say, "No, I can't take on this extra burden." In most cases these are minor sicknesses that last just long enough to give them a chance to catch their breath and start the cycle all over again. Only in rare cases do the ailments become serious or chronic. President Franklin D. Roosevelt (see his chart in Volume I) is one of the more drastic examples; he had Aquarius on the cusp of the 6th and Uranus in Virgo in the 12th, making only one aspect, a trine to Neptune.

Many people with this placement like to work in seclusion, by themselves, privately or behind the scenes, such as writers, composers or artists. But just as often it signifies a person who has many hidden or unknown strengths which he can use in the type of work he does.

Pope John Paul II, prince of the Roman Catholic Church, a typical 12th house institution, has Scorpio on the 6th house cusp and Pluto in the 12th house. The Pope has a rather challenging chart (see page 12) and the only trine and sextile in the horoscope are to Pluto.

You may also be very interested in research, work in such fields as oceanography or marine biology, be a nurse or a doctor, or work in one of the counseling fields.

Lesson 7
Seventh House Rulers

This is the first nonpersonal house; the "I" of the 1st house becomes the "you" of the 7th. Aries reaches out and realizes that he is not alone in this world. The 7th house is angular and a house of face-to-face or one-to-one relationships. Libra is its natural sign and Venus its natural ruler. Libra and Venus are both social in nature, therefore, this is the house where you relate to others and which describes your attitude toward marital or business partnerships as well as lawyers or agents acting in your behalf. Since it is an angular house, its actions are open and public; traditionally it is considered the house of your open enemies, the public, and your dealings with the public. The "enemies" derive from the fact that this house is in opposition to your personal embodiment, namely the Ascendant. As such it shows what you look for in others, the qualities you need to complement your strengths and weaknesses.

Ruler of the 7th in the 1st: You are a person who needs to identify strongly with a partner or the public before you can function completely as an individual. Normally a leader, unless the planet is Venus, the Moon or Neptune, you gain confidence from your ability to show other people how to do things. Often you are an exceptional teacher. Other areas where you may function well are the entertainment, sales and political fields.

Mohandas Gandhi, (see chart in Volume II), India's spiritual and political leader had Aries on the 7th house cusp and Mars in the 1st house in Scorpio. Mars was involved in a powerful T-square conjunct Venus, opposed to Jupiter and Pluto in the 7th, and square the Moon in Leo in the 10th. The trine to Uranus in the 9th house gave the necessary flow and ease for him to use all of the energy manifested through the T-square to negotiate passively and peacefully and serve as a beloved and respected leader to his people.

Some very glamorous screen stars have this placement. Elke Sommer has Pisces on the 7th and Neptune in Virgo in the 1st trine her Moon, which explains her quick rise to fame and public acceptance. Ageless Merle Oberon had Leo on the 7th cusp and the Sun in the 1st house, as does Kim Novak. Carole Landis, ill-fated glamour girl of the forties had Gemini on the 7th and an unaspected Mercury in Sagittarius in the 1st house.

Ruler of the 7th in the 2nd: This is frequently the placement of the person who marries for money or security. Certainly your partner must share your value system. This may be an indication that you earn money through the legal field or in face-to-face confrontation like heavyweight champ Max Baer who had Aries on the 7th house cusp and Mars in Sagittarius in the 2nd house opposed to Pluto.

People who have this placement often earn large salaries because of their popular public appeal. You and your partner may earn money together such as actor Paul Newman who has Cancer on the 7th house cusp and the Moon in the 2nd in Pisces. He works with his wife Joanne Woodward. Joe Namath, with Sagittarius on the 7th and Jupiter in Cancer in the 2nd is another good example. (See his chart in Volume II.)

If the planet is well integrated into the chart, you usually marry someone who earns well or is a good money manager. There is always the chance that your partner may inherit money, since your 2nd house is their 8th.

Ruler of the 7th in the 3rd: This can be the placement of a person who marries their childhood sweetheart or even a distant relative, or someone they meet through a sister or brother. You feel you must have good lines of communication with your partner and the aspects to the planet will indicate just how intellectually compatible you are.

Paul McCartney, who wrote such beautiful and enduring music with his partner, fellow Beatle John Lennon, has Virgo on the 7th house cusp and Mercury in Gemini in the 3rd house. Charles Lindbergh (see his chart in Volume II), who became famous for his solo flight to Paris, later flew all over the country with his wife photographing the terrain for map makers. One flew the plane while the other operated the camera. He had Mercury in Pisces in the 3rd house ruling his 7th cusp, and traveling with his wife was very rewarding for him. His wife Anne Morrow Lindbergh is a writer (3rd house communication), as was Robert Browning, whose wife, Elizabeth Barrett Browning, had Pisces on the 7th house and Neptune in Sagittarius in the 3rd house. They wrote to and for each other and the world. These examples all illustrate the need of communication with a partner that this placement seems to call for. (See Browning charts below and on page 61).

Ruler of the 7th in the 4th: You are a person who seeks security through partnership of some kind. Often you may marry late or not at all, because you find such contentment and happiness in your parental home and you tend to make a partner of one of your parents. However, if the energy is not properly applied, you may deny yourself the opportunity for marriage because of a sense of duty and obligation to a very demanding parent, or you may seek to replace a parent with your marriage partner.

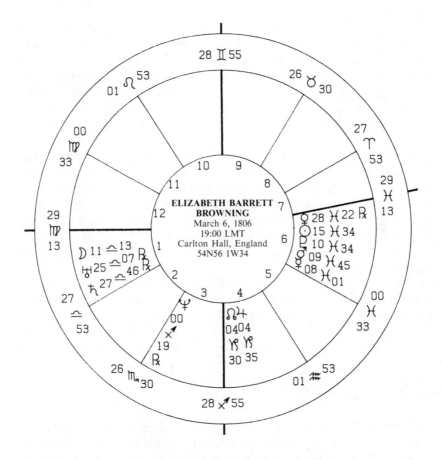

You could be a person who marries happily but whose work or public contacts take you far from your partner and that partner maintains the home while you're out doing your own thing. General George Patton (whose chart is on page 124) is a good example. He had Sagittarius on the 7th cusp and

Jupiter in Virgo in the 4th house. While he was fighting wars in foreign countries, his devoted wife maintained the home and raised the children.

Often this placement indicates a partner who stays in the background and provides the comfort, stability and haven that a very public person needs.

Ruler of the 7th in the 5th: Many really romantic people have this placement. With the ruler of the house of marriage in the romantic, creative, idealistic 5th house, you usually marry for love — sometimes in the face of adversity as did Robert Browning (see his chart on page 61) who had Mercury in Taurus in the 5th ruling his Gemini 7th cusp. In spite of her family's objections, he persisted in his suit for Elizabeth Barrett and eventually they married and were very happy together.

Then again, you may have stars in your eyes like Elizabeth Taylor who has Aries on the 7th house cusp and Mars in Pisces in the 5th. (See her chart on page 69.) Seven times she has married for love. Needless to say, her Mars opposes Neptune and squares Jupiter, and it has taken her some time to integrate all that energy in a constructive way. On another level, your creative (5th house) energy may be well received by the public (7th house), or you may be creative with a partner either in business or in the arts.

Ruler of the 7th in the 6th: Often you meet your life's partner through or at your work. Or you may marry and then go into a business together. This can be the placement of someone who enjoys working in partnership with one or more people, or giving service in some way through legal or psychological counseling. Sigmund Freud (see his chart in Volume II) had Taurus on the 7th house cusp and Venus in Aries in the 6th, and he founded psychoanalysis — the means of helping others by counseling them through the free association of ideas.

We have as clients a young couple who both have the ruler of the 7th in the 6th; they met at work and have since opened their own very successful business where they spend 10 hours a day working together.

With stressful aspects, this planetary placement may indicate an attraction to someone who has health problems, either physical or mental, thus affording you the opportunity to be supportive and helpful. Or your attitude toward partnership could be one of "all work and no play," especially if Saturn is involved.

Ruler of the 7th in the 7th: At your best, you identify strongly with your partner and seek a meaningful and enduring relationship; but if you aren't using the planetary energy in its most positive way, you may flit from one partner to another, seeking personal gratification in the quantity not the quality of the contacts you make.

This placement seems to indicate a need for an involvement with public adulation and approbation. It often brings you before the public in a capacity

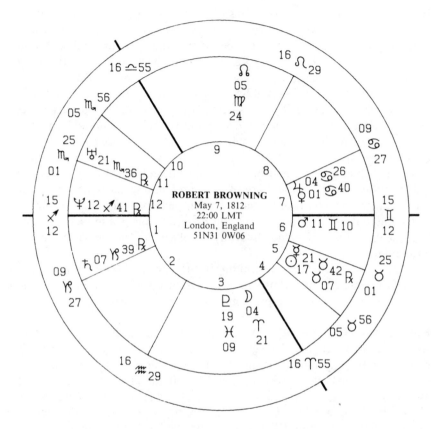

ROBERT BROWNING
May 7, 1812
22:00 LMT
London, England
51N31 0W06

of leadership. Both Adolf Hitler and John F. Kennedy (whose charts are in Volume II), had Aries on the 7th house cusp and Mars in Taurus in the 7th. Jacqueline Kennedy Onassis also has Taurus on the 7th and Venus in Gemini there. Since Venus is opposed to Saturn, it's understandable that she did not seek the limelight; rather it was thrust upon her through her relationship with her partners.

If the ruler of the 7th house is the Sun, Uranus or Pluto, you tend to seek a strong and dominating partner, a "take charge" person, and if the aspects to the planet are challenging, there is a never ending contest of wills. If the planet that rules the house is the Moon, Neptune or Venus, you are generally attracted to a more submissive type person, one whom you feel at home with. If the planet is Saturn, you seek steadiness and often find this with a mature person or even someone you've known for a long time. Jupiter or Mercury ruling the 7th and in it, tends to draw you to people who espouse the same philosophy as you and to those with whom you find it easy to communicate.

Ruler of the 7th in the 8th: This often is a very political placement indicating that others will back your ideas and goals with their financial and moral support. Josef Stalin had Cancer on the 7th house cusp and the Moon in Virgo in the 8th, as does Ted Kennedy. (See charts in Volume II.) They both achieved high position through the support of the public.

You seek help and financial backing from your partner and whether or not you receive it is judged by the aspects to the planet in question. Sometimes your marriage is based primarily on a good sex relationship and you and your partner have little else in common. This placement seems to give a lot of public sex appeal. Actor Clint Eastwood has Venus in Cancer in the 8th ruling his 7th house cusp and singer Linda Ronstadt has Mercury in Leo in the 8th ruling her 7th house; both of them present a sexual and charismatic public image. (See charts in Volume II.) This placement also gives an ability to handle money for other people; you may function as a money manager in some capacity and are nearly always in charge of balancing the family checkbook.

We have a client with Gemini on the 7th cusp and Mercury in Cancer in the 8th house conjunct Pluto and trine Uranus. He is a psychologist who deals with clients who have problems of a sexual nature.

Ruler of the 7th in the 9th: You frequently seek a partner of a different social, ethnic or religious background than yours and may even meet this person in a foreign country. If the planet is working well in your chart, you have a good relationship with your in-laws. If the planet has challenging aspects, your liaison with a partner from such a different milieu may prove difficult and unrewarding. Barbara Hutton, the repeatedly married heiress (see her chart in Volume II), had Libra on the 7th house cusp and Venus in Sagittarius in the 9th house opposing Pluto and inconjunct Neptune, showing quite plainly her difficulty in relating to some of the foreign men she married.

With this planet well integrated into the chart, you may be a very good courtroom lawyer or a teacher who entrances your students with tales of inspiration and aspiration. You could enjoy traveling with your partner or, like one of our clients, run a travel agency with your mate.

Ruler of the 7th in the 10th: You have the potential for public recognition in the field of politics, entertainment, the arts or anything where you can make yourself heard. A partner may be very helpful to your career, promoting and prodding you to forge ahead. Quite often if Saturn is involved, the contrary occurs and you'll do anything to prove to yourself and the world that you can achieve your goals without the help of a partner or a mate.

Walt Disney and Vittorio De Sica, a couple of prominent movie makers, have Pisces on the 7th house cusp and Neptune in the 10th creating an illusion for the public. (See Disney chart in Volume II.) Helen Hayes, the extraordinary dramatic actress, also has Pisces on the 7th and illusionary Neptune in the 10th house and she was certainly encouraged by her husband, newspaperman Charlie MacArthur (Neptune sextile Venus). However, she was required to make some personal sacrifices to achieve her success (Neptune opposed Saturn). (See her chart below.)

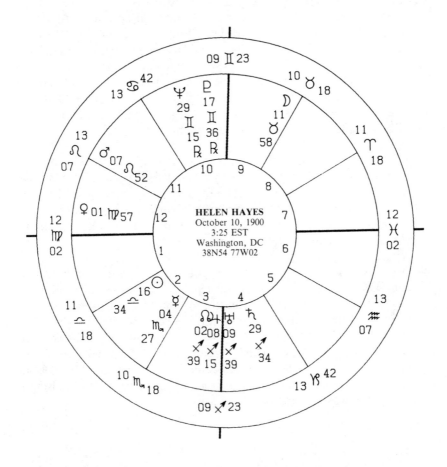

HELEN HAYES
October 10, 1900
3:25 EST
Washington, DC
38N54 77W02

You are ambitious to have your marriage succeed and seem to want a partner you can look up to; or you could seek a successful or notorious partner. Depending on the aspects to the planet, how you fare in this quest is determined from the way the energy is integrated in the chart.

Ruler of the 7th in the 11th: Your main requirement from a partner is friendship; the give and take kind because you have the need to be yourself in the partnership. You may be attracted to someone who has children that you can look after. This is frequently the placement of a person who goes into business with a friend. With different kinds of aspects, it may indicate that you are a loner who doesn't feel the need to be tied down to a marriage situation. Therefore you are quite independent as for example the famous pianist Liberace who has Cancer on the 7th house cusp and the Moon in Sagittarius in the 11th house. He is very charming and entertaining, but very self-contained and does everything as an individualist.

The other side of the coin is the often married person who feels incomplete without a partner; the "love received" attitude of the 11th house is never quite satisfied. Zsa Zsa Gabor, who has been married six times, has Neptune in Leo ruling the 7th house cusp and Mickey Rooney, at last count, married eight times, has Mercury in the 11th in Libra. It rules his 7th cusp, squares Pluto and trines the Moon, accounting in part for his ability to attract the ladies and then his impatience after he gets what he thinks he wants. (The Rooney and Gabor charts are in Volume II.)

Ruler of the 7th in the 12th: No matter how happily married you are, you always need some time and space to yourself. If the planet has challenging aspects there may often be some doubt or suspicion connected with your partner's actions and needs. Once you learn to handle these questions in your own mind, you can have a rewarding commitment; but if you let your doubt hold sway, it can ruin the relationship.

You are often the backup person in a partnership, the power behind the throne, the confidante upon whom your mate depends and uses as a sounding board. A couple of prominent political wives serve as good examples. Rosalynn Carter (see her chart in Volume II) has Pisces on the 7th house cusp and Neptune in Leo in the 12th. She was always there when Jimmy needed her and he often admittedly sought her advice. Cornelia Wallace also has Pisces on the 7th cusp and Neptune is in Virgo in the 12th. When she and George were married, he often deferred to her firsthand knowledge of political ins and outs; knowledge learned at her uncle Big Jim Folsom's knee when she was a youngster at the governor's mansion.

Lesson 8
Eighth House Rulers

The keywords usually associated with the 8th house are sex, death and transformation. This can be attributed to the fact that Scorpio is the sign we are dealing with, and in mythology as well as in astrology it is given three symbols: the lowly scorpion, representing the lower nature of man (sex); the eagle, representing a higher species ready to take wing and leave earth (death) and the phoenix, a magical bird that rises from the ashes and transforms itself. We realize that sex can represent many qualities — it can represent pure lust, for the purpose of reproduction, or a demonstration of a deep feeling of love. Death, too, has many meanings and does not always mean the death of a person; just as often it represents an idea, a thought, an act or even an illness which dies or is transformed. Surgery is also a facet of this house and often an operation brings the end (death) of a virulent disease.

Since the 8th house is the 2nd house from the 7th, it also signifies the financial, moral, spiritual or physical support you can receive from a partner or the public. It indicates legacies, wills, trusts, taxes and insurance as well as occult matters, sleep and deep research. It is succedent, a house of endings. The natural ruler is Pluto, and the co-ruler is Mars.

Ruler of the 8th in the 1st: You have a great need to show the world how you feel about 8th house matters. If you have occult leanings, you may want to demonstrate your expertise like Uri Geller, Israel's psychokinetic wonder boy who bends spoons without touching them, restarts broken clocks, etc. He has Taurus on the 8th and the ruler Venus in Scorpio in the 1st. Many people with this placement have built-in sex appeal. You don't quite know what it is, but that certain magnetic, charismatic appeal is ever present. If the ruler has many challenging aspects, you may even flaunt your sexuality at the world. Movie star Marilyn Monroe had Pisces on her 8th house cusp, and the ruler Neptune in the 1st opposed both Jupiter and the Moon and squared Saturn; this strong T-square gave her trouble throughout most of her short life. (Her chart is on page 111).

Many people with this position talk a lot about death and may even seem to court it. They are not afraid of it but it occupies their thinking. Writer Ernest Hemingway (see his chart on page 140) devoted a lot of words to death and dying and ended his life by his own hand. Three students of ours went to a seminar by Elisabeth Kubler-Ross on "dying with dignity." Not only did they go, but all of us had to listen to their dissertations on the subject again and again. All three have the ruler of the 8th in the 1st.

Ruler of the 8th in the 2nd: Unless the ruler is very difficult to integrate, other people will support you not only with words but also with financial backing, if that is your need or wish. With hard aspects your sexual excesses could cost you quite a bit of money and you would be wise to reevaluate your value system or priorities before your self worth becomes damaged.

You may gain through a partner or an inheritance and also you could be quite lucky in collecting debts, especially if Jupiter or Saturn is involved and if there are flowing aspects to the ruler of the 2nd or 8th. Many people with this position seem to be well taken care of even after a divorce, through alimony or by still working with the former partner's resources. We have two clients with this placement who are divorced. One is a banker and his former wife wants him to handle her and "their" money; Saturn which rules his 8th house is in Leo in his 2nd house. The other one owns a restaurant with his wife. Since both are good at their work, they decided to keep the business and work in it together though they are now divorced. She runs the lunch shift and he is in charge of dinner; she does most of the buying and he supervises the kitchen. He has Cancer on the 8th and his Moon is in Capricorn in the 2nd.

Anita Bryant, who has Pisces on the 8th and Neptune in Virgo in the 2nd opposed to Mercury, is an example of a person who is outspoken in her views against homosexuality (8th) which offends her sense of values (2nd).

Ruler of the 8th in the 3rd: Much like the ruler of the 8th in the 1st, you feel a need to express some of your 8th house concerns. This time, however, they are not so much part of the way you package yourself; instead, you will talk, sing, paint or write about them. For example, Elisabeth Kubler-Ross has lectured all over the world on her experiences with death and dying and that people have the right to die with dignity. She has written a book and many articles on the subject of euthanasia and has delved deeply into the possibility of life after death. She has Libra on the 8th and the ruler Venus in the 3rd. (Her chart can be found below.)

You may be the life of the party because you excel at telling risque stories or slightly off-color jokes. You could have what is commonly referred to as a "bedroom voice," that certain husky quality that sounds like a constant sexy come-on. There are other ways of expressing sex appeal, as Frank Sinatra does through his singing (see his chart in Volume II). He has Scorpio on the 8th house cusp and Pluto in Cancer in the 3rd, sextile to Mars in Leo in the 5th house of creativity and romance.

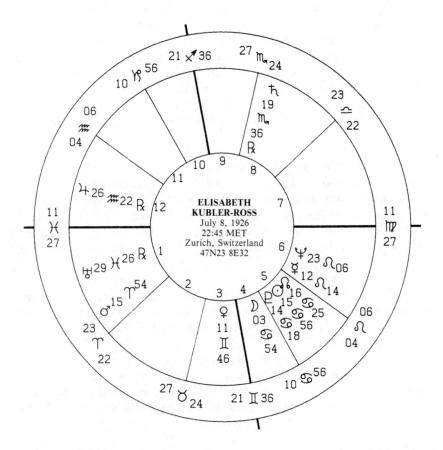

Ruler of the 8th in the 4th: One of your parents will play a large role in shaping your attitude toward sex. If you are a man and the 4th represents your mother, you may have over idealized her and may therefore demand too much of any female you encounter. This is sometimes called the "madonna complex." In a female chart this position often produces very strong women who feel they do not need a man to prove themselves, and consequently they can be ground breakers in new areas, as is the first professional female jockey Robyn Smith-Astaire (see her chart in Volume II). Another example is black revolutionary Angela Davis who brought a whole university campus into upheaval in the late sixties. Jupiter in Leo in the 4th rules her 8th house and opposes her Moon in Aquarius in the 10th; but it also trines her Venus and sextiles Saturn and she did get a lot of support in those hectic days.

Quite a few people with this placement seem to be active in real estate, either investing for themselves or earning their livelihood through it. They deal with other people's resources (8th house) and do it with land, houses or in other 4th house areas. One of our students who has Capricorn on her 8th house cusp and Saturn in Virgo in the 4th received an inheritance and immediately bought a small farm. She is still paying it off and it does not bother her, since she expects to spend most of her life there — after she is married to someone who will help her run it!

Since the 8th house shows your death and the 4th the end of your life, it is quite conceivable that if your 8th house ruler is in your 4th, you will die at home.

Ruler of the 8th in the 5th: This is the perfect example of people who present sex in a romantic and glamorous way. Many beautiful film stars have this placement, such as Marlene Dietrich (see her chart on page 8) and Zsa Zsa Gabor (see her chart in Volume II). Richard Chamberlain (see his chart in Volume II) with Venus in Aquarius in the 5th house ruling his 8th, exemplifies the male counterpart, as does Hugh Hefner whose chart is on page 69.

Jim Jones of the "People's Temple" used sex, religion, his strong power of persuasion and his magnetic personality to cajole 900 people into committing suicide with him in Guyana in 1980. The Sun rules his 8th house and is in Taurus in the 5th square Mars in Leo in the 8th. Many of the victims were children (5th).

Your children may play an important role in the way you change and transform yourself, more so than your parents, mate or career. It is as if you realize what life is all about only after they are born, and then your entire outlook changes. We have noticed this with both male and female clients and with students who have this placement.

Ruler of the 8th in the 6th: You may put a lot of work into handling your mate's resources or those of other people. Many times you work with a partner in the same place of business but are handling another aspect of it, so it is not a one-to-one relationship. If the ruler is very tension producing and you have not learned to handle the aspects, you may develop

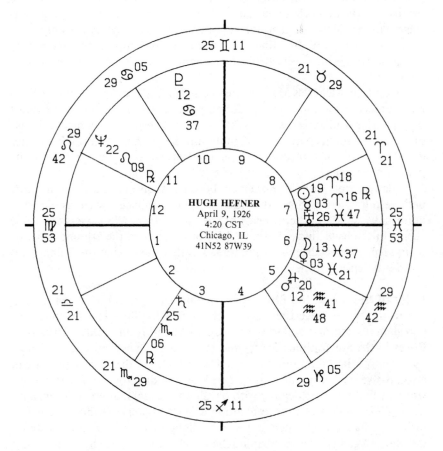

25 ♊ 11

29 ♋ 05

♇ 12 ♋ 37

21 ♉ 29

29 ♌ 42

♆ 22 ♌ 09 ℞

21 ♈ 21

25 ♍ 53

☉ 19 ♈ 18
☿ 03 ♈ 16 ℞
⚷ 26 ♓ 47

25 ♓ 53

10   9

8

HUGH HEFNER
April 9, 1926
4:20 CST
Chicago, IL
41N52 87W39

7

11

12

1

2

6   ☽ 13 ♓ 37
♀ 03 ♓ 21

3   4

5   ♃ 20
♂ 12 ♒ 41
♒ 48

29 ♒ 42

21 ♎ 21

♄ 25 ♏ 06 ℞

21 ♏ 29

25 ♐ 11

29 ♑ 05

elimination problems or your health may play tricks on you. A good sex life is important to your physical and psychological well-being and if the ruler is in a strong position, you will do almost anything to fulfill your needs. The Duke of Windsor had Virgo on the 8th house and Mercury in Cancer in the 6th; he gave up a country and a crown to attain sexual fulfillment with his duchess. Charles Chaplin had Gemini on his 8th house cusp and Mercury in Aries in the 6th opposed to Uranus. He pursued many women, wooed many more and married quite a few.

You may be involved in some form of research and work hard in your investigative capacity, yet this may not be your career but something you do on the side as a service or to help others. We have two clients with this placement and they spend much of their free time helping in an astrological research project, but they earn a living at something else. One is a computer analyst, and the other is a salesperson.

Ruler of the 8th in the 7th: Your sexual attitude may be quite prim and prudish, to the point that you can really enjoy yourself only with your marriage partner. Since the scorpion, the eagle and the phoenix are only steps of development, you may find that your own growth potential and ability to transform becomes very dependent upon the relationship you have with your mate.

Cult leader Charles Manson created a "family" and was "married" to many of its members — marriage for purposes of sex only. Jupiter, the planet of expansion and excess is in his 7th house in Scorpio ruling his 8th house of death. He got his partners to commit murder for him. Manson is a rather drastic example of someone who has not learned to properly integrate the planetary energies.

Many people with this placement become involved in handling the partner's resources. In business they are the money managers whereas the partner usually handles other aspects of the partnership. We have quite a few clients in the legal field who have 8th house rulers in the 7th and most of them seem to specialize in corporate law rather than being the flamboyant murder defense attorneys seen on television.

Ruler of the 8th in the 8th: Many people who present a certain sex image to the public have the ruler of the 8th in the 8th. That includes the sex/glamour prototype like Ava Gardner (Aquarius on the 8th, Uranus in Pisces in the 8th conjunct Mars) and strip teaser Gypsy Rose Lee (Cancer on the cusp, the Moon in Leo in the 8th house). On the other hand, it can also involve you in occult dealings, or like film director Roman Polanski, you may make movies dealing with occult and sexual matters. (*Rosemary's Baby, Chinatown* and *Tess* to mention a few.) Polanski's whole life is full of bizarre happenings, such as the cult killing of his wife Sharon Tate by the Manson gang, his own escaping the gas chamber in Auschwitz as a child and his involvement with young women (minors) which caused him to flee the United States. He has Cancer on the 8th and the Moon in Cancer in the 8th in close conjunction to Pluto; both are involved in a T-square to Mars and Uranus. (See his chart on next page.)

This placement can work in a totally opposite way if the ruler has many inconjuncts. Perhaps you just can't bother to adjust yourself to all the sexual needs of a partner or you may consider that sex and the whole aura surrounding it are exaggerated out of proportion and that you can just as well do without it. If you have many challenging aspects to the ruler, you should be particularly cautious in filling out your income tax returns — it seems the Internal Revenue catches you at everything.

Ruler of the 8th in the 9th: A certain optimism and idealism pervades all your 8th house attitudes. Any occult or mystic tendencies will become imbued or involved with religion and vice versa. Pope John Paul II has this placement (his chart in on page 12). So does author Christopher Isherwood. He has Capricorn on the 8th house and the ruler Saturn in Aquarius in the 9th. His early fame came from a book called *Berlin Stories*, later translated into the musical and film *Cabaret*. He has since written many books dealing with the search for truth and his latest book, *My Guru and His Disciple* tells about his years at the Vedanta Center in Hollywood where he has been actively supporting the Ramakrishna/Vivekananda interpretation of the Vedas.

Your higher mind can play an important role in your transformation as it did with seer Edgar Cayce, who had Pisces on the 8th and Neptune in Taurus in the 9th. With difficult aspects you may not be able to complete your higher education, because of a lack of financial backing or because in your overly optimistic appraisal you did not lay the proper foundation. This may prevent you from utilizing all your abilities for handling other people's resources. In our clientele we have a few examples of people with this placement who are bookkeepers instead of CPA's, bank tellers instead of bank

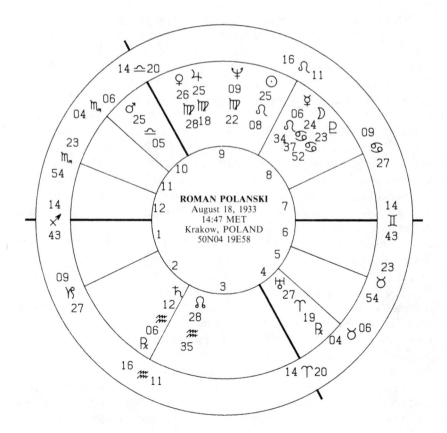

managers, etc. Some of these people go back to school at a certain point in their life, usually when by progression they have good Pluto, Uranus or Saturn aspects to the ruler of the 8th.

Ruler of the 8th in the 10th: This is the classic position of the successful politician who receives support from others in order to achieve his career goals. Presidents Roosevelt, Carter and Kennedy and Queen Beatrix of Holland have this placement (most of these charts can be found in Volumes I and II). Many other public figures, too numerous to mention, also have this placement. Just as numerous are actors and actresses who have received public support.

Sometimes you may be a person whose sex life becomes very public and if any challenging aspects to the ruler have not been resolved, scandals may ensue. Or you can, like actress Liv Ullman, write about your personal life, including the fact that she had a long standing affair with director/producer Ingmar Bergman and bore his illegitimate child. She has Uranus in the 10th ruling her 8th house, opposed to Pluto.

Quite often it signifies that your death, when it occurs, will be in a public place. Again President Kennedy serves as an example, as does his brother Robert whose Jupiter ruling his 8th house was in Capricorn in the 10th, conjunct the Moon, opposite Pluto in the 3rd and inconjunct Neptune in the 5th.

You may choose an 8th house profession such as undertaking, embalming, surgery, prostitution, the sex shop owner and so on.

Ruler of the 8th in the 11th: Friends may give you much support and you may do a lot with your friend's resources. We can cite two pertinent examples from our own files. The first is a woman, now over 75 years old, who has never worked a day in her life and yet she lives like a princess. She has a small annuity her husband left her, but it is really small since he died 40 years ago when money was worth much more than it is today. The rest of her income comes from friends who put her up, pay for trips she takes, pamper and spoil her, and never seem to feel that she may be a user. She has a Cancer stellium in the 8th (including the Sun) and the Moon in Libra in her 11th.

The other example is a man who does all sorts of odd investing jobs; one day he finds a possible future oil well or he hears of a small shopping center waiting for some backers to be built. In all cases he not only uses his own money, but gets all his friends to join him in the venture. So far he has tripled both his investments and theirs. He has Sagittarius on the 8th house cusp and Jupiter in Aries in the 11th, trine Saturn in Leo in the 4th.

Many of your 8th house feelings are very goal oriented. You don't just study astrology for the fun of it but in order to achieve certain aims you set for yourself. The same applies to any occult fields you feel like delving into. Or you may be into some form of research, yet your motivation is based on a future goal or the hope of fulfilling a future ambition; this may prevent you from really enjoying what you are doing while you are doing it.

Your sexual attitudes could depend on how much you feel loved, a typical 11th house matter. If you don't feel loved, you cannot enjoy sex. This by the way does not mean that you have to love the person; just to feel needed, wanted and desired is what matters to you, especially if the Moon, Venus or Saturn are involved.

Ruler of the 8th in the 12th: You have a hard time showing your true sexual nature, as if you are afraid of being too vulnerable if you ever open up. But under certain conditions the opposite takes place, and you have plenty of affairs going on, but most of them are secret. If the aspects are very difficult, you may put too much emphasis on sex, and all the problems it brings you are detrimental to your relationships.

Your feelings are very deep, especially if the Moon, Sun, Mars or Pluto are involved and whatever changes take place over the years are from within, and an integral part of you. Your death, when it happens, may take place in a hospital. At times this placement may bring a fear of death without your understanding the cause.

Much of the time other people's resources are available to you, unless the aspects to the ruler have not been integrated into the chart; yet you may not be aware of it or may not wish others to be aware and therefore keep the fact pretty much under wraps. Oil millionaire J. Paul Getty for example, never wanted anyone to know how rich he was, what resources were open to him, where the money came from, etc. He had Leo on the cusp of the 8th, and his Sun was in Sagittarius in the 12th.

Interestingly enough Igor Stravinsky, the Russian composer whose famous ballet music *The Firebird* is based on the story of the phoenix, had Aries on the 8th and the ruler Mars in Leo in the 12th, square Neptune and Saturn in Taurus in the 9th. He had to leave his native country and was considered a great loner in his adopted country, the United States. That did not stop him from composing more beautiful music, much of it totally different from his previous works composed in Russia.

Lesson 9
Ninth House Rulers

Cadent and a house of life, the 9th is represented by Sagittarius and naturally ruled by Jupiter. The warmth and outreach of Sagittarius' fire combines
with the optimistic and expansive attitude of Jupiter to make this the house
of your higher mind and your philosophical and idealistic approach to life.
Despite Jupiter's wish to grow and expand and despite Sagittarius' need to
aim that arrow toward the stars, the aspirations are held within the traditional bounds of your upbringing. (The 9th is opposite your 3rd house of
early schooling and environment.) Since it is on the western side of the meridian, where you are involved with others and are often dependent on them,
the steps you take will be only as big as people around you will support.
Unless Uranus or Pluto rule this house, or the ruler is so challenged that
you become a rebel with a cause, you will aspire to your goals and try to
realize them. If the ruler has strong aspects to Jupiter, religion will play an
important role or give guidelines to support you.

As the arrow symbolizing Sagittarius implies, the 9th house aims are
far and wide; therefore long distance travel and foreign transactions show
here. Since the 9th is the 3rd house from the 7th which represents your marital
partner, it is considered the house of your in-laws. By the same logic, it is
the 5th house from the 5th, or the children of your children — namely your
grandchildren.

Ruler of the 9th in the 1st: You are the kind of person who has your own philosophy of life and you don't hesitate in making your ideas known to people with whom you come into contact. If other things in the chart support it, you will seek a good education and may even choose to air your thoughts through teaching. If the planet is Jupiter, Neptune or the Moon, you may be quite religious and may even opt for that type of lifestyle, becoming a priest, nun, minister or rabbi.

Two examples of people who have influenced others with their philosophy are pacifist Indian leader Mohandas Gandhi (see chart in Volume II), who had Gemini on the 9th house cusp and Mercury in Scorpio in the 1st and Werner Erhardt, the founder of *EST,* the philosophy that tries to teach self-improvement through self awareness and self acceptance. He has Cancer on the 9th and the Moon in the 1st house in the philosophical sign of Sagittarius. His Moon squares the Sun, Saturn and Neptune, providing plenty of drive and indicating the impact he has on other people's thinking and concepts. The sextile to Mercury which rules the Midheaven provides the avenue of expression through a career.

With a strong Sun, Mars or 5th house, sports may appeal to you and with the proper application of energy you could excel in this field. You may choose a legal profession but if the planet is severely challenged, you may run afoul of the law.

Ruler of the 9th in the 2nd: One might say of you that you "put your money where you mouth is." Either your philosophies are quite materialistic or you are more than willing to use your income to back your theories and concepts, as did movie producer Sam Goldwyn (see chart in Volume II), who spared no expense to bring his dreams before the public. On another level, you may earn your living through travel, foreign commerce or possibly through teaching or religion. We have the charts of a priest and a rabbi in our files, both of whom have Sagittarius on the 9th cusp and Jupiter in the 2nd. The priest has Jupiter in Gemini and the rabbi has it in Taurus. They both earn their living by spreading the word of God.

Another example is economist Sylvia Porter (see her chart on next page) who has the Moon in Sagittarius in the 2nd ruling the 9th. She has made quite a name for herself by publishing (9th house) her financial theories and advice (2nd house). Although her Moon opposes her Sun and Pluto, it also trines Mars providing the integration of energy necessary to make her tops in her field.

Most of your traveling will be done under the heading of business and many of your expenses will be reimbursed or you can use them as tax deductions.

Ruler of the 9th in the 3rd: This is the classic placement of the writer and teacher because it links the house of ideas (9th) with the house of communication (3rd); if other factors in the chart support this, it is easy for you

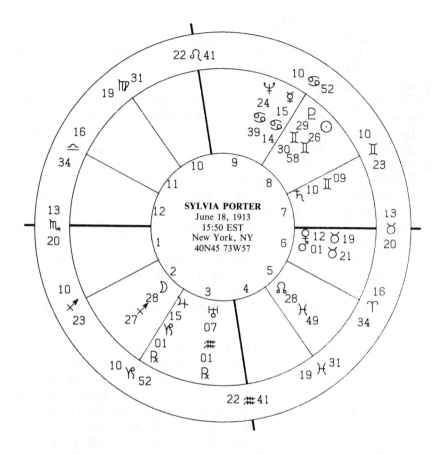

to impart knowledge and to even pen the books that bring your subject to your students. Unless the ruler's aspects are very difficult, you love to travel and are always ready to pack and go at the drop of a hat. Billy Mitchell who commanded the American-European Forces in World War I, had Pluto in Taurus in the 3rd and Scorpio on the 9th house cusp. His Pluto opposed Venus in the 9th and he was later court-martialed for insubordination because of his criticism of the War and Navy Departments. Convicted and sentenced to suspension from the service for five years, he resigned and devoted the rest of his life to writing. The connection between the 3rd and 9th houses shows his interest in what was at that time a distant and unique form of travel. It also points up his communicating ability as well as problems with the law.

Quite often this placement makes you the missionary since you need to communicate your beliefs, especially to those in far away places.

Ruler of the 9th in the 4th: You will most likely at sometime in your life live in a foreign country. You have a deep interest in foreign cultures, people and affairs and tend to get along well with those of diverse interests. With challenging aspects, you may run into legal difficulties in establishing your estate. It is remotely possible that because of not obeying the law, you would live in a state of confinement, especially if the planet involved is Mars, Uranus or Saturn.

Theodore Bundy, the accused rapist who left a trail of terror behind him, has Aries on the 9th house with Mars in Sagittarius in the 4th opposed to Uranus which rules the other legal house, the 7th. He has been a guest of the law for several years, and since his conviction is for life, this demonstrates the misuse of this 9th house/4th house energy.

Among the many who have made their home in a foreign country are French humanist Albert Schweitzer, British archeologist, soldier and writer T. E. Lawrence, glamour girl Zsa Zsa Gabor (all of whose charts are in Volume II) General George Patton (whose chart is on page 124) and operatic tenor Lauritz Melchior.

The philosophy or religion you were imbued with in your family home will most likely be what you believe in all your life, unless Uranus is the 9th house ruler and it is very challenged. Even then it may only indicate that you were brought up in a very free thinking home and allowed to seek answers to your many questions.

Ruler of the 9th in the 5th: Yours is a "live and let live" philosophy and you may even have a sort of devil-may-care attitude much like actor, world traveler and *bon vivant* Errol Flynn (see his chart in Volume II) Flynn had Libra on the 9th and Venus in Cancer in the 5th conjunct Neptune and opposed to Uranus. A romantic adventurer until the day he died, Flynn — by his own admission — let nothing anyone else ever did or said faze him.

You could espouse your own philosophy through your creative endeavors in either the musical field like Henry Mancini, the movies like Walt Disney (see their charts in Volume II), or writing like John D. MacDonald, (see his chart on next page). He conceived and created fictional philosopher/salvage man/private eye Travis McGee. MacDonald has Libra on the 9th cusp and Venus in Cancer conjunct Pluto in the 5th. Venus squares Mars in the 8th and MacDonald's alter ego McGee, philosophizes on everything including sex, death and taxes.

On another level you could be a teacher of religion or philosophy, or you could excel in the sports field because you are combining the Sun energy of the 5th house with the expansive Jupiter energy of the 9th house. Basketball super star Kareem Abdul Jabbar, who has Cancer on the 9th and the Moon in Pisces in the 5th, attended college on an athletic scholarship.

Ruler of the 9th in the 6th: Yours is an everyday philosophy, a practical religion — one that is simple enough for you to live with comfortably. It may be expressed in many different ways, but is always easy and workable, rarely deep and profound and often tinged with humor. You may work as

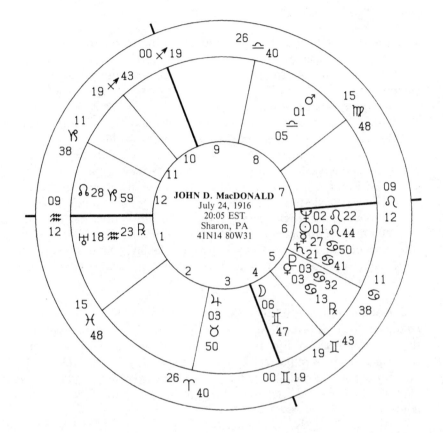

a teacher, lecturer or in the import-export business. We have three clients, all men who have the 9th house ruler in the 6th and they are all long haul truckers. One, who has Cancer on the 9th and the Moon in Aries in the 6th, is a long distance mover.

Your work may be connected with foreign countries, and you may even travel to out of the way places to work, like one of our clients who is a geologist and travels all over the world testing earth samples. He has Capricorn on the 9th and Saturn in the 6th in probing Scorpio. Another client is a steam fitter and he also has to travel in connection with his work. He has Libra on the 9th and Venus in Cancer in the 6th. Venus conjuncts Mercury which rules his 4th and he has never lived longer than three years in any one place.

Ogden Nash, the humorist/poet (whose chart is in Volume II), has Aquarius on the 9th house cusp and Uranus in Sagittarius in the 6th. Uranus opposes Pluto in the 12th giving the necessary drive to accomplish his solitary work; it has a wide trine to his Leo Sun in the 2nd indicating the ability to make money from his wry and witty poetry.

Ruler of the 9th in the 7th:　It is very important to you to have a partner who shares your ideological opinions and background. Yet if the planet is Uranus, Pluto or Mars, you may deliberately choose someone whose philosophies are totally different from yours — someone with whom you can do some verbal and mental fencing to sharpen and define your own outlook. Or, on another level, your philosophical outlook is influenced or determined by your partner and your relationship to him or her.

This is often the placement of people having to do with the law — making it, breaking it or enforcing it. The ministry may attract you as it did evangelist Kathryn Kuhlman, who had Gemini on the 9th house (religion) with an unaspected Mercury in Taurus in the 7th house (public). It was easy for her to share her religious beliefs with her wildly enthusiastic audiences.

You may be attracted to a partner of a different nationality and very often you are socially active with your partner's family, your in-laws. Whether you and they get along well together is determined by the aspects to the planet in question.

Ruler of the 9th in the 8th:　Your philosophy of life could very well be connected with the metaphysical or occult. Certainly you are intrigued with the deeper mysteries of life and the hereafter. Strongly intuitive and perceptive, especially if Neptune or the Moon is involved, you seem able to "tune in." If the planet is well integrated in your chart, you may find that if you play your hunches and listen to the "still small voice within," you unerringly make the right decisions and choose your best path.

Mary Baker Eddy, the founder of Christian Science, had Mercury in Leo in the 8th ruling her Virgo 9th house cusp. She was able to combine the metaphysical, spiritual and religious to present a new religion to the world — a doctrine based on spiritual healing. She is the only woman to have founded a major religion. (See her chart on page 81.)

Ralph Waldo Emerson had Taurus on the 9th house cusp and Venus in Aries in the 8th, sextile Mercury in the 10th and in a yod with Jupiter and Neptune. He studied for the ministry (9th), but because of his religious doubts he gradually formed his own transcendental philosophy, which views the world of phenomena as a symbol of inner life and which emphasizes individual freedom and self-reliance (8th). He wrote, lectured and traveled widely to promote his beliefs.

Ruler of the 9th in the 9th:　Three quite famous law breakers have this placement. Arthur Bremer who attempted to assassinate presidential candidate George Wallace has the Sun in Leo in the 9th house ruling the cusp and opposing Jupiter, the planet of law and order. Lt. William Calley of

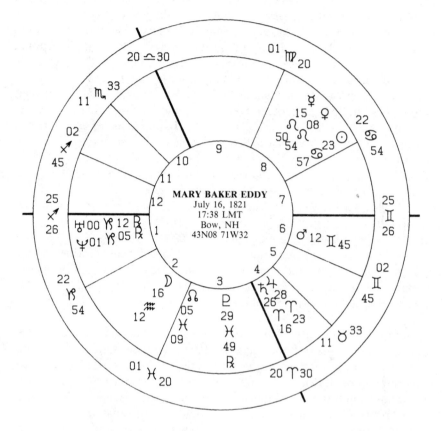

Mi-Lai infamy has Cancer on the 9th with the Moon in Leo in the 9th, square
Mercury in Taurus in the 7th (the other legal house). Roman Polanski (see
his chart on page 71), the Polish movie director who has been in and out
of trouble with the law because of his attraction to under age nymphets, has
Leo on the 9th with the Sun in Leo in the 9th. The trine to Uranus seems
to provide the opportunity for him to avoid punishment.

On the positive level this placement may indicate that you are an exceptional teacher — one who is able to tune in to your students' mind and communicate on their wavelength. This is particularly true if the planet is Mercury, Uranus, Neptune or the Moon. You may be a traveler or explorer,
always seeking new worlds to conquer like astronaut Tom Stafford with Venus
in Scorpio ruling his Libra 9th house cusp.

Ruler of the 9th in the 10th: Very often you find yourself in a career
that involves travel — possibly to foreign countries. You seem to have an

affinity for foreign affairs and if other things in the chart support it, you could do well as an ambassador, diplomat or embassy attache.

Several of the U.S. astronauts share this placement. Buzz Aldrin has Aquarius on the 9th and Uranus in the 10th in Aries. Both Charles Conrad and Ed White have Cancer on the cusp of the 9th house and the Moon in Leo and Virgo respectively, in the 10th. Gordon Cooper has Aries on the 9th and Mars in the 10th in Gemini. You could certainly say that their careers required some long distance travel; in a typically 9th house/Sagittarian fashion, they reached for the stars. Richard Byrd, the polar explorer, had Virgo on the 9th and Mercury in Scorpio in the 10th. Mercury square Saturn afforded him the tenacity and staying power he needed to achieve his discovery. He was also an author of note, which is another avenue for the person who has the 9th house ruler in the 10th.

If the planet is Mercury, Jupiter, the Sun or the Moon, you could have a successful career in some field and then instruct others in your area of expertise. When the energy is expressed in its most physical way, you may be a sports super star or an entertainer. Your philosophy could influence your government and you could play a vital role in world politics as did Jawaharlal Nehru (India), Napoleon Bonaparte (France) and Josef Stalin (USSR). (See Nehru and Stalin charts in Volume II.)

Ruler of the 9th in the 11th: Many of your friends come from the same background and general upbringing and have the same outlook on life that you have, especially if the ruling planet has flowing aspects. If it is challenged, you seem to be drawn to those whose views are diametrically opposed to yours which in turn may stimulate you to learn and broaden your outlook. With proper application of energy, you could be a diplomat or tactician performing a service for your government. On another level you could use your legal expertise as an entry into politics, especially if the ruling planet is the Sun, Moon or Mercury.

When the energy is misapplied, there could be a tendency for you to waste your talent in a round of partying and social affairs — traveling here and there with your friends and never actually settling down to any accomplishment.

The chart of Queen Beatrix of the Netherlands (see Volume II) is a good example of the practical application of this placement. She has Sagittarius on the 9th house and Jupiter in Aquarius in the 11th conjunct the Sun, Moon and Venus and exactly square Uranus. She became Queen rather suddenly (Uranus) when her mother announced her abdication on Beatrix' 42nd birthday. It will be interesting to watch how she handles Holland's affairs in the next few years.

Ruler of the 9th in the 12th: Your philosophy is built on your own deepest feelings and on the strength you draw from your own convictions. You feel that you don't need input from outside influences to shape your beliefs. This may be expressed in writing which is a very private occupation well in keeping with the 12th house, or in deep research, possibly in the medical field. An example is scientist Werner von Braun, who worked so diligently on the U.S. space program. He had Capricorn on the 9th and Saturn conjunct the 12th house cusp in Taurus.

If the energy is not properly integrated into the chart, you may have great self-doubt in relation to your precepts and beliefs and you could spend time in psychoanalysis dealing with your emotional and spiritual attitudes to find out who you really are.

Even though other indications in the chart may show that you are outgoing, gregarious and even flighty, there is a side to your nature that remains hidden and reserved. You may journey to distant places to study and learn philosophy, the occult or metaphysical lore. Always a seeker, you want to learn all that life has to offer.

Lesson 10
Tenth House Rulers

Angular, a house of substance and represented by Capricorn, the 10th house is naturally ruled by Saturn, the planet of ambition. Wherever Saturn rules or is placed, you may feel insecure or lacking and wherever you feel inadequate, you tend to overcompensate. Therefore the 10th house which relates to achievement will be an area where you will try particularly hard to prove yourself. The 10th is the highest house in the chart, the southernmost point, emphasizing that this is the area of culmination, the most you can strive for. That is why traditionally it shows your profession, status, reputation and psychologically your real ego needs.

Since the 4th house is your home, the 10th house (opposite the 4th) is your world, your community or however far your sphere of influence reaches. The 4th represents one of the parents, often the more nurturing one; the 10th shows the other parent, the one who carries more authority, who sets the limits when you are a child. In later years it will stand for anyone else who represents that authoritarian pattern, such as your employer, the government, etc. Where the 6th house shows the kind of work you do, the 10th indicates your career or profession, the highest you can reach.

Ruler of the 10th in the 1st: Whatever you achieve in life, you'll have to do it on your own. You may coast along on someone else's coattails, but eventually to get the ego satisfaction you need, the effort has to come from you. The ruler and its aspects will indicate how long it may take and how hard you have to work to get there. With this placement you usually desire the limelight; to be a behind-the-scenes manipulator such as a producer or director is not enough for you. For this reason many politicians as well as theater and movie people have the ruler of the 10th in the 1st.

President Carter has Cancer on his Midheaven and the Moon in Scorpio in the 1st, so does his former Vice President, Walter Mondale (see his chart is on page 54). This house placement which they have in common often gives an innate compatibility, a mute understanding. Mondale has Sagittarius on the 10th house cusp and Jupiter in Pisces conjunct the Sun, both in the 1st house. Jupiter is the focal point of a T-square to the Moon and Mars, giving him the emphasis and challenge not always associated with the Sagittarius/Pisces combination. Other politicians who come to mind with this position are presidential candidate John Anderson, Vice President Nelson Rockefeller (also a presidential candidate) and French president Charles de Gaulle.

Since so much personal effort is involved in achieving your highest potential, you must guard against becoming too self-centered or ego oriented, especially if Mars is the planet in question. With flowing or well integrated aspects, success may come easily, but may not necessarily mean as much to you as the accomplishments earned by the sweat of your brow.

Ruler of the 10th in the 2nd: Chances are that you will make money through your career; how much income you earn and how important it will be to you can be seen by how prominent the ruler is in the chart and if you have learned to integrate the aspects to their greatest advantage. Your resources and values play an important role in the type of profession you choose.

In our clientele two cases illustrate what we are referring to. The first is a man with Taurus on the Midheaven or 10th house cusp and the ruler Venus in Libra in the 2nd, conjunct Neptune and sextile Jupiter. He loves beautiful things, including some of the luxuries that only money can buy, so he wants to earn a good living, but not at the cost of doing "dirty" work. He is a very talented artist, yet that provides a very uncertain income; so he also owns an art gallery and does extremely well. The other case is a woman with Virgo on her 10th and Mercury in Capricorn in the 2nd. Money is very important to her security. She first tried to get it through a husband (Saturn which rules the 2nd is in Cancer in the 8th), but when the marriage failed and she could not live on her alimony, she buckled down and went to work and became a very successful insurance broker.

Singer/actress Judy Garland had Pisces on the Midheaven and Neptune in Leo in the 2nd house. Judy had trouble realizing her true ego needs most of her life. She utilized the Pisces/Neptune in Leo to express her many talents, helped by Neptune's sextile to the Sun and Jupiter and the trine to Mars; but she never really adjusted to the exact Neptune inconjunct to Uranus in the 10th house. Instead, she fell prey to the most negative use of Pisces and Neptune — drugs and alcohol. (Her chart is in Volume I.)

Ruler of the 10th in the 3rd: Your career should include some form of communication since you feel a great need to express yourself. This is not so much the placement of actors and actresses who portray a role where someone else's opinion or feeling is stated, rather, it indicates those who need to express their ego through a definite statement of their own attitude. Ruler of the 3rd in the 10th is typified by Betty Friedan, vocal and feisty fighter for women's liberation; she has Libra on the Midheaven and Venus in Aries in the 3rd as the focal point of a T-square, with the Moon in Capricorn in the 1st and Pluto in Cancer in the 7th. Venus is also in rather wide (8° orb) conjunction to Mars, a combative Venus to say the least, which well explains part of her actions. (See her chart below.)

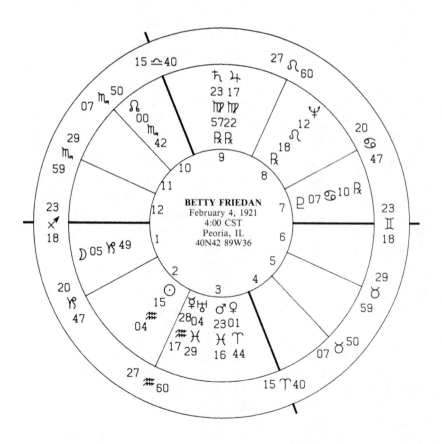

Quite often with this position your profession is dependent on or involved with a relative. Such as Walt Disney whose brother Roy ran all the business aspects of the Disney Productions, giving Walt a chance to concentrate on the artistic and creative end. His Mercury in Scorpio ruled his Gemini 10th house and made a close sextile to Venus in the 5th house of creativity and children. (See his chart in Volume II.)

Your career may necessitate a lot of commuting, in fact, among our students we can think of at least eight who cover quite a bit of mileage. Two of them are salesmen with extended territories, both of them have Aries on the Midheaven and Mars in Virgo and Libra respectively. Three of them are models and are required to pose in many locations all over the city and its environs.

Ruler of the 10th in the 4th: This is the classic position for writers or any of the professions that can be managed out of the home. For example, one of our clients runs a typing service from her home. People send her manuscripts, legal briefs, et al. Since she had polio as a youngster and is restricted to a wheelchair, this is an ideal career solution. She has Cancer on the 10th house cusp and the Moon in Capricorn in the 4th. Very often you will embrace a career that is earth or land connected, such as farming, archeology, geology or real estate. You could also be working with one or both of your parents or you might take over their business.

You may decide to do something where you can show your love for your country the only way you know how. German General Erwin Rommel, known as the "Desert Fox," picked a career where he could defend his country. He had Scorpio on the Midheaven and Pluto in Gemini in the 4th, exactly conjunct Neptune, both of them exactly squaring Jupiter and opposing Venus, a very potent T-square. Other examples of those serving their country are Russian leader Josef Stalin (see his chart in Volume II) and President Richard Nixon who has Gemini on his 10th house and Mercury in the 4th conjunct Mars and Jupiter, opposed to Pluto in the 10th and inconjunct Saturn in the 9th.

Ruler of the 10th in the 5th: Many people involved with the theater or motion pictures have this position. They bring their innate artistic talents and creativity (5th) to their career (10th). Rudolf Bing, former general manager of the Metropolitan Opera in New York, has Scorpio on his Midheaven and Pluto in Gemini in the 5th. He was quite a controversial manager whose Martian personality at times got him into fights with many of his divas, including Maria Callas who was rarely allowed to sing at the Met while he was in charge. Bing's Pluto is the finger of a Yod to the Midheaven and he has a tight stellium of the Sun, Mercury, Jupiter and Saturn in Capricorn, all hovering around his Ascendant. Actress Jane Fonda is another good example. She has Taurus on the 10th house cusp and Venus in Sagittarius in the 5th trining the Ascendant in Leo. Sometimes you may not become famous, but your children do, or you help your children with their career. Many stage mothers fit that description. We have a client with three children and she has pushed all of them into work practically since they were born. They posed for baby food pictures and later modeled children's clothes. She has Leo on the 10th and the Sun in Aries in the 5th. Quite often your hobby becomes your career, and many times you excel in the sports field like tennis star Billie Jean King and boxers Jack Dempsey and George Foreman.

Ruler of the 10th in the 6th: When the ruler of your professional life is in the house of work, your work more often than not becomes your professional life. You may be a bookkeeper in order to pay the rent, finish your schooling, take an exam and become a CPA. Or like one of our clients, work as a secretary in a real estate office, take your sales and then your brokers exam, become a licensed broker, make good money at it and end up owning your own real estate office. This client has Capricorn on the 10th house and Saturn in Libra in the 6th conjunct Jupiter. Her Sun is in Capricorn in the 10th house. As this planetary picture would indicate, she is very ambitious, very hard working and with Jupiter involved, not satisfied with "just" being a broker!

Since the 6th is also the house of health, many doctors and hospital workers have this placement, as do people involved in the nutritional or hygiene field. Sometimes you don't follow a career, but enjoy giving service and your standing in the community is geared to working in local and community affairs. You may have a career in the military service, like Dwight D. Eisenhower. Here we have the army officer, great wartime general and finally U.S. president who served his government (10th house) in many ways. His Capricorn Midheaven was ruled by Saturn in Virgo in the 6th trine Mars in Capricorn in the 10th.

Ruler of the 10th in the 7th: You may enjoy a very public career or be professionally involved with a partner. An example is composer Richard Rodgers who worked first with lyricist Lorenz Hart and then with Oscar Hammerstein II. They collaborated on such classics as *On Your Toes, Babes in Arms, Pal Joey, Oklahoma, Carousel, South Pacific* and *The King and I*, to mention just a few! Rodgers has Aquarius on the Midheaven and Uranus in Sagittarius in the 7th. The ruler is opposed to Mars in the 1st and it sextiles Jupiter in the 10th. (See his chart on next page.)

Your marriage partner may play a very important role in your career. Actor Paul Newman works with his wife Joanne Woodward; both of them acting together or he directing her in a movie or television production. He has Scorpio on the 10th and Pluto in the 7th involved in a grand water trine with Saturn and Uranus.

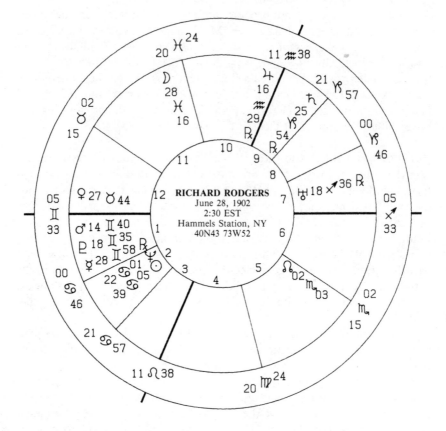

Republican Senator and majority leader Howard Baker also was helped by his wife. She is the daughter of former majority leader Everett Dirksen, a man known for his smooth voice and quick wit. She opened many government doors for her husband; his own ability took him the rest of the way. Baker has a Capricorn Midheaven and Saturn in Scorpio in the 7th exactly conjunct the Moon and closely conjunct the Sun.

Dealing with people on a one-to-one basis in your profession is another aspect of this position. Psychoanalyst Sigmund Freud had Leo on the Midheaven and the Sun in Taurus in the 7th conjunct Uranus and sextile Neptune. (See his chart in Volume II.) You have a need for give and take with the public and some extremely successful sales people have this placement.

Ruler of the 10th in the 8th: Unless the ruler's aspects are very difficult to integrate, you will receive support from outside sources, from your partner or from the public, especially if you deal in some public commodity. This is an excellent position for any occupation that necessitates such support: The playwright who needs financial backing to get his play produced, the actor who needs the public's applause and approval or the politician who needs other people's money for his campaign and the public's vote in order to get elected.

Actresses Lauren Bacall and Sophia Loren have this placement; Bacall with Aries on the 10th and Mars in Aquarius in the 8th, trine Saturn and opposed to Neptune; Loren with Libra on the Midheaven and Venus in Virgo in the 8th, conjunct Neptune. In each case the ruler is involved with Neptune, one indication of a career related to some artistic or creative field. Both ladies are also known for their beauty and sex appeal, another facet of a 10th house ruler placed in the 8th house.

Often you don't have to work for a living, but your career is one of charitable works, since your mate's money is sufficient for both of you to live on, or your partner may be deceased and have left enough money to enable you to enjoy a good social standing.

Ruler of the 10th in the 9th: Your ego needs are imbued with your philosophy of life and regardless of what you do, you rarely compromise your ideas or ideals. If the ruler is Saturn and Jupiter rules the 9th, religion may play a very important role. One of our clients has Sagittarius on the 9th house cusp and Capricorn on the 10th; Saturn is in Capricorn in the 9th trine the Moon in Virgo and square the Sun in Aries. She is a missionary in Oman (Middle East), lives a very interesting but spartan life and would not change it for anything. She will try to convert you or anyone at the drop of a hat.

With the ruler of the 10th in the 9th travel is always important to you and you may choose a career where you can do plenty of it, such as owning or working for a travel bureau, the military if Mars is involved or flying, especially with Uranus strong in the chart. Quite a few stewards and stewardesses have this placement.

Since the 9th house is also the house of higher learning, this position is frequently found among university professors and teachers on all levels. Many times you may teach in a field where you have been successful before; for instance the retired engineer who now teaches an adult engineering class at a local high school. It is also the house of publishing, and publisher Bennett Cerf serves as a good example with Gemini on his Midheaven and Mercury in Taurus in the 9th.

Ruler of the 10th in the 10th: Much of your life may revolve around the need to prove to yourself and others that you are somebody, that you count, that you can, will and must achieve. You may do this in many ways, since the possibilities are as diverse as there are people — it's the fact that this

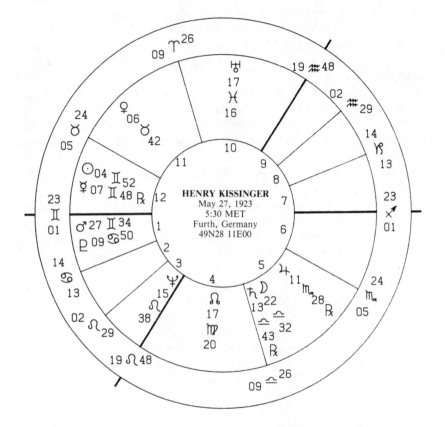

is your life's motivation which makes you different from others. To give a few pertinent examples: former Secretary of State Henry Kissinger, whose ambition is legion as is his passion for work; conductor Zubin Mehta who is in charge of the New York Philharmonic and the Israel Philharmonic and who gives his time to innumerable other musical endeavors at the cost of his private life; and Jean Claude Killy who did the same and who single-mindedly pursued his skiing medals at an age when most young men like to do other things. Killy has Aries on the 10th and Mars in early Gemini in the 10th. Mehta has Jupiter in Sagittarius in the 10th ruling it. (Both Killy's and Mehta's charts are in Volume II.) Kissinger has Uranus in Pisces in the 10th ruling the Aquarius Midheaven. It is involved in a grand water trine with Jupiter and Pluto and it is the finger of a yod to Neptune and Saturn. This prominent position of Uranus helps to explain in part the force always propelling him on. (His chart is above.)

Since the 10th house represents one of your parents, your career may be the result of parental guidance or help. You could be the son or daughter who follows in the footsteps of your parents by taking over a family business. Just as often we have seen the contrary where you spend your life proving to an absent parent that you can do without him or her. This is particularly true in the case of divorced parents where custody is given to the mother and where the son tries to prove to her that he can provide as well or better than the father did. The more challenging the aspects to the ruler, the harder he will try.

Ruler of the 10th in the 11th: Your career or social standing could be very group oriented. Many people who frequent the society pages and have made a career of belonging to all kinds of organizations have this placement. So do certain politicians like congressmen, senators, assemblymen, etc., who work in well-established groups like the Senate, the House of Representatives, the different State houses or Parliament in many foreign countries. You may also be involved in group work such as in unions, as was labor leader James Hoffa with Sagittarius on the 10th and Jupiter in Capricorn in the 11th.

Friends usually play a very important role in your professional life, you may work with a friend or a friend may have been your backer, either morally or financially. Two clients have the ruler of the 10th in the 11th; one has Aquarius on the Midheaven and Uranus in Aries in the 11th trine Saturn in the 7th opposition the Moon in the 5th. He always finds a woman to romance (Moon in the 5th — love given). She becomes his friend (11th house of friends and love received) and convinces her husband to go into partnership with him. The husband provides the money (Saturn in the 7th) and our client does the work. So far he has succeeded at this game three times, each time in a different country; the husbands don't fare badly either, our client has never yet lost their money or taken away their wives for more than just a fling.

The other client has Sagittarius on the Midheaven and Jupiter in Capricorn in the 11th, sextile Saturn in the 1st, trine Neptune in the 7th and opposite Pluto in the 5th. He came to the United States as an immigrant and went to work at anything and everything while he attended school to learn English. Outgoing and personable (Sun in Aries Pisces rising), he made many friends who were so impressed with his drive and willingness to work, that they gave him a large financial loan to buy a market. He now owns a chain of eight markets.

Ruler of the 10th in the 12th: Much of your professional activity may take place behind the scenes, such as directors, producers or any of the many people who make motion pictures or stage plays but who are never seen "out front." You could be involved in a 12th house career; these careers include medicine, nursing and prison work, to cite a few. We have several doctors in our clientele who have this position in their charts.

This is also a rather typical placement for writers, since much of their work is done in private, if possible behind closed doors. Ernest Hemingway, whose chart is delineated in depth in this book (see page 140) serves as one example; Mercury in Leo in the 12th rules his Gemini Midheaven.

Often you are the power behind the throne, the person who makes many suggestions and decisions but who is not really seen by the public, since the pronouncements are all made by the power on the throne. In olden days people like Cardinal Richelieu were the inspiration or advisers to the kings; in modern days we have Rosalynn Carter, former first lady and trusted advisor to her husband, president Jimmy Carter. She has Gemini on the Midheaven and Mercury in Leo in the 12th. (Her chart is in Volume II.)

This placement frequently indicates that you are very private if not actually secretive about your career, like someone who works for the CIA. On a psychological level you may not wish to reveal your true ego needs.

Lesson 11
Eleventh House Rulers

A part of the day side (above the horizon) of the horoscope, the 11th house is on the eastern side of the meridian and is the last of the three houses of relationships. True to its natural sign Aquarius and ruler Uranus, it represents social and mental relationships, those you select for shared interests; in other words, your friends. As the house following the highest you can achieve, the 10th, it shows the results of your ambition and goal orientation; it describes the ends and aims you hope to reach through your career or status (10th). As a succedent house it does not initiate but rather follows through whatever you started in the 10th. Since Aquarius prefers group involvement to one-to-one contact, the 11th shows organizations and associations with friends. The 5th house is where you give love, so the 11th, opposite the 5th is where you receive it. Similarly, the 5th is where you take risks deliberately; the 11th indicates circumstances over which you have little or no control.

Another reason the 11th represents circumstances beyond your control is that Uranus is the planet of the unexpected; thus you can never be really sure of how you will react to its energy. Uranus represents your freedom urge and the 11th house reflects this need.

Ruler of the 11th in the 1st: With this placement your friends are important to you. You rarely lose sight of your goals and with challenging aspects you may rush in where angels fear to tread. Essentially quite goal oriented, you often choose your life's path early and forge steadily ahead brooking no interference, even if it takes you a while to integrate the energy into your lifestyle.

With difficult aspects you may have the tendency to ride roughshod over others until you learn that you can get where you're going by using tact, diplomacy and a bit of charm. Sometimes, to achieve your ends, you will close your eyes to what you don't want to see like Watergate figure John Dean who has Sagittarius on the 10th and 11th houses and Jupiter in Aquarius in the 1st in a grand trine with Mercury and the Moon. He was able to achieve recognition at a relatively young age. Jupiter, however, squares Uranus in his 3rd and has an exact inconjunct to Neptune in the 8th, so that in his "blind ambition" Dean overlooked the value of honesty and was a victim of deception.

Friends may play an important role in your life and if the planet is Neptune and it has challenging aspects, you should guard against fair-weather friends who may be prone to mislead you.

Ruler of the 11th in the 2nd: It is possible that you will be in business with a friend at some time in your life. This placement also indicates that you could earn your living through working for a large organization and if the planet is Jupiter or Neptune it could be a religious group — church or charity.

Conversely, you may not work at all, and your value system may depend completely on the people you associate most with. If other areas in the chart back this, you may be easily influenced by your peers and have the need to work at developing your own values, inner talents and resources.

The opportunity to develop a government associated career is highly likely, since the 11th house represents the Congress in the U.S. government and parliament in many other countries. Eugene McCarthy who has devoted so much of his life to good government, has Sagittarius on the 11th cusp and Jupiter in Aries in his 2nd house conjunct the Sun, square Saturn and trine Mars and the Moon. His value system is well established and he functions easily within this framework.

Ruler of the 11th in the 3rd: You will most likely choose your friends from among your neighbors, schoolmates and everyday acquaintances. Unless the planet ruling the 11th has very challenging aspects, you are generally on good terms with your sisters and brothers and maintain friendly relations with them throughout your life.

Your aims and ambitions may be associated with the fields of travel and communication and the aspects involved will indicate the ways for you to succeed in your endeavors. Several prominent sports figures have this placement. Among them are pro golfer Jack Nicklaus with Libra on the 11th and Venus in Pisces in the 3rd, Brazilian soccer star Pele, whose Mercury in Scorpio in the 3rd rules his 11th house Gemini cusp; lady bullfighter Portia Porter, who has Pisces on the 11th and Neptune in Leo in the 3rd; and lovely ice-skating champion Linda Fratianne, with Cancer on the 11th cusp and the Moon in Sagittarius in the 3rd. Their dedication to the pursuit of their aims causes quite a lonely life and perhaps not as much social contact as they would like.

Ruler of the 11th in the 4th: Invariably your friends spend a lot of time in your home and you visit in theirs frequently. In our files are many charts from the "flower child" generation of people who have this position. They were quite content with communal living and enjoyed the day-to-day prox-imity with their friends.

It is possible you will live in a home provided by the government. General George Patton (whose chart is on page 124) lived in Army quarters provided by the U.S. government almost all his life starting with his early days at West Point. He had Mars in Virgo in the 4th ruling his Aries 11th house cusp. The fact that it was Mars and that Jupiter was also in the 4th indicates that his was a military home which was provided.

Your hopes, wishes and goals may be directly connected with owning your own home, properties or estate. Several of our students who share this placement are employed in the real estate investment business. Quite often the parent represented by the 4th house is also your friend or the one who urges you to achieve your goals.

Ruler of the 11th in the 5th: You really love your friends and the feeling is reciprocated, especially if the planet is working well in the chart. Again, many people whose aims have to do with sports have this placement. Golfer Lee Trevino has Pisces on the 11th and Neptune in Virgo in the 5th. The skiing Mahre twins, Phil and Steve, also have Neptune in the 5th in Scorpio ruling the 11th; so does jockey Robyn Smith Astaire (see chart in Volume II), however, her Neptune is in Libra.

Your goals may be closely aligned with the creative and entertainment fields, as were Jack Benny's who had Pluto in Gemini in the 5th ruling his 11th. (See his chart in Volume II.) Several well known pop singers have this position, including Cass Elliott (Neptune in Virgo), Sara Vaughan (Mercury in Aries), Eartha Kitt (Sun in Aquarius), and Mary Wilson of the Supremes (Neptune in Libra). In the operatic field examples include tenors Enrico Caruso (Mars in Scorpio) and Lauritz Melchior (Mars in Sagittarius).

Unless the ruler is very challenged your children will bring you happiness and often your social life is involved with them. A student of ours has Aries on the 11th house cusp and Mars in Libra in the 5th. She is a Cub Scout leader, coach of her daughter's softball team and Vice President of the local PTA. To top it off, she teaches Sunday school. She admits that all these activities comprise most of her social life.

Ruler of the 11th in the 6th: Yours is the classic placement of the person who is caught up in selfless giving — of yourself and your services. Many times you work for a charitable organization, sometimes in a paid capacity but often just donating your time and energy to help others. You may be the bingo caller at the local VFW chapter or the grand master of the Elks or the president of the PTA. On another level you could work for the government in some capacity — for instance in civil service. We have many charts in our files of career Army or Navy personnel with the ruler of the 11th in the 6th. A lot of you may find yourselves in the restaurant or bartending business.

A typical example of a person who worked for a large organization was FBI chief J. Edgar Hoover, who had Scorpio on the cusp of the 11th and Pluto in Gemini in the 6th. Adolf Hitler, who formed his own National Socialistic Worker's Movement (the Nazi party), is another with this placement. (See chart in Volume II.) He had Virgo on the 11th and Mercury in Aries in the 6th opposing both Uranus and his Ascendant. His need to give service to his country got somewhat out of hand due in part to the stressful position of Mercury in his chart. The opposition to Uranus may explain his erratic thinking processes and Mercury conjunct his Sun in Taurus made him very dogmatic, autocratic and domineering. This clearly shows how planetary energy may be misapplied.

Ruler of the 11th in the 7th: Your interest in new and far-reaching ideas may be applied to some type of public crusade, much like Betty Friedan who has Scorpio on the 11th and Pluto in the 7th. She founded the National Organization of Women (NOW) based on the right of women to apply for jobs for which they were qualified and on their right to receive equal pay for equal work. (See her chart on page 87.)

You seek a partner with whom you can relate on a friendly basis; equal give and take are as important to you as security might be to someone else. If the planet is Uranus, Pluto or Mars, the give and take might be 20-80 at times and 80-20 at others, but a spirit of camaraderie is always important in any sustained relationship.

Mike Douglas, the popular television host, has Scorpio on the 11th and Pluto in Cancer in his 7th house along with a Cancer Moon and Mercury in Leo and he has the easy rapport with the public (7th) that we can expect with this position. (See his chart in Volume II.)

You have the ability to make your friends feel that they are the most important people in your world. Often you are a representative for a charitable or nonprofit organization, because when you integrate the ruling planet into your chart, you can charm the socks off the public.

Ruler of the 11th in the 8th: You may be the lucky recipient of an inheritance from a friend. With very difficult aspects you could find yourself uprooted by one means or another from a comfortable social position. Or you may be the victim of gossip or unkind remarks from people you thought were your best friends. Until you learn to handle these challenges, your associates may take advantage of you; if you don't assert yourself, you may find it easy to follow along some undesirable paths because you take the way of least resistance. Of course, there would have to be other indications in your chart that you were heavily dependent on others.

Friendship is important to you and you seek support from your intimates; if the planet is well aspected, they back you in every way they can. If the Moon, Venus, Mars or Pluto are involved, your need to receive love may be very dependent on sexual involvements, in which case the 8th house position (sex) is stronger than the 11th house (friends and love received).

Since the 11th is the house of circumstances over which we have no control and the 8th is the house of death, this placement can indicate an untimely or accidental death.

Ruler of the 11th in the 9th: You seek friends with the same outlook that you have; someone who shares your moral and ethical principles. Yet often your friends come from foreign countries and you may even live away from your place of birth, enjoying alien cultures and experiencing different and stimulating home situations.

Frequently the money from your career (the 11th is 2nd from the 10th) is connected with distant countries. Author Pearl Buck (whose chart is on page 100) had Leo on the 11th house cusp and the Sun in Cancer in the 9th conjunct Mercury of communication and trine Uranus, the planet of the unusual. She was raised in China, the daughter of missionaries. Her unique writing ability and her depiction of life in China through her books *The Good Earth, Sons* and *A House Divided*, just to mention a few, won her both a Pulitzer and Nobel Prize for literature.

Your goals and hopes may be focused on getting a good education and the legal profession or ministry could attract you. If the planet is Jupiter or Venus, you find it easy to relate to your in-laws and you are usually quite friendly with them. We have a student with this position who was best friends with her husband's sister long before she ever met him. Twenty-five years later they are still bosom buddies.

Ruler of the 11th in the 10th: Often your career is linked in some way to the government. A lot of senators and congressmen have this position, including Communist hunter Joseph McCarthy who had Uranus in Capricorn in his 10th ruling Aquarius on the 11th cusp. Governor Jerry Brown of California has Gemini on the 11th and Mercury in Aries in the 10th. Franklin D. Roosevelt (see Volume I) had the Moon in Cancer in the 10th ruling the 11th. All of them were ambitious men whose aims were directly related to positions of responsibility and authority.

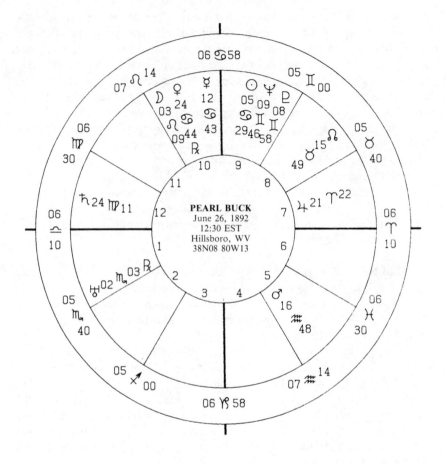

You may choose your friends for what you feel they can do to help you in your career but if you are using this placement in a positive way, your friends and acquaintances will go out of their way to help you up the ladder to success. You in turn will aid them to achieve their hopes and wishes. Most of your friends will be met through your profession or career.

With very challenging aspects or misuse of the energy, you may rise to the top only to fall again through unforeseen circumstances. Chiang Kai Shek, the Chinese leader with a history of governmental ups and downs, had Sagittarius on the 11th and Jupiter in the 10th in Scorpio conjunct the Midheaven but square the Nodes.

Ruler of the 11th in the 11th: You are very determined to reach your goals if the aspects are stimulating. If they're not, you may drift and dream idly through life. Life does seem to smile on you, especially if the planet is Jupiter or Venus and you are often attracted to the arts and are generally

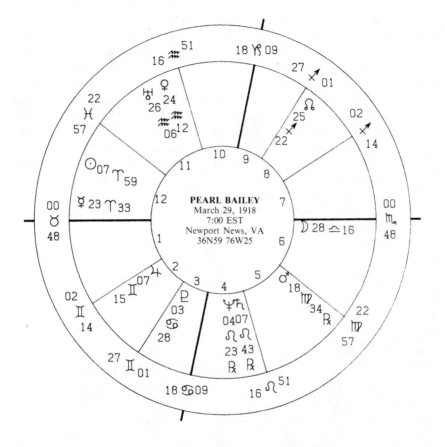

quite successful. A wide variety of people have this position. Among them are pianist Wilhelm Backhaus (Venus in Taurus), baritone Nelson Eddy (Saturn in Capricorn), actors Orson Welles (Mars in Aries) and Mickey Rooney (Venus in Libra), and entertainer Pearl Bailey (Uranus in Aquarius). (See Welles and Rooney charts in Volume II and Bailey's chart above.) As you can see, most of the time the planet is dignified and this seems to assist these people in achieving their aims.

Friends play an important role in your life and you identify strongly with them. You are quite social and philanthropic and can nearly always be called upon to contribute to a good cause, either financially or with your time. Depending on the aspects, of course, you may be drawn to controversial or unusual friends, much as Frank Sinatra, who has been questioned repeatedly about his ties with the Cosa Nostra. Uranus in Aquarius is in and ruling his 11th house. Since it is sextile to Mercury, he is always able to talk his way out of any difficulty. (See his chart in Volume II.)

Ruler of the 11th in the 12th: Your aims and goals may have to do with the medical profession, research or in operating behind the scenes in some fashion. Several writers have this placement. Faith Baldwin who has Virgo on the 11th and Mercury in Libra, wrote over a hundred romantic novels, most of them with a 12th house theme. Her Mercury trines both Neptune and Pluto in the 8th. (See her chart below.) Arthur Conan Doyle the master of suspense and intrigue, has Aries on the 11th and Mars in communicating Gemini in the 12th. He and his friends got very involved in ESP and parapsychology, forming research groups and sponsoring seances. French novelist and playwright Alexandre Dumas had Gemini on the 11th house cusp and Mercury in Cancer in the 12th house. Dumas worked with many of his friends as collaborators again showing the link with the 11th house.

Timothy Leary (see his chart in Volume II) is another example. His Venus in Scorpio in the 12th rules his 11th and he and his friends (11th) did drug research (12th) using themselves as guinea pigs.

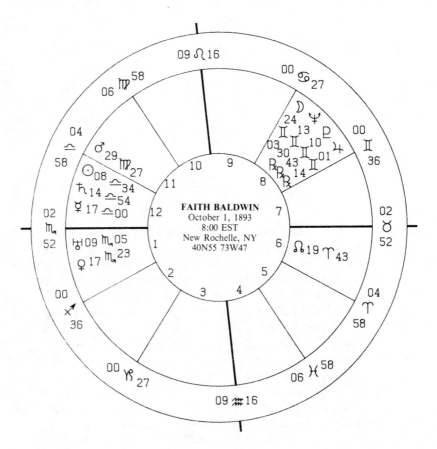

With challenging aspects you may not choose your friends carefully and they may prove to be deceitful or envious of your position. Even though you are quite socially oriented, you seem to need time to yourself every day to recharge your batteries and to get in touch with yourself. This is especially true if other indications in the chart support it.

Lesson 12
Twelfth House Rulers

This is the last house of the zodiac. It is cadent and a house of endings, its natural sign is Pisces and its natural ruler is Neptune. Because Neptune is the planet of illusion and illumination, spiritual or escapist urges, we sense a certain mystery in the 12th house. Pisces is sensitive, intuitive, compassionate and sacrificing, so some of this combines to make the 12th house the most inspirational one of all. But we need to remember that this is the house before the Ascendant. The Ascendant describes your outer body, it is out there for everyone to see; the 12th is the hidden part of you, the area where you can fool the world and yourself. In the psychological sense it is your subconscious, that which is within and stored in its memory bank are the traumas and delights of all that's happened to you since birth. Whether you will use the right key to face your innermost self is a decision only you can make.

Certain charts have an easier time or a deeper need to look within, but basically everyone is free to be cognizant or to stay ignorant. In a practical or daily living sense the 12th house can show many of your behind-the-scenes activities, things that you do by yourself or in total privacy; it can also indicate if you give service or work in a serving profession, such as a hospital worker, doctor, nurse and so on. Twelfth house service is more giving or sacrificial than 6th house type service; such as charitable work that you may be involved in. It also describes places of confinement or institutions where in you are imprisoned or locked away from reality. In its most positive sense it shows the area where you can find your real self, where you find inspiration and belief.

Ruler of the 12th in the 1st: With this house position more than with any other, you feel a deep need to look within, as if you realize that only by knowing yourself can you portray the role you have chosen as your image. That does not necessarily mean that you will honestly face your subconscious, just that you feel the urge to explore what lies beneath the surface. Mahatma Gandhi (see his chart in Volume II) serves as a good example of the practical and philosophical application of this placement. Mercury, ruling his Virgo 12th cusp, is in Scorpio in the 1st house. It has no major aspects to any other planet in the chart giving it additional strength of will and purpose. Gandhi spent most of his life fighting for the independence of India in a nonviolent way. He served many years in prison and just as many looking for the Atman and the answers to life and death within.

Ruler of the 12th in the 2nd: Of course each planetary position in astrology can be used positively or negatively, but sometimes it becomes very obvious which of the two we are using. This placement is such a case. The positive use helps you find your true values, utilize your talents and resources and enjoy your possessions as things that make life more fun. The negative use gives the effect of having Saturn in the 2nd house — always worried that you will end up in the poorhouse — making money or material objects the end instead of the means. One of our clients has Libra on the 12th and Venus in Capricorn in the 2nd. Every time she goes through a personal crisis she immediately remodels her home, purchases a new wardrobe or goes on a trip — anything to avoid looking within and facing her real needs. Her Venus is in a grand trine with Jupiter and the Moon and has no challenging aspects to force her into introspection.

Arturo Toscanini is an example of the more positive application of this placement. This fiery Italian conductor knew his values and also knew that his inner self could not live under fascism and dictatorship; upon Mussolini's ascent as the "Duce," Toscanini left his beloved Italy and immigrated to the United States. He has Sagittarius on the 12th house; his Jupiter is in Aquarius in the 2nd house, conjunct Venus, square the Moon and Saturn. (See his chart in Volume II.)

Ruler of the 12th in the 3rd: Your need to communicate your innermost thoughts to the world is one way this placement expresses itself and a lot of writers have this position. Many times though it works exactly the opposite way: You use your sensitive nature and deep insight to let others communicate with you. We have three psychologists in our clientele who have the ruler of the 12th in the 3rd. Most of them also have the 7th house emphasized to show their involvement in one-to-one relationships.

Sometimes you are the behind-the-scenes manipulator, speaking and somehow communicating through others. Some ghost writers have this position as does Jimmy Carter's right-hand man, former White House assistant Hamilton Jordan; he has Aquarius on the 12th and Uranus in Gemini in the 3rd, exactly square to Jupiter and opposition the Midheaven. He did a good job in managing some of the president's affairs, but he often put his foot in his mouth when it came to handling his personal life. Uranus in the 3rd loves to do unusual things and people still talk of the drink he poured down a lady's decolletage, saying that it reminded him of the river Nile.

There can be secret involvements which nearly always come to public notice, since the 3rd is an open house of free communication. Such was the case with former Attorney General John Mitchell (his chart is on page 14) whose Watergate entanglement became public knowledge and cost him his career as a public servant. The Moon in Scorpio in the 3rd rules his 12th.

Ruler of the 12th in the 4th: The need to be yourself is strongly evident in your nature as is the need to have time to yourself, or at least a place — a corner in the home — that you can call your own. You are a very private person and unless you have a fiery Ascendant, people think of you as quiet and even shy. Often you retire into your own world, especially if Neptune, Venus, Pluto or the Moon rule your 12th house. You may also be a homebody and even try to incorporate your work or career into the home. Sometimes this position burdens you with the responsibility of taking care of the parent represented by the 4th house.

Lawrence of Arabia, (whose chart is in Volume II), had Cancer on the 12th house and the Moon in Sagittarius in the 4th. He did not stay at home, on the contrary, he fled his homeland in order to "hide" his true identity among alien tribes in the desert. He preferred the safety of his innermost self, his psychological roots, to the more superficial security of the four walls of a house. Albert Schweitzer illustrates the same premise. (See chart in Volume II.) He too left his homeland for a faraway country, Africa, to establish new roots. But Schweitzer incorporated other 12th house principles since his new home was a hospital, the only place of refuge for thousands of natives. He had Virgo on the cusp of the 12th and Mercury in the 4th in Capricorn, exactly conjunct the Sun, square Neptune, the Moon and Jupiter; Mercury was the focal planet of an angular, cardinal T-square.

Ruler of the 12th in the 5th: The most obvious practical application of this position is the fact that you may have some secret love affairs. Whether you enjoy them or can keep them secret can only be determined by looking at the whole chart. Sometimes this acts contrarily. We have students and clients who have 12th house rulers in the 5th, but the planets have not been well integrated into the chart and they shy away from any romantic involvements, calling romance immature or childish. Instead they use the energy for sports, work or both. One client, a man, has Sagittarius on the 12th and Jupiter in Gemini in the 5th, in a grand trine to the Sun and Mars and a boomerang with Jupiter opposed to Pluto and sextile Neptune. Both Neptune and Jupiter inconjunct Mercury. His wife is constantly complaining about his cool and unromantic, even harsh approach; but he takes every occasion to go skiing, fishing, running, hiking and roller skating.

Another example is Federico Fellini (see his chart below). As a movie director he is much felt, much heard but never seen, always working behind the scenes in a typically 12th house fashion, expressing his creativity and imagination in a 5th house way. He has Leo on his 12th cusp and the Sun in Capricorn in the 5th, conjunct the Moon and square Mars in Libra in the 2nd.

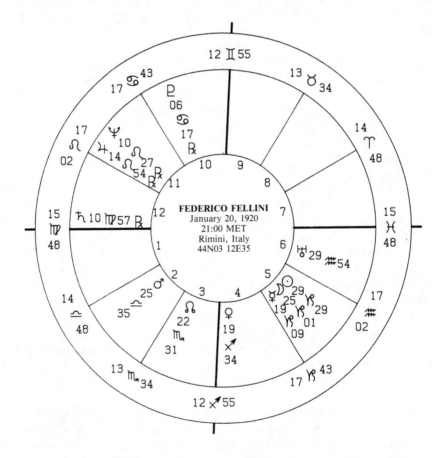

FEDERICO FELLINI
January 20, 1920
21:00 MET
Rimini, Italy
44N03 12E35

You may experience some disappointments through your children, or as is quite often the case, you are too strong for them and they as a result, cannot live up to your expectations or demands.

Ruler of the 12th in the 6th: You may be a workhorse trying to run away from your inner self by being too busy to ever find the time to look within. If it is not actual work, it can be volunteer service. A client comes to mind who has Taurus on the 12th and Venus in Sagittarius in the 6th. Venus squares the Moon, opposes Jupiter, trines Saturn and sextiles Uranus. She is forever leading a youth group, heading the drive for this or that, serving as a chairman for innumerable charitable groups; yet she has deep marital problems and just cannot find the time to see a psychologist or attend some marriage counseling sessions with her husband.

Sometimes, especially if the ruler is not strong in your chart, you may decide that work is not for you; instead you may retire early (at age 32 like one of our students) or you may just do enough work to survive and spend the rest of your time pursuing deeper subjects. Some of the work you perform may be involved with taking care of a sick or handicapped person, or like Eleanor Roosevelt who at a certain point in her life had to fill in for her husband Franklin who had polio. She had Scorpio on the 12th house and Pluto in Gemini in the 6th, square Jupiter and Venus and trine Uranus and Mercury. (Her chart is on next page.)

If the planet ruling the 12th is very tension producing, you need to find some work or hobby to integrate the energies and use them in a positive way or illness could result.

Ruler of the 12th in the 7th: A partner could be the key to your understanding of yourself and, depending on the aspects, facing yourself and your needs honestly. If Saturn or Pluto is involved, a partnership can go to the depth of your being and the bond broken only through death. An example is Charles Lindbergh (see chart in Volume II), who has Scorpio on the 12th and Pluto in Gemini in the 7th. His wife Anne Morrow Lindbergh was his mainstay, support and friend throughout the difficult years following the kidnapping of their baby and his early endorsement of Hitler at the beginning of World War II.

As happens so often in astrology, the opposite can result when more lighthearted or fickle planets rule the 12th house. The great actor/director Charlie Chaplin had Libra on the cusp of the 12th and Venus in Taurus in the 7th, conjunct Mars and square Saturn. Somehow he always needed more reassurance than one woman could give him. This also was true of the beautiful but ill-fated actress Marilyn Monroe. Her 7th house Moon in Aquarius ruled her 12th, conjuncted Jupiter, squared Saturn and opposed Neptune, forming a strong T-square. The tidal swings of the Moon in restless Aquarius accentuated the insecurity of the Saturn square and the conjunction to Jupiter may have given her false optimism. The Neptune opposition clouded any clear thinking she may have done on the subject of who she

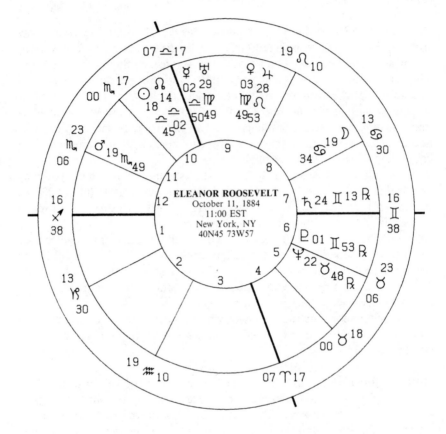

ELEANOR ROOSEVELT
October 11, 1884
11:00 EST
New York, NY
40N45 73W57

was and where she wanted to go. (Her chart is on page 111.)

Ruler of the 12th in the 8th: In the old texts it simply said: "Trouble with inheritance or death of secret enemies." Our approach to astrology certainly has changed over the years. Inheritances may play a role, but there does not have to be any trouble with them; in fact, they may enable you to pursue some of your deeper needs or wishes. One of our students was having quite a few psychological problems because she learned in her late teens that she had been adopted. Her grandmother passed away, leaving her enough money to get some very good counseling and to trace her real parents through a competent lawyer. She has Sagittarius on the 12th and Jupiter in Leo in the 8th.

Quite a few of the astronauts have this placement: Buzz Aldrin, Gordon Cooper and John Glenn, to mention just three. It is possible that zero gravity has a similar effect to an out-of-body experience. Aldrin (Taurus on

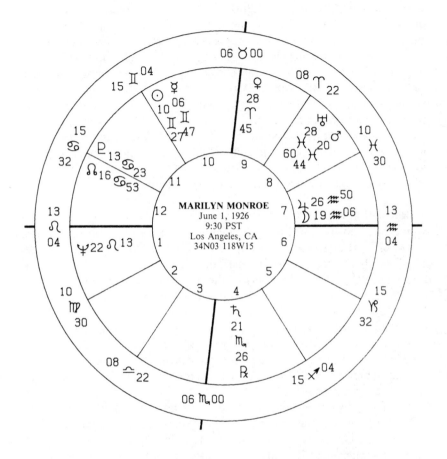

06 ♉ 00

15 ♊ 04
☉ ☿ 06
10
♊ ♊
2 47

♀ 28 ♈ 45

08 ♈ 22

⛢ 28 ♂ 20
♓ 60 ♓ 44 10 ♓ 30

15 ♋ 32
♇ 13 ♋ 23
♌ 16 ♋ 53
10   9
11
12
1

MARILYN MONROE
June 1, 1926
9:30 PST
Los Angeles, CA
34N03 118W15

8
7
6

♃ 26 ♒ 50
☽ 19 ♒ 06
13 ♒ 04

13 ♌ 04
♅ 22 ♌ 13

10 ♍ 30
08 ♎ 22

2
3
4
5

♄ 21 ♏ 26 ℞

15 ♐ 04

15 ♑ 32

06 ♏ 00

the 12th, Venus in Capricorn in the 8th) stated that he came back a transformed man and most of the astronauts who have flown in outer space have
gone through transformation and tremendous inner changes of attitude.

Timothy Leary (see chart in Volume II) also had some "out-of-body"
experiences, only they were drug induced and part of the research he was
doing on the effects of such substances as LSD. All very Neptunian/12th
and 8th house involvements.

You could get support (8th house) from hidden sources or secret societies
like the Mafia.

Ruler of the 12th in the 9th: Much of your inner sustenance can be found
through religion and charts of many religious leaders have this placement.
One good example is Vivekananda, the great Indian swami who went to
foreign countries like the U.S. and England (9th house) to teach his religion
and philosophy (9th) in order to find his own true calling and gain more

insight into his subconscious (12th). (See his chart on page 11.) Another example is Edgar Cayce, the sleeping prophet, who gave help and support to others while he was in a subconscious (12th house) or super conscious (9th house) state. The Moon rules his 12th and is in the 9th in Taurus. In Cayce's case the wide conjunction of the Moon to Neptune served as illumination rather than illusion; the trine to Mars gave practical application to his creativity and the sextiles to Mercury, Saturn and Venus provided the opportunity to utilize his talents and resources.

A negative use of this position is exemplified by the chart of Lt. William Calley who was tried and found guilty of killing innocent women and children in Mi-Lai. He has Libra on the 12th and Venus in Leo in the 9th conjunct Pluto. A foreign country (9th) became his self undoing (12th).

Ruler of the 12th in the 10th: The most obvious interpretation is that your career may have a 12th house orientation as in medical, nursing or prison work, or in church work like Pope John Paul II (whose chart is on page 12). The obvious conclusion is that your career can help you gain insight into yourself, particularly in any of the psychological fields where you not only are trained to help others, but first of all go through analysis yourself. How much of the learning you apply to your needs and how much of your subconscious self you really want to face, depends upon the integration of your chart and your decision of how you will use it. Scientist Albert Einstein used both insight and intuition in order to develop his Theory of Relativity. He had Gemini on the 12th and Mercury in the 10th in Aries conjunct Saturn. (See his chart on page 52.)

In many instances your life's work can give you inner assurance and a purpose, but you may also use it as an excuse for not facing yourself — the usual alibi of being too busy or having to live up to obligations. In this respect the placement is similar to the ruler of the 12th in the 6th. We have found that many of our students and clients who have this position cannot get away with any behind-the-scenes or secret actions. Whatever they try to do in hiding (12th house) comes out in the open or becomes common knowledge in the community (10th house).

Ruler of the 12th in the 11th: Friends can become the pivotal point in your ability to face yourself and to learn to like what you see, unless the ruler is Neptune or the aspects are such that you have great problems working with the chart; then you need to guard against fair-weather friends. One of our clients has Libra on the 12th house cusp and Venus in Virgo conjunct Neptune in the 11th; it opposes the Moon in Pisces and squares Mars in Sagittarius in the 2nd. She has lost out three times so far in deals she has entered into with friends. She has lost money when she loaned it to them and she feels that her friends withdraw their support when she most needs it.

You could be a behind-the-scenes manipulator for some large organization such as the CIA or similar secret groups. Or you could be the master of secret negotiations like Henry Kissinger, former Secretary of State. He has Taurus on his 12th and Venus in Taurus in the 11th opposed Jupiter in the 5th. (See his chart on page 92.) From our observation the most common occurrence for this position affects your goals (11th) which you keep under tight wraps (12th) or your hopes and wishes (11th) are very nebulous and need better insight (12th).

Ruler of the 12th in the 12th: This position more than any other gives you innate strength like a well from which you can draw water whenever you need it. You don't necessarily understand your subconscious motivations or needs, but when the chips are down you know instinctively what to do. This is one of the most intuitive placements for the ruler of the 12th.

We can use the planetary energies in many given ways; however, the negative utilization is often easier than the positive one. Murderess Susan Atkins who participated in the cold blooded killing of Sharon Tate and her companions under the supposedly hypnotic spell of Charles Manson, has Jupiter in Sagittarius ruling her 12th house and situated in the 12th; Jupiter opposes both Venus and Uranus, trines Mars and inconjuncts Mercury. The easy vanity and self-indulgence of the opposition to Venus and the lack of moderation of the Uranus opposition did not help to stabilize the escapist tendencies of a 12th house Jupiter inconjunct Mercury.

Some people who found inspiration and belief through their 12th house rulerships are Henry Mancini (the inspiration of music) and Rosalynn Carter (the belief in country and husband) (charts are in Volume II) and of Margaret Mead (intuitive understanding) (chart is on page 30).

PART II

Introduction
The "Art" of Chart Interpretation

This is not a tongue-in-cheek expression: To truly look at a horoscope — to take some planets, signs, house placements and aspects and from that mass of glyphs understand who this person is, how he or she reacts to life, love and the pursuit of happiness — is an "art."

There are probably as many ways of approaching this subject as there are astrologers. After a while you and everyone else will discover a way of delineating which is uniquely yours, and that is the way it should be. But until you have reached that kind of proficiency you need a few guidelines to help you look without overlooking and to see with understanding.

In Volume II of *The Only Way to . . . Learn Astrology* we end with Lesson 20 entitled "Steps to Delineation." In this book we make practical use of those steps. The overview is always necessary in order to understand the synthesis of the whole, to realize what makes the native unique, and to find the main pull or direction. Then we dissect the horoscope into many facets — the Sun, the Moon, the Ascendant and so on; but as we look at each little piece we always remember the total picture seen in overview.

In this volume we show you four distinct ways of interpreting a chart. Though Joan McEvers and Marion March see eye to eye in every facet of teaching astrology, each has developed her own style of delineating. Joan starts with the overview and then goes right to the Ascendant and first house, then the second and third houses and so on around the wheel. She uses the decanates and dwads when interpreting the Sun, Moon and Ascendant. She delineates each planet as she gets to the particular house the planet occupies. She looks at the planet's sign, then the house it is placed in, the aspects made and where the planet rules. As she goes around the wheel, she delineates each cusp and then looks to where the rulers of the cusp are located. The interpretation of General George Patton's chart is a good illustration of the Joan McEvers approach.

Marion also starts with the overview. She then proceeds to the Sun and delineates it by sign and house, blending it with the sign and house of the ruler, and finally interprets the aspects to the Sun. She uses the same procedure for the Moon and Ascendant and the chart ruler (Ascendant ruler). She then works her way around the chart, house by house, interpreting planets as they are found in the houses. Once in a while a chart seems to call for an early delineation of Mercury or Venus. The interpretation of the charts of Ernest Hemingway and Princess Diana are good examples of Marion's techniques.

Joan always uses Mars as the co-ruler of Scorpio; Marion refers to it as "the former ruler" and does not use it that way in natal chart delineation.

As explained in Volume II, there are two kinds of nodes: the Mean Nodes and the True Nodes. Neither kind is better than the other. Joan owns a computer that stores the Mean Nodes on its disc. Marion uses Neil Michelsen's *American Ephemeris for the 20th Century* which happens to list the True Nodes.

Many astrologers have different methods of figuring the final (or chart) signature. Joan uses the ten planets and brings the Ascendant into play only when she needs a tie breaker. Marion uses the ten planets plus the Ascendant and Midheaven. Some astrologers give different values to the luminaries, such as 1 for each of the planets but 2 for the Sun, Moon and Ascendant and **none** for the Midheaven. Or 1 for each planet and the Midheaven, 2 for the Ascendant and Moon, and 3 for the Sun. Here again each of you will find your own way. The only important factor is that the signature has to match or resemble the character of the person in question, however you may arrive at it.

Another area in which you need to find your own answers concerns the question of orbs when aspecting. We can only recommend that you keep fairly tight orbs, since the average person always reacts to tight orbs (under 5°), nearly always to average orbs (8° or less), and only sometimes to wide orbs (over 8°). Our delineation uses major aspects only (conjunction, sextile, square, trine, inconjunct and opposition). Please note that we include the inconjunct (quincunx) as one of the major aspects and allow a 5° orb. We have found that these six aspects form the basic character and are the mainstay to understanding the innate needs, urges, potentials and talents of a human being. Minor aspects are very important in daily living. They concern the habit pattern, the small irritations and the minor pleasures that make life what it is; but they do not shape the early personality that makes you what you are. We will teach you more about minor aspects in a later book.

We want you to have a wide exposure to diverse methods of delineating, so we show you not only different approaches but also different purposes. With Ernest Hemingway's chart we give you a hindsight interpretation, using a step by step in-depth method and substantiating it all the way with biographical data. The delineation for Princess Diana's chart is also in depth but in her case we have only the facts as of this date and do not know how the Princess will handle herself or use her potential in years to come. The approach for General George Patton is again in depth and methodical, but handled with a different technique and using just enough biographical substantiation of this fascinating man to make your learning meaningful and interesting. With Barbra Streisand's horoscope we use a totally different technique which we call "zooming in"; although all facets of the chart (each planet, house and aspect) are covered and explained, it is not done by methodically going from house to house, but by concentrating on areas as they stand out: configuration, chart pattern, a lack, an overabundance, etc. To show some additional interpretive techniques, we use various steps to give you further insight, such as Arabian Parts and Fixed Stars to mention two. (See Volume II, Part 3.)

In part III of this book we show you another way of zooming in on a chart — this time to look for specifics, such as vocational aptitude, appearance, relationship needs and physical strengths and weaknesses.

You can and probably will devise your own technique of chart interpretation. To demonstrate how easy it is to adapt something to your own way, here's a method used by Gloria Stein, one of Aquarius Workshops' most able teachers. She starts with the overview as outlined in "Steps to Delineation" in Volume II. She then delineates the Sun and Moon, their signs, houses, rulers, decanates and aspects. Her next step is to interpret the conception of the self; this she finds by looking at the Ascendant, its sign, decanate, ruler and aspects to both. Planets in the 1st house give added emphasis to the self-image.

For the foundation, roots and attitude toward the inner self, she delineates the 4th house cusp, its ruler, aspects to the ruler and planets in the 4th house. Her next concern is the reasoning and communicative ability, which she finds by interpreting Mercury by position, sign and aspect, then by judging the 3rd house (here she also considers early conditioning and siblings) and the 9th house where she looks not only for the higher mind expression but also for the philosophies and higher consciousness.

Her next goal is to determine what the person wants to do and achieve. She looks to the 10th house and its ruler for status, recognition and career; and to the 6th house and ruler for the work ethics and drive in order to realize what the 10th promises. The 2nd house tells her about the person's ability to earn money, their inner resources and their sense of values, while she reads the 8th house for joint support and business ventures and the partner's or other people's resources.

She interprets attitudes toward relationships by checking the 7th house for one-to-one relationships, the 11th house for group activities and friends and the 5th house for love affairs and children. Though she may already have delineated Venus and Mars as rulers of some previously examined houses, she will describe them again in the context of love and sex; she will also refer back to the 8th house, this time for sexual attitudes. Last but not least, Gloria will interpret the 12th house for the innermost or hidden part of the nature.

Gloria, like Joan and Marion, describes all houses, planets and aspects, only the order in which she looks at them is different; that difference is suited to her personality. We hope that each of you will find your method of chart interpretation.

In the four delineations that follow, we base the entire interpretation on our own keywords and key phrases as they are found in Volumes I and II of *The Only Way to . . . Learn Astrology* and in Part I of this volume. In certain cases we may have changed a word or phrase to fit our vocabulary and sometimes we incorporated the sentences verbatim. At times we used less than half the written material because not all of it was applicable to the horoscope at hand — which is what the art or judgment of chart interpretation is all about.

For those of you who still feel insecure about using your own words, just follow our delineations by referring back to the proper sections in Volumes I, II and III. To illustrate: General George Patton's overview states that: "The 4 above — 6 below division indicates a person who is somewhat more subjective than objective, one who is inwardly oriented." On page 43 of Volume I, Lesson 4, "The Houses/The Meridians," it states: "If you have many planets below the horizon, especially if these include the Sun and the Moon, you will be somewhat subjective and content to work behind the scenes." Patton has only a slight predominance of planets below the horizon, and only the Sun is included, therefore the sentence needs to be toned down. With Saturn, Mars, Jupiter, Uranus and Venus angular, the Sun in the 5th house and some strong configurations, Patton will not be content to stay behind the scenes; but he will be quite introspective and inwardly oriented, especially with Pluto in the 12th house, the Sun in Scorpio and the Moon in the 8th house.

To give you another example: In the Hemingway delineation we state that the 11th house Sun "is generally goal oriented." In Volume I on page 92, "Sun in the 11th House," the text states: "You do your own thing and generally achieve what you want." As you can see, this is the same idea put into slightly different words. To continue, the book says: "You are either very social with many friends or you can be the loner who goes your own way.'' We felt that the Hemingway chart showed both sides of this sentence, but rather than just throwing it in at this point, we wanted to elaborate (and did) as we delineated the 11th and 12th houses. The book goes on: ''Good at meeting challenges, you are usually an excellent organizer who can inspire others to help you in all your undertakings.'' We paraphrased: ''An excellent organizer, he loved to be in charge of arranging trips, safaris and hunts. His Virgo Ascendant and Capricorn Moon confirmed this tendency .'' The book continues: ''You are often the leader in some new field or involved with service on a large scale. The Sun in the 11th house and the Sun in Aquarius operate similarly.'' We say: ''As often in the case with the Sun in the Aquarian 11th house, he was a leader in his field, initiating a style of writing never before tried in the United States.''

In the Barbra Streisand delineation we even put quotation marks around some words or phrases to show you that they were lifted verbatim from our books.

Now study the different delineations and see if you come up with similar interpretations.

Lesson 13
GENERAL GEORGE S. PATTON:
A Modern Gladiator

United States Army officer George Smith Patton, Jr. was born November 11, 1885, at 6:38 PM on the 1800-acre Wilson-Patton ranch in San Marino, California. The event was recorded in his mother's Bible, but he regarded his birth date as merely another link in an historic chain. He believed his life had spanned the ages; he recalled incidents that had occurred centuries before in which he, in earlier incarnations, had played a part.

He graduated from West Point and served in the cavalry as an aide to General Pershing. Patton was the first man detailed to the tank corps in World War I. He commanded the 2nd armored division in World War I; he was major general in command under Eisenhower's U.S. forces in Morocco; he commanded the 2nd Army corps in Tunisia; he commanded the 7th Army in Western Europe. He died December 9, 1945, in Italy from injuries sustained in a jeep accident.

In delineating Patton's horoscope we will start with the **overview** in the lower right-hand corner of the chart. He has three planets east of the meridian and seven planets west; four planets above the horizon and six below. The four above/six below division indicates a person who is somewhat more subjective than objective, one who is inwardly oriented. With seven planets west of the meridian, we see that his life would be closely bound up with the destinies of others. Both the Sun and Moon are included in the setting planets, which emphasizes the fact that he would choose a lifestyle where

GEORGE PATTON
November 11, 1885
18:38 PST
San Marino, CA
34N07 118W06

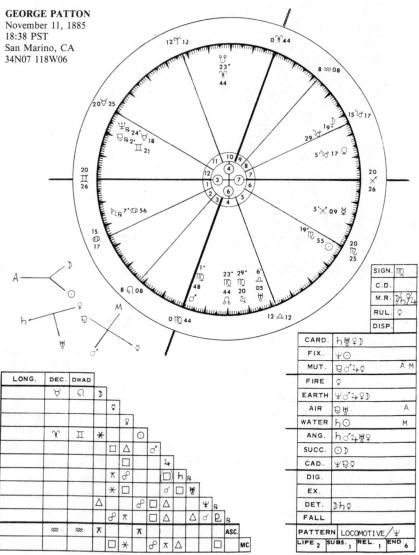

he would not always be able to demonstrate his own free will. With a Scorpio Sun and Capricorn Moon, this was not easy for him but was among the many lessons he had to learn.

His planets are rather equally divided by quality with four cardinal, two fixed and four plus the Ascendant in mutable signs. He had only one planet in fire, five in earth, two plus the Ascendant in air and two in water; therefore, his chart signature was Virgo (predominance of mutable and earth). His Sun was in Scorpio and he had a Gemini Ascendant. This is a powerful combination that needs positive direction if it is to work well. Scientific and inventive, he accomplished a great deal. Many astrologers feel that Scorpio and Gemini are not compatible as they have nothing in common, sharing neither quality nor element.

Scorpio is passive and Gemini is active. Since Scorpio is probing and Gemini curious, he was able to use the energy inventively and productively; but there was a cruel streak in his personality due to the frustration of not always finding the key to integrate the Scorpio/Gemini diversity. The Moon in Capricorn added detachment and the need to be recognized as an important and powerful person.

To all of this we must add some Virgo qualities because of the Virgo signature. Usually the signature, if there is one, is a backup to the Sun, Moon or Ascendant sign; but in Patton's case it provides some different insight into his character and personality. To the Scorpio incisiveness, the Capricorn ambition and the Gemini versatility, we must add Virgo discrimination, industriousness, the ability to criticize and a certain melancholy.

The single planet in a fire sign is somewhat compensated for by two planets in the houses of life. One of these, the Sun, is accidently dignified in the fifth house, so he was not lacking in drive and enthusiasm, the qualities of fire. The Moon in Capricorn, Saturn in Cancer and Mercury in Sagittarius are all in detriment, indicating that they would not operate at full strength in his horoscope. This does not mean that he was not emotional (Moon) only that his emotions were controlled (Capricorn); not that he was not disciplined (Saturn) only that his discipline was dependent upon his feelings (Cancer); not that he could not communicate (Mercury) only that his communication was colored by his idealism (Sagittarius). The Moon and Saturn are in mutual reception, as are Jupiter and Mercury. This means that each pair of planets work well together; therefore it was easy for him to integrate them into the chart and use them more positively than was first thought when we observed that three of the four are in detriment.

The chart pattern is a locomotive. All ten planets are placed within two thirds of the zodiac and leave an empty trine between the Moon and Neptune. The locomotive gives a certain balance but also a strong sense of lack which forced him to achieve. Neptune is the engine planet, indicating that his achievement could come through behind-the-scenes activity (12th house), inspiration and trusting his own feelings and hunches (Neptune), and applying his perceptions practically (Neptune in Taurus).

The chart ruler Mercury governs his Gemini Ascendant and is placed in the 6th house. It shows that service, routine and method were important to him. Since his chart signature is Virgo, the natural 6th house sign, it is easy to understand the devotion of his whole life to giving service to his country, his attention to detail and his reputation for meticulousness.

At this point we look to see if Patton has any configurations. There is a cardinal T-square with Saturn in Cancer in the 1st house opposing Venus in Capricorn in the 7th, both square Uranus in Libra in the 4th. This indicates that he needed to develop an awareness (opposition) of other people's values and feelings (Venus in the 7th) in relationship to his own attitudes of form and responsibility (Saturn in the 1st). The square from Saturn to Uranus shows that he had to learn the art of compromise and to develop the ability to cope with his feelings of insecurity stemming from his home life and early upbringing (Uranus in the 4th). The square from Venus to Uranus shows that there might be a separation from his partner at some time in his life and that he would be determined to have his own way, resent authority and feel a need to be different. Much of this worked out through his 10th house of career, the area opposite Uranus in the 4th which is the focal point of the T-square.

As a military man Patton was colorful, legendary and paradoxical. His rise was due to his own will to achieve; this was instilled from early childhood through the reminiscences of his grandfather Smith and his cronies, who were always around telling Civil War stories when Georgie was growing up. The eccentricity of Saturn square Uranus is verified by the fact that young Patton did not attend school, because his father did not believe in formal education. Tutored by his father, he quickly learned to read and was an accomplished writer (Gemini rising); but he never learned to spell — as he put it, "I have trouble with the A and B and — what do you call that other letter?"

The second configuration is a mutable grand cross with Mars in the 4th house opposing the Midheaven, squaring Mercury in Sagittarius in the 6th and Pluto in Gemini in the 12th. Mercury and Pluto oppose each other. This reemphasizes the importance of his early training and background (Mars in the 4th) in his subsequent military achievement and recognition (Midheaven/10th house). Mars square Mercury accentuates curiosity but creates restlessness, making him combative and the square to Pluto indicated a need to deal with violence. What better way to deal with violence than within the acceptable confines of war? The opposition of Mercury to Pluto contributed to his ability to tell it like it is.

The yod from the Ascendant to the Sun and Moon is the third configuration and indicated the belief he held in the mystique of greatness. His perceptive ability is shown by the Sun in Scorpio sextile the Moon in the 8th

(Scorpio) house. The necessary adjustment (inconjunct) of the Sun in the 5th (creativity) but conjunct the 6th house cusp (service given) to the projection of his personality (Ascendant) and the reorganization of his emotions (Moon) pointed the way for him to live this out; as he wrote in 1926, "Truly in war, men are nothing, a man is everything."

We have learned a great deal about Patton's intrinsic personality from the overview of the chart. Now we will proceed to take the chart apart house by house.

Gemini rising is restless, curious, expressive, inventive, changeable, clever and can be conniving. Most of these qualities will surface through his work, since the ruler Mercury is in the 6th house. His Ascendant degree is in the Aquarian decanate of Gemini; this adds an independent streak, broadens his intellectuality, emphasizes his ability for detachment and highlights his inventiveness. Since the dwad is also in Aquarius, you might consider the Aquarian qualities to be doubled, so to speak. Gemini is never at a loss for words and Patton was known for his outspoken, direct, often blunt and profane use of language (Mercury is in Sagittarius). His biographer Martin Blumenson states: "He was unpredictable, capricious, at the same time dependable, loyal. He was brutal yet sensitive. He was gregarious and a loner. Enthusiastic and buoyant, he suffered from inner anguish." That certainly sounds as though he was describing a Scorpio with Gemini rising.

Saturn in Cancer in the **1st house** gives a need to take on responsibility and the desire for power because of childhood conditioning. Serious and dedicated, his sense of melancholy, conscientiousness and a feeling of personal insecurity spurred him to great achievement. Since Saturn ruled his 8th house and opposed Venus in the 7th, he undoubtedly had sexual problems (8th) and separations from his partner (7th) that caused stress and difficulty in showing his true feelings. Saturn inconjunct Mercury in the 6th house indicates a desperate need for approval but also a tendency to ruthlessness, especially as far as his work was concerned. The wide sextile to Mars (6°) provided a marvelous sense of timing; the ability to know when to fight and when to run, certainly contributed to his penchant for the military. Since Mars is in the 4th house, home and family and earning their respect were important to him. The square to Uranus added to his know-it-all attitude and again shows his need for approval. It is almost as though he proved his masculinity by demonstrating his authority to his father and grandfather, as well as to those in command over him in later years.

Saturn trine the Midheaven contributed to his rise in his profession, added to his method and organization and pointed up his dedication to achieving his goals. This also demonstrates the loner quality that people sensed in him. Saturn is retrograde in his chart and at an early age Patton knew who he was and where he was going, which is the most positive use of a retrograde Saturn. Deliberate in attaining his goals, he had a well developed sense of humor, most of the time self-directed.

With **Cancer** on the **2nd house** cusp, he was most likely economical, security conscious and able to build up a nice estate. The Moon that rules the 2nd house is in Capricorn in the 8th and has positive, flowing aspects, so undoubtedly money was never a problem for him. He came from a well to do background and married well (Moon in the 8th). His values were closely linked with home, tradition and patriotism, all Cancer qualities. The 2nd house shows how you earn your income, and with the Moon in the 8th house, Patton chose to earn his through 8th house matters (death and destruction).

The **3rd house** shows how we communicate. With **Leo** here Patton was a good conversationalist and had excellent powers of self-expression. With the Sun in Scorpio and Mercury in Sagittarius, he was known to be good copy — profane, blustering but never at a loss for words. Ambitious and enterprising, with a good and clear-thinking mind, he was eager in his pursuit of knowledge and was an avid reader and always well informed. In spite of the active 4th house, he had a happy childhood and got along quite well with his two younger sisters. This is confirmed by the Sun, ruler of the 3rd house of early environment, sextile the Moon. Leo on the 3rd always gives the ability to dramatize, and Patton was no exception. The Sun's opposition to Neptune surely enhanced this.

Obviously the **4th house** is a very important one in Patton's chart. With **Virgo** on the cusp, he felt that work kept him young and he was always willing to serve — in this case not just his family, but also his country. He did not so much work from his home as he lived where he worked. This position added to his somewhat schizophrenic personality indicated by the Scorpio Sun and Gemini Ascendant. The fact that the ruler of the 4th, Mercury is in the 6th house, again shows how he was raised, with the idea of giving service; it also indicates the comfort of his early upbringing and the fact that he had servants (Mercury trine Jupiter in the 4th). Even in his army career, Patton always had aides around to carry out his orders.

Mars in Virgo in the **4th house** tells us that he was cool, logical and scientific, loved to work and contributed a lot of enthusiastic effort to his career. Thorough and painstaking, routine as such did not bother him and his orderliness and attention to detail carried over into his home life and appearance. He was well known for his ivory-handled revolvers and for changing into clean shirts three times a day. He had an aggressive need for security and since Mars rules the 11th house, that security came through large organizations such as the U.S. government.

With Mars in the 4th house, you may do well away from the place of your birth and Patton was no exception to this; his most striking victories came half way around the world from where he was born. This Mars placement often indicates a military background which was true in his case. Grandfather Smith and his cronies had been in the Civil War and they were always around while Georgie was growing up, spinning fanciful tales of service life. Surely this intrigued and influenced Patton in his ambition for a military career.

Mars square Mercury in the 6th house contributed to his impulsiveness and tendency to leap to conclusions; but it also provided the mental energy necessary for his amazing military strategy and single-minded devotion to his work. The trine to Venus in the 7th shows the devotion and loyalty of his wife, Beatrice. It also added warmth and affection to his otherwise rather austere nature. Though he was away from home so much of the time due to his career demands, Patton always knew that Bea was there providing the needed security for him to return to.

Mars square Neptune gave a strong imagination and contributed to the prophetic dreams, visions and foreknowledge in which he saw himself as Caesar, Hannibal and Alexander. This aspect undoubtedly contributed to the unsavory legend that grew about his pistol carrying, swashbuckling, cavalier attitude that the newspapers — always hungry for headlines — printed about him. Neptune rules his Midheaven.

Forceful and aggressive, he came on strong, as Mars square Pluto often does. He never quite learned to control his tendency to ride roughshod over others, but his need for physical violence found an adequate outlet in the games of war. Mars opposite the Midheaven increased his need to dominate those around him; fortunately, his choice of a career provided an acceptable way of doing so. With this aspect, nothing stops you from getting ahead and "undaunted" is a good word to describe the person who has this aspect. George certainly lived up to this image. Tact and diplomacy eluded him all the days of his life. Even after he became secure in his self worth, he did not overcome his strong need to override others and their ideas.

If the **North Node** signifies the area of growth in this lifetime, then Patton with his North Node in the 4th house was supposed to work on security, home and family affairs and his psychological roots and private life. From what we know of his life, this was an area he had difficulty facing, and he found it much easier to escape through his **South Node** in the 10th house to his career and the fame and notoriety that it brought about.

Jupiter in Virgo in the **4th house** gives the ability to gain the cooperation of others. This certainly was important to Patton. He was a natural scholar, in spite of his unorthodox schooling. His lofty ideals did indeed lead him to expect too much from others (Jupiter rules the 7th house). Cleanliness and order were very important to him; he was a fanatic about his clothes and always dressed to the teeth with polished boots and saber. He was devoted to his home and family, even though he was away from them so much of the time and as often happens with Jupiter in the 4th, he came from a financially secure background. His enjoyment of open spaces surfaced most often on the battlefield where he really seemed at home. The militant background was in evidence, not so much in his childhood as during his adult years, by his own choice.

Restless and disliking restriction (Jupiter conjunct Uranus), Patton was definitely his own person; he showed a deep respect for knowledge and was most likely a genius in his field of expertise. He was interested in anything new and progressive and had a very strong belief in the occult. The opportunities for travel that a Jupiter/Uranus conjunction gives were also very evident in his life. Jupiter's wide sextile to Mercury gave him great command of language (in spite of the fact that he could not spell), good comprehension and great integrity. He spoke fluent French and was able to read Latin. Travel was rewarding for him and he was honorable, fair and philosophical.

The square from Jupiter to Venus contributed to his reputation for being vain, conceited and overly emotional. He certainly did have a tendency to exaggerate in action as well as with words, but his intuition did flourish and he used the challenges of this aspect pretty well. The trine from Jupiter to Neptune enhanced his spiritual and mystical beliefs and he used his psychic ability in a beneficial way. He truly believed that he had lived in the time of Caesar, Augustus and Alexander the Great, and his knowledge of their military strategy contributed directly to his stunning victories in North Africa and Sicily in World War II. Exuberant, enthusiastic and ambitious, he encouraged others to explore their potentials and he had the great organizational skills that we expect from someone with a Jupiter/Pluto trine.

Uranus in Libra gives tremendous charm and personal magnetism and allows a person to get away with wild notions without being offensive. Since Uranus is the focal point of a T-square in Patton's chart, he was very independent and self-willed; but because of the conjunction to Jupiter, he was more than willing to accept the responsibility for his actions. Uranus in the 4th house promises unexpected ups and downs in one's home life. According to his biographer, Ladislas Farago, his upbringing though unusual, was loving and solid.

The sextile from Uranus to Mercury stressed his near genius while it contributed to his brilliance, talent, independence and originality. A spellbinding speaker, he was eloquent, unique, enterprising, had an excellent memory, was impatient with ignorance and had great dramatic sense. Spectacular and swaggering, he was America's most flamboyant fighting leader, idolized and vilified, loved and hated.

The square from Uranus to Venus shows his tendency to be spoiled and used to having his own way; but he was able to make his point with charm when he felt like it! Self-centered and egotistic, he was magnetic in his dealings with others (Venus in the 7th house). He was touchy and willful and there were many rumors about his sexual exploits, which this aspect indicates may not all have been rumors, especially with Saturn opposing Venus and squaring Uranus confirming possible problems. He had a strong desire nature, resented authority and liked to shock others. Many times people with this aspect like to act differently and draw attention to themselves in order to cover up a deep inferiority complex. In Patton's case this does not seem to be true. He really believed he was invincible.

Uranus also trines Pluto. This is a generational aspect, but it plays an important part in Patton's chart because his Sun is in Scorpio, ruled by Pluto and Uranus is angular. The trine gives endurance and strength which he demonstrated admirably. It also indicates the true idealist which George certainly was. Uranus rules his 9th cusp and with Aquarius there, you are interested in establishing your own philosophy. This was easy for George because of the trine.

Romance, poetry, music and involvement with others is important to the person who has **Libra** on the **5th house** cusp and with Venus in the 7th in Capricorn, we can assume this was true of Patton. Since Venus has some challenging aspects, this was a side of his nature that only his intimates were aware of. He met his future wife Beatrice Ayer when he was seventeen and she was just fifteen; they corresponded for three years, during which time he graduated from Pasadena High School (not without difficulty — Sun, ruler of the 3rd opposing Neptune — too much dreaming) and spent a year at Virginia Military Institute. They met again when he went to West Point, but it wasn't until May 26, 1910, that they were married. He never courted another girl, and she never had another beau. She was well able to keep up with him in sailing and riding. She shared his love of horses and when they were living near Washington, D.C. in his early years in the Army, they maintained their own stable.

In 1912 when George went to the Olympic Games in Stockholm to appear in the pentathlon, Bea and his mother went with him at his own expense. He came in fifth in a field of 32 contestants. Venus ruling his 5th house and square to Uranus contributed to his need to take chances and be daring.

Determined, aggressive and shrewd, the **Sun** in Scorpio is rarely passive or neutral about anything. George's nature was deep and he was often quite secretive, in spite of his boisterousness; many times he was jealous, sometimes resentful and often vengeful. He had keen judgment and penetrating insight and, of course, these qualities put him in a position where he was able to exercise authority over others. Willpower and persistence definitely were his strong points and he was certainly able to be direct and outspoken — too much so at times. Since his Sun was in the Pisces decanate, we must add the intuition, mystical attitudes and the love of poetry that Pisces provides.

The Gemini dwad reinforced his Gemini Ascendant and added to his innate curiosity and communicative abilities. Not only did he recite poetry, he also wrote it. The Sun in the 5th house gave him strength, creativity and made him popular and self-indulgent. He had a great interest in his children (two girls and a boy) even though, due to his work he could not spend much time with them during their formative years (Venus, ruler of the 5th square Uranus in the 4th). The Sun's placement here added to his ability to dramatize situations and magnified his need for attention.

Since the Sun is close to the 6th house cusp, we have to delineate its action through the 6th as well as the 5th house. The Sun in the 6th fits the description of Patton as a capable and good organizer who took pride in his achievements. He had high regard for diet, health and hygiene and observed a regular routine whenever possible. He did very well in the service field and was also an active and successful sportsman. His favorite pastime was polo, and when he was living in the United States, he owned a string of polo ponies and played every chance he got.

The Sun in Scorpio is often involved with death which Patton surely was in his role as an army officer. He was also interested in the occult and life after death, and even had a premonition of his own death in the late fall of 1945 (Sun opposed to Neptune in the 12th). He ransacked his memories and took stock of his life and put his thoughts down on paper in a kind of professional memoir he called "Retrospect." He prefaced it by musing that, "War is an ancient subject and I, an ancient man, have studied and practiced it for over 40 years." (Page 97 Patton/Farago.)

The Sun opposed to Neptune often involves you in situations where others depend upon you. This was true of Patton with all his men relying on his abilities on the battlefield. This aspect gives psychic ability, but the person does not always use it in a positive way. In Patton's case, since Neptune was dignified by house (12th), trine the Moon and Jupiter, he was able to use his insight, perception and intuition through his career because Neptune ruled his Midheaven.

The sextile from the Sun in Scorpio to the Moon in Capricorn in the 8th house brought success without much struggle and created a harmonious balance between his ego (Sun) and emotions (Moon). He received help from those he served under — Generals Pershing, Bradley and Eisenhower, to name a few — who, though they disliked his personality, admired his ability.

With a T-square, and a grand cross, he was not apathetic in any area. The Sun has a very close inconjunct to the Ascendant and this provided an inordinate amount of drive, but his achievements were reached by the trial and error method. His strong personality definitely needed toning down to enable others to interact with him. Since the Sun ruled his 3rd house, much of the toning down had to do with his verbalization of his ideas and attitudes toward others. Patton never really learned to make this adjustment; his arrogance, ruthlessness and flamboyance always managed to keep him in hot water with his superiors, the press and the public.

Scorpio on the **6th house** cusp has great professional integrity. Those with this placement pride themselves on their conscientiousness and resistance to fatigue. Patton was no exception. He was a driven man when it came to his routine. Order and method, perseverance and persistence were gods to him. He was a tireless worker who loved his work. The dedication he gave to everything and the integrity he expected from others indeed made him difficult to get along with, but only if these others did not adhere to his principles. With Pluto, the ruler of the 6th in Gemini in the 12th, it is easy to see how he was able to rely on his intuition in his work. He always took on more than he should, much to the awe of those who worked with and for him. His hidden strength, his interest in historical research and his indefatigable and untiring ability to forge ahead may all be attributed to this placement. With the co-ruler Mars in the 4th house, it is obvious that he either worked at home or lived where he worked. Pluto in the 12th in Gemini tells us that he relied on his subconscious to a great extent in his daily functions and that he was not averse to speaking of his feelings. He was well known for his poetry writing and his ability to quote from the Bible when it served his purpose.

Mercury in Sagittarius is sincere, has a dry sense of humor, is impulsive and speaks without regard for the circumstances. Patton was renowned for all of these traits. He did not scatter his mental energies (Mercury is opposed to Pluto) and his mind was sharp and direct — almost too much so. Generous, progressive and honest, deception was alien to him. It would have been to his benefit if he could have applied a little more of Scorpio's ability to dissemble; but with the challenging aspects to Mercury, he was always blunt and to the point — HIS. This placement showed his interest in philosophy, religion and intellectual stimulation. He really loved to travel, was at home among strangers and was indeed a nonstop talker at times. His co-workers felt that he had a tendency toward moral sermonizing and being overly pedantic, all Mercury in Sagittarius in the 6th house traits.

This was especially evident in his chastisement of a soldier at the 15th Evacuation Hospital in Messina, Sicily. The first slapping went unnoticed and unreported. But his nervous temper (Mercury square Mars) got him into deep trouble the second time he slapped a soldier. Pvt. Paul Bennett was suffering from nervous exhaustion. He was in the hospital to be evacuated from his unit because sedatives had not had any effect on him; his case was considered to be that of battle fatigue. Patton, who was paying an impromptu visit to encourage the soldiers when he encountered Pvt. Bennett, took offense (Mercury involved in a grand cross) at what seemed to him to be the

babying of a coward. He slapped Bennett. Minutes afterward he was con-
trite, to the point of breaking into sobs. He turned to Colonel Currier, com-
manding officer of the hospital and said, "I can't help it. It makes me break
down to see brave boys and think of a yellow bastard being babied."

He commented later that he was ashamed and that he hoped the whole
thing could be forgotten; but the incident had attracted too much attention
and had become common gossip all over the 7th Army. When a detailed
report reached Eisenhower's headquarters, that was it. Patton was sent to
England after having to apologize publicly to everyone involved. Since Mercury squares the Midheaven, we can see how his mouth endangered his career.
With Mercury opposed to Pluto, he "told it like it was," his speech was incisive; but he rarely exhibited tact and diplomacy and this aspect probably
contributed to his accident proneness. He often fell from his horse while playing polo and during his years in the cavalry, he was thrown, butted, kicked
and rolled over by horses. Biographer Blumenson says, "He probably
developed what doctors now call subdurmal (*sic*) hemotoma . . ., an injury
and shock around the head (which) may prompt changes in personality."
Since Pluto is in his 12th house ruling his Sun and Mercury rules his Ascendant, the challenging aspect between these two planets from health houses
contributed in some measure to his physical accidents.

With **Sagittarius** on the cusp of the **7th house**, Patton sought in partnership someone who was independent, companionable and understanding;
also, someone who came from the same general background that he did, who
understood his need for independence, and who was able to stand on her
own two feet and maintain the family home while he was off in foreign countries fighting wars. This is illustrated by Jupiter, ruler of the 7th in the 4th
house. Companionship was more important in a marriage relationship than
sex; though he found his ideal mate early, they did not rush into marriage
and thus it lasted all of his life. Obviously his partner was a very understanding person who could handle the long separations and the rumors that came
back to her.

In spite of any sexual peccadillos, George always came back to Bea and
in all his letters he idealized her. To him she was a beacon in the dark, the
light of his soul. She was a strong woman who fought to keep George under
control when he was near her. She, more than anyone, could turn away his
wrath with a soft word and calm him down when he became obstreperous.

When he was a colonel in World War I, Patton disobeyed orders and
though he weathered the storm with only a formal reprimand, his command-
ing officer — knowing that George knuckled under to only one person,
Bea — wrote her a note telling her to admonish her wayward husband. Mrs.
Patton, knowing how accident prone George was (Pluto and Mercury square
Mars), spent years of their marriage in constant agony trembling for her husband, not merely when he went to war, but even when he was driving his

own car at reckless speed or riding his horses over his chosen obstacles. He was very headstrong but he knew how worried she was and always tried to keep his more risky escapades from coming to her attention.

Venus in Capricorn is somewhat insecure and tries to compensate for this sense of inadequacy with ambition and status seeking. Instead of being cold and calculating in partnership, this placement of Venus in the 7th house (where it is accidentally dignified) seems to confirm the fact that George spent much time away from his wife and family. Proud and reserved in his public behavior, he was certainly successful, but the square of Venus to Uranus and the opposition to Saturn most likely contributed to his ignominious removal as the head of his forces in Sicily after the soldier-slapping incident. This Venus position indicates outward repression of emotions and sensitivity but an inward lustiness and sensuality. This is backed up by the Sun in Scorpio in the 5th house. Though Bea was not a great deal older or younger than George, as is so often the case with Venus in Capricorn, she was mature and a very stabilizing influence in his life. Certainly she was loyal and dedicated and he was happy in his marriage (Venus in the 7th trine to Mars).

The challenging aspects to Venus did cause him to build up resentments. This was very evident in his attitude toward British Field Marshall Montgomery. In Africa, Sicily and Germany, Patton felt that he was in direct competition with Montgomery. They were both stubborn, egotistical and headstrong personalities, and disagreed completely on methods of pursuing their warring tactics. It is quite possible that the position of Venus in Patton's chart, as ruler of the 12th house, led to a near persecution complex. When General Eisenhower backed Montgomery's decisions over Patton's tactical ideas, he felt that he was being used, misused and taken advantage of. He wrote in his diary on April 15, 1943, "War is very simple, direct and ruthless. It takes a simple, direct and ruthless man to wage war." He had no doubt that he was such a man and that Monty was not.

The inconjunct from Venus to Pluto indicated a need for Patton to learn moderation in his relationships, but he seemed incapable of that. This aspect also contributed to his belief in the occult and reincarnation and enhanced his excellent communication abilities in both writing and speaking. But it did not tone down his need to express profanely. With Venus sextile the Midheaven he was generally well thought of in his career. His fellow officers knew him to be capable and dependable.

Capricorn on the **8th house** cusp gives courage and the ability to stand strong in the face of adversity and Patton demonstrated this often. Usually this position promises a long life and rarely a sudden death, but the many other indications in Patton's chart rebutted this. Saturn, the ruler of the 8th placed in the 1st and squaring Uranus in the 4th house (which indicates the end of life), shows that he would most likely die unexpectedly in an accident; this is borne out by Mercury which rules the 4th, opposed to Pluto and square Mars.

The **Moon** in Capricorn has a need to be recognized as an important and powerful person. Though emotionally supersensitive, Patton was very critical of others as well as himself, but he was untiring and considerate when he was interested or involved. This lunar position emphasizes reserve and coldness and caused him to be overly sensitive to real or fancied slights. He sought to justify himself by acting with great personal dignity. His great ambition to succeed was realized by the Moon's very good aspects (trine Neptune, sextile the Sun).

Fanatic and obsessive, he achieved the popularity and notoriety that this placement of the Moon seems determined to have. We find that the Moon in Capricorn often gives a strong tie with a grandparent and this proved true in Patton's case (his grandfather Smith). The good lunar aspects gave him leadership and administrative ability, but they and the inconjunct to the Ascendant also contributed to his need to achieve power at any cost and without concern for others. He made enemies easily and this caused problems with his reputation.

His mother was quite traditional and conservative, practical and efficient, but she was also very socially oriented. Since the Moon in a man's chart shows his needs in a wife, these qualities were present in Bea also. She furthered his social ambitions, ran a comfortable home and balanced the family checkbook.

The Moon in the 8th house gives an inherent need for security which George achieved through his military career. Affection, love and sex were important to him but on his terms, not so much because of the Moon's aspects but because of the general tenor of the chart. The Moon's trine to Neptune in the 12th house enhanced his ability to use his psychic talent to further his career (Neptune rules the 10th), and it also indicates some unusual desires, the tendency to excessively idealize and fool himself, and it shows his attraction to poetry, literature and art.

In the years since his death, several of his biographers have indicated that he had homosexual tendencies. In examining his horoscope, this does show as a definite possibility. Saturn, ruler of the 8th house is square Uranus. It opposes Venus, ruler of the 5th house and Pluto is in the 12th. All of these placements are considered to be a possible signature of the homosexual. He also has the Sun opposed to Neptune which can be an added indicator. However, Venus in Capricorn is usually fairly straitlaced and Jupiter, the ruler of the 7th house trines Neptune, which makes him rather idealistic regarding his partner.

With the Moon inconjunct the Ascendant, he was too touchy and it was difficult for him to sublimate his feelings, therefore it was hard for him to get along with others. He never really learned to handle his anger without giving way to his emotions and he never overcame his hot temper and sarcastic tongue.

The Moon is in the Taurus decanate; and Venus (ruler of Taurus) is in his 7th house, verifying his close association with, and his devotion to his wife. The Moon is in the Leo dwad, which emphasizes his emotional need for recognition and his contempt for danger (Sun in the 5th, Moon in the 8th).

Aquarius on the **9th house** gives a vivid imagination. Though Patton was not a professional writer, he had great communicative ability and could express himself lucidly and succinctly, either orally or on paper. He was very curious about life and never stopped learning. A voracious reader, his favorite subjects were history and philosophy. Foreign cultures fascinated him and when he wanted to do so he could charm people right out of their shoes. Uranus, ruler of the 9th in the 4th, indicates that he would make his home in a foreign country at some time in his life.

With **Pisces** on the cusp of the **10th house** he had great vision as far as his career was concerned, and since Neptune trines both Jupiter and the Moon, his success is strongly indicated. Neptune in the 12th house shows that he was very good at tactics and behind-the-scenes maneuvering and of course, verifies his intuitive and occult tendencies. The **South Node** in the 10th house made it simple for him to assume a position of command and it was easy for him to escape the vicissitudes of life by keeping himself constantly busy through assuming a position of authority and responsibility.

Aries on the **11th house** involved him with large organizations (the Army) and he found his friends among the military. Mars ruling the 11th from the 4th house, enhanced his ability to assume authority over others and it was easy for him to become a leader. He managed his leadership well; the men who served with and under him admired and respected him, even though they never knew what old "Georgie" would do next. Although he was known to his close friends and family as Georgie, he never encouraged this form of address from his contemporaries. In fact, the men permitted to call him Georgie to his face comprised a rather select company.

With Mars ruling the house of circumstances over which you have little or no control, Patton was often at the mercy of others. Mars has very challenging aspects and as his biographer Farago put it, "Glory was to Patton that bright tragic thing which meant dominion. . . . He had so much of it and expected so much more. . . . It happened to him so often. He was not allowed to follow up his victory in Sicily with a much greater triumph in Italy. And when in 1944 he opened a path to Paris, another man was given the honor of entering the liberated city."

With **Taurus** on the **12th house** cusp, Venus in Capricorn and Gemini rising, the key to Patton's subconscious was through common sense and logic, not emotion. He had a stubborn streak that caused him to resist change; but since the ruler, Venus, trines Mars in Virgo, logic and tactics appealed to him, and he could logically justify his reasoning most of the time. His greatest strength was his ability to be practical and calculating, to trust his insight and prophetic dreams, and, in a sense, to rely on his stubbornness.

Neptune in Taurus gives an aesthetic approach to both the sciences and the arts, and this was definitely evident in Patton's makeup. He responded to beauty, music and poetry; also we can say that he had an innate business sense, especially as it pertained to the waging of war. There is no record that he was careless with his money, but with Neptune opposed to the Sun, this could have been so. He was always very comfortable financially, so this is not really important in our delineation. The placement of Neptune in the 12th house made him very sensitive to his subconscious and his psyche, and as long as he applied this practically, his intuitive insight helped him face reality. Despite the lifestyle he chose for himself, he was very much a loner, and at times suffered from deep-seated loneliness.

Neptune in his chart was retrograde, indicating that inward action could produce tremendous personal insight and that he could use his talents easily and at a relatively early age. This placement also enhanced a tendency to martyrdom which his unconsidered action and remarks contributed to.

Pluto in Gemini indicates a restless personality, one who is impetuous and this is especially noticeable in Patton's personality because Pluto rules his Sun in Scorpio. He searched for new ways to express himself and to expand his intellect; but because Pluto was in the 12th house and retrograde, the avenues open to him were through his subconscious and prophetic dreams. He "knew" he had experienced all these events before. The challenging aspects to this placement of Pluto provided George Patton with his love of war, his hatred of mediocrity and his belief that he could do well in life only in a specialized profession like soldiering.

Lesson 14
ERNEST HEMINGWAY:
An American Original

He was one of the great writers of the 20th century. He was born on July 21, 1899 and for 62 years he experienced the joys and sorrows of existence to the fullest. Yet the proud little 2-year-old boy who yelled "fraid of nothing" learned that there was quite a bit to fear and endure. One day he changed his life's motto from *"Il faut d'abord durer"* (one must first of all endure) to *"Il faut apres tout mourir"* (one must after all die) and on July 2, 1961, he put a shotgun to his head and killed himself. His name was Ernest Hemingway.

This "American Original," as he was often called, did most of his great work while living in foreign countries as one of the "Expatriates" (with Gertrude Stein, Scott Fitzgerald, Ezra Pound and others) in Paris, while he recuperated in Italy, resisting the Franco forces in Spain, and while living on his *Finca* (home) in Cuba. This flamboyant man who pursued danger and adventure as others do a good night's sleep, was basically a shy, sensitive and even gentle man. This master of words and language was a sloppy letter writer who had trouble spelling and who worked all his life to overcome a slight speech impediment. (His l's and r's sounded like w's.) This man who defined pride as "a deadly sin," strutted his manhood, his athletic skills, his capacity for drinking, his prowess as a hunter and fisherman. This fierce individualist whose physical presence never went unnoticed, feared anyone who assumed a proprietary interest in him. He had four wives and though he wanted everyone to call him

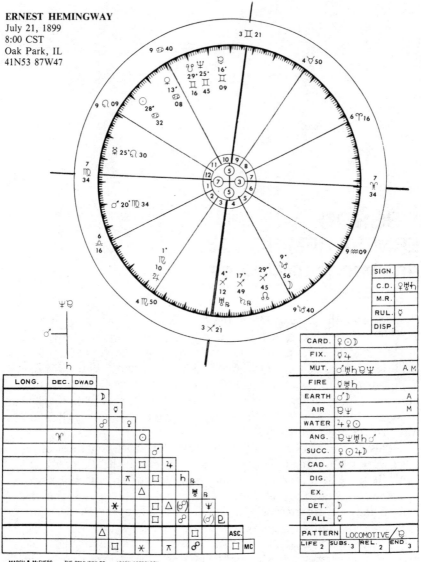

ERNEST HEMINGWAY
July 21, 1899
8:00 CST
Oak Park, IL
41N53 87W47

SIGN.	
C.D.	♀⚥♄
M.R.	
RUL.	♀
DISP.	

CARD.	♀☉☽
FIX.	♀♃
MUT.	♂⚥♄♀♆ A M
FIRE	♀⚥♄
EARTH	♂☽ A
AIR	♀♆ M
WATER	♃♀☉
ANG.	♀♆⚥♄♂
SUCC.	♀☉♃☽
CAD.	♀
DIG.	
EX.	
DET.	☽
FALL	♀
PATTERN	LOCOMOTIVE/♀
LIFE 2	SUBS. 3	REL. 2	END 3

LONG.	DEC.	DWAD												
			☽											
				⚥										
					♂	♀								
	♈					☉								
							♂							
			□				♃							
			⊼	□				♄R						
				△				♅R					
			✶		□	△	⚹		♆					
					□	♂	⚹		♂♇					
		△					□				ASC.		
			□	✶	⊼	♂					□	MC	

"Papa," he was not a very devoted father to his three sons. He always wanted a girl and addressed all pretty women as "daughter."

Much has been written about Ernest Hemingway, so it will be easy to substantiate what we find in the horoscope. Our biographical references are *Ernest Hemingway — A Life Story* and *Ernest Hemingway: Selected Letters 1917-1961*, by Carlos Baker; *Papa Hemingway* by A. E. Hotchner; *How it Was,* by Mary Welsh Hemingway and some personal knowledge through mutual friends.

A biographical sketch of Hemingway's life would probably read thus: Born on July 21, 1899 at 8 AM CST in Oak Park, Illinois, just outside of Chicago, the second of six children. His father was a doctor, his mother a singer who gave up her career for marriage. He left home before age 18, wangled a reporting job on the *Kansas City Star* and at 19, despite rejection by the U.S. Army because of defective eyesight, volunteered as an ambulance driver on the Italian front where he was severely wounded. In 1920 he married Hadley Richardson who bore him a son christened John but nicknamed Bumby. They lived in Paris where he wrote *The Sun also Rises*. They divorced in 1927 and he married *Paris Vogue* writer Pauline Pfeiffer who became the mother of his two other sons Patrick and Gregory, nicknamed Monsy and Gigi respectively. They bought a home in Key West, Florida, where he wrote *A Farewell to Arms, To Have and Have Not* and numerous short stories.

He went to Spain as a special correspondent during the Civil War and his experiences there were the basis of *For Whom the Bell Tolls*. Pauline divorced him so he could marry writer Martha Gellhorn who in 1946 was replaced by writer Mary Welsh. He served as a World War II correspondent and received a bronze star in 1948. He lived on his *Finca* in Cuba until Castro forced him out; then he settled in Ketchum, Idaho. His book *The Old Man and the Sea* won a Pulitzer prize in 1953 and in 1954 he received the Nobel prize for literature. In between books he traveled far and wide, fished for tuna and marlin, hunted big game, followed the bulls and suffered numerous injuries and accidents, including two nearly fatal plane crashes.

How does an astrological synopsis look? (See chart on page 140.) As stressed in Volume I and outlined in Lesson 20 "Steps to Delineation" of Volume II of *The Only Way to . . . Learn Astrology*, we start with an **overview.**

Hemingway has an even division of planets **above** and **below** the horizon, showing a good balance between outgoingness and a need to rise above his position at birth versus subjectivity and instinct. He has seven planets **east** and three **west** of the meridian, indicating an ability and wish to take charge of his own life and exercise his own free will.

The **locomotive pattern** (all planets placed within 2/3rds, leaving an empty 120° segment in the horoscope) often describes a person who brings much power to bear in order to achieve. Pluto (the engine) motivates Hemingway into action and plays a very important role in this chart because it is also the most elevated planet and part of a strong mutable T-square. This Plutonian drive was constant (Pluto has only challenging aspects) and seemingly forced Hemingway to prove himself to be in charge or boss, whether he was wrestling with a marlin on his beloved boat *Pilar*, shooting lions on an African safari, or training lions for a circus. As A.E. Hotchner tells it:

I noticed Ernest had 3 long deep scratches on his forearm and asked about them. "Cotsies" he said. "They had a circus pitched near here with two good 5 year old cats. It was wonderful to hear them roar in the morning. Made friends with the trainer and he let me work them with a rolled up newspaper — but you have to be careful not to turn your back!" I said lion bating was a rather dangerous pursuit for a writer who wanted to continue practicing his trade. "Miss Mary agrees with you" Ernest said. "Promised her I wouldn't work cotsies any more til the book is finished. But know of no other place as good to lay it on the line!

Pluto likes to "lay it all on the line," all or nothing — and Gemini loves to tell the tale!

The **house emphasis** is well balanced in this chart with two planets in the houses of life, three in houses of substance, two in houses of relationships and three in houses of endings. The only emphasis would be that five planets are in angular houses, confirming Hemingway's potential for dynamic action and his need to be the initiator and doer.

The elements are evenly divided and there is no **final signature**; but the qualities show that with five planets plus the Ascendant and Midheaven in mutable signs, Hemingway was very versatile, often changeable, sympathetic and imbued with great intuition. His mind could be flexible and ingenious. As Carlos Baker describes him:

The sentimentalist quick to tears and the bully who used his anger like a club; the perpetual student, the omnivorous reader, the brilliant naturalist, the curious questioner, the retentive observer, careful expositor and temperamental teacher.

There is no **final dispositor** or **mutual reception**, but the **chart ruler**, Mercury in Leo in the 12th house tells much of the story. It shows a man who is innately withdrawn, devoted to private life and the unknown, yet the Leo quality calls for drama, status, romance, pride, dignity, creativity and a drive to shine. These divergent feelings made Hemingway a complex person who struggled with his own dichotomies all his life. Says Hotchner:

For all of his courageous exploits and formidable outward appearance, Ernest was a shy man. He refused to speak publicly because of his intense shyness; his graceful Nobel Prize acceptance speech was read at Stockholm by the U.S. Ambassador to Sweden.

One of the keys to this chart is the **T-square** with Pluto and Neptune in Gemini in the 10th house opposing Saturn in Sagittarius in the 4th house and all three square to Mars in Virgo in the 1st house. A mutable T-square makes for an idea and people-oriented person. The indecision or wavering often found with strong mutability will be minimized here, since this T-square is angular and therefore totally action oriented. With Mars as the focal planet, Hemingway had plenty of coping energy; but Mars has three squares and no outlets (sextiles or trines) so we can expect much steam (Mars is a fire planet, Pluto and Neptune are water planets) and lots of dust (Mars/fire — Saturn/earth).

The empty arm of the T-square is always a very sensitive point; in Hemingway's case it was the 7th house, partially explaining his need to relate on a one-to-one basis and making four stabs at it. The T-square assumes even greater importance when we realize that there are very few interplanetary aspects; the fewer aspects, the more directional are the existing ones. We will analyze the T-square in more detail as we proceed, but this OVERVIEW already gives you good insight into Hemingway, the man.

We can at this point add a few more refinements. You may note that Pluto at 16° Gemini is on the **fixed star** Rigel which promises "artistic ability"; Venus at 13° Cancer is conjunct Sirius suggesting "ambition, pride, wealth and fame"; Mars at 21° Virgo is on Denebola giving the ability to be "critical and persevering." Additional emphasis can be given to Venus, Uranus and Saturn since they are on **critical degrees**. Venus is the planet in **oriental appearance** making the Venusian principles of love, affection, partners, art, beauty, values and social urges a most integral part of the Hemingway personality. All these points will be confirmed as we now dissect the chart. (Fixed stars, critical degrees, planets in oriental appearance and more are all found in Volume II.)

As we dig a little deeper, we start with the "inner individuality" — the **Sun** which is **in Cancer in the 11th** house. The ruler is the Moon located in Capricorn in the 5th house. Though attached to home and family, the 11th house position made Hemingway quite social and less maternal. Imaginative, conscientious and receptive, he deeply cared what others thought about him. He needed to feel needed, illustrated by his repeated recounting of how he saved his wife Mary's life after she'd been given up by the doctors and by his love of and caring for stray animals. Recounts Hotchner:

In his garage Ernest established headquarters for the wounded owl. He set up a box for him and fitted a cane into the box for a perch. Ernest was deeply concerned about his eating and trapped mice every night so he'd have a fresh breakfast, and at noon he was given duck and rabbit heads, because he needed furs and feathers for roughage. Then Ernest shifted his concern to whether Owl would eliminate properly. "Eating's one thing, crapping's another"; only after there were significant droppings for proof did he begin to relax. Owl and Ernest became great pals; he talked him into sitting on his hand and only once in a while did Owl get crabby and try to take a chunk out of his finger.

Even more touching and descriptive of the peaceful, caring and Cancerian side of Hemingway's nature is this Hotchner vignette:

Black Dog, who was mostly a springer spaniel, had wandered into Ernest's ¬Sun Valley ski cabin one afternoon, cold, starved, fear-ridden and sub-dog in complex — a hunting dog who was scared stiff of gun fire. Ernest had brought him back to Cuba and patiently and lovingly built up his weight, confidence and affection to the point that Black Dog believed he was an accomplished author himself. "He needs 10 hours sleep but is always exhausted because he faithfully follows my schedule. When I'm between books he's happy, but when I'm working he takes it very hard. He sticks with me from first light on and he keeps his eyes open loyally, but he doesn't like it."

Emotional security, especially with the ruler of the Sun in Capricorn, was one of the prime needs in Hemingway's life and he pursued it diligently by trying to be somebody and manipulatively by trying to get from his wives the love he felt his mother withheld from him; but most of all he would find security in creativity, love affairs, romance, pleasures, amusement and games — all **5th house** matters where the **ruler** of the Sun is located. As Hotchner points out:

Ernest worked hard when he was writing, and when he was not writing he practiced the art of relaxation with equal dedication. He was never in too much of a hurry to savor the pleasures around him.

The **Capricorn overlay** to his Sun added ambition and serious dedication to whatever he undertook. As he himself said, "You need the devotion to your work that a priest of God has for his."

The **Pisces decanate** of the Sun gives additional credence to Hemingway's sensitivity, a side of his character seen only by his friends (Sun in the 11th). For example his intuitive grasp of Scott Fitzgerald's problems as he wrote to their mutual editor Max Perkins:

It was a terrible thing for him to love youth so much that he jumped straight from youth to senility without going through manhood. Work would help him, noncommercial work — a paragraph at a time. But he judged a paragraph by how much money it made him and ditched his juice into that channel because it gave him instant satisfaction.

And to Fitzgerald he wrote:

Forget your personal tragedy. We are all bitched from the start and you especially have to hurt like hell before you can write seriously. But when you get the damned hurt, use it — don't cheat with it. Be faithful to it as a scientist. . . .

Such concern and perception was an integral part of Hemingway, but rarely seen by the world around him.

An **11th house Sun** is generally goal oriented, and Hemingway was no exception. Good at meeting challenges, he created them if they failed to manifest often enough. An excellent organizer, he loved to be in charge of arranging trips, safaris and hunts. His Virgo Ascendant and Capricorn Moon confirmed this tendency. As is often the case with the Sun in the Aquarian 11th house, he was a leader in his field, initiating a style of writing never before tried in the United States.

The **Sun square Jupiter** contributed to his egotistical nature, also shown by his chart ruler in Leo. Since Jupiter always exaggerates and overdoes, it can blow up the need to be somebody as well as the physique and it often causes you to indulge in food, sex and drink. Hemingway had weight problems all his life. Six feet tall, he rarely weighed less than 210 pounds and some times as much as 260. To get down to 170 pounds was a real achievement (at the end of his life he managed it by eating hospital food), and he was usually delighted to get down to 190 pounds. His temperament was such that he found it nearly impossible to diet. In Cuba in 1952, as he writes in a letter to Harry Breit, he felt depressed, found a crony in his favorite joint, the "Floridita," and in the course of the afternoon consumed 2 steak sandwiches and 18 double "Papa" special (no sugar) frozen daiquiris. That is 72 ounces of rum! He then went home, took a few vitamin B tablets and read all night. As he wrote to his publisher Charles Scribner:

> "I can't cut out sweets and starches, because I never do eat them; I get enough sugar from the alcohol I consume."

Hemingway was a steady drinker who occasionally went on binges and then turned to massive doses of vitamins with the conviction that they would counteract the effect and prevent him from becoming a sad alcoholic like his old pal Scott Fitzgerald.

The **Sun trine Uranus** contributed to his popularity and it also indicates a person with great enthusiasm and unusual talents, in Hemingway's case confirmed by Mercury sextile Neptune, Mars square Neptune and Jupiter trine Neptune. This trine can make you quite cause oriented and Hemingway had his share of causes. He hated all politicians, bureaucracy, propaganda and most of all tyranny. He believed that the government is best which governs least. He resented the incursions of modern civilization upon the shrinking wilderness and fought these intrusions in word and deed.

With the **Sun sextile** the **Midheaven** success came relatively easy in his chosen field once he decided on his goals and priorities; and success did come, when he decided to quit working as a reporter and dedicate himself to writing.

The Sun is the heart of the chart — the main expression of the individual.

Where you find the Sun is where you want to shine and Hemingway wanted to shine among his friends and in social situations; yet what people saw was only partly the Sun — it has to be blended with the other planets and especially the Ascendant. To illustrate, here is Hemingway's version of how he met Marlene Dietrich:

> You know how we met, the Kraut and me? Back in my broke days I was crossing cabin [economy] on the *Ile* [luxury liner *Ile de France*], but a pal of mine who was traveling first [class] loaned me his reserve tux and smuggled me in for meals. One night we're having dinner when there appears at the top of the staircase this unbelievable spectacle in white. The Kraut of course. A long, tight white-beaded gown over that body, in the area of what's known as the Dramatic Pause, she can give lessons to anybody. So she gives it that Dramatic Pause on the staircase, then slowly slithers down the stairs and across the floor to where Jock Whitney was having a "fawncy" dinner party. Of course no one in that dining room has touched food to lips since her entrance. The Kraut gets to the table and all the men hop up and her chair is held at the ready, but she's counting — twelve. Of course she apologizes and backs off and says she's sorry but she's very superstitious about being 13 at anything and with that turns to go — but I have naturally risen to the occasion and grandly offer to save the party by being the 14th. That was how we met. Pretty romantic, eh? Maybe I ought to sell it to Darryl F. Panic.

This story is quite indicative of an 11th house Sun with the chart ruler in Leo and the ruler of the Sun in the 5th house. But here's how Marlene "the Kraut" tells it:

> "This nice young man offered to save my dilemma, then sat down at the table and never said another word all evening."

Virgo rising with the ruler in the 12th as seen by Marlene versus the Hemingway version.

The next step is to understand the emotional personality; so we look to the **Moon** which is in **Capricorn** in the 5th house and the ruler Saturn is in Sagittarius in the 4th. To understand emotions, we need to understand the basic needs and desires. How we feel about ourselves, our self-image, our ability to project feelings and emotions is to a great extent based on our parental perception. Did we feel loved by them? Did they give us as much tenderness and attention as we felt entitled to? In astrology the Sun and the Moon represent the father and mother respectively. The 4th and 10th houses also denote the parents as do Venus and Saturn and we will discuss those areas as we go along. But before we look at the emotional personality, we should understand what kind of parental role model the native had and how he perceived the parents. By first looking at the archetypal role of the Sun and Moon we can better interpret the other lunar functions.

In Hemingway's case the **Sun** is in Cancer and he perceived his **father** as loving, nurturing and caring. With the Sun square Jupiter, he saw his father as a larger-than-life figure and the trine to Uranus made him seem imaginative, intuitive and fun to be with. Add the image of a man who knows where he is going (Sun sextile Midheaven), is serious and dedicated (ruler in Capricorn), and at the same time full of fun and interested in recreation and relaxation (ruler in the 5th house). Since the Sun is in the 11th house, he saw his father as a friend, a team player, an idealist with high hopes for life and a strong sense of justice (Aquarian traits).

According to all the biographies, Hemingway adored his father and all his early writings were based on his youthful remembrances of outings with his father, the Nick Adams series being the best known. It was his father who taught him to shoot, to row, to fish, to listen, to be quiet and to feel nature.

His **mother**, seen as the **Moon** in Capricorn in the 5th, seems a bit cold and demanding, disciplinarian and traditional, even conservative regarding child rearing. The 5th house position made her dramatic, fun to be with at times. Since the ruler Saturn is in Sagittarius in the 4th house, she assumed a large role in Hemingway's early upbringing, imbuing him with strict yet honorable moral codes and intellectual demands. We must remember though, that Saturn is the second male principle and therefore also describes some demands Hemingway felt his father made of him. The other female principle is Venus which opposes the Moon, indicating an alienation from the mother. In Hemingway's mind his mother was too possessive, demanding and she somehow made him feel that he could not live up to her expectations. Yet the trine to the Ascendant indicates that his mother was an important factor, supporting him and giving him a good start in life. These mixed feelings he held about his mother played a large role in his later approach to the women in his life.

Looking at the other lunar functions, we note that with the **Moon in Capricorn** he wanted to be recognized as important and powerful. Though very sensitive, he was critical of others yet very considerate when personally interested or involved. Shy and insecure about his own worth, he had many subconscious fears and was overly sensitive to real or fancied slights. His mind reacted quickly to sense impressions, but as often with anger and antagonism as with love or affection. As Baker states:

> "He could be the most loyal friend or pick quarrels for no reason; he would switch from being warm and generous to being a ruthless and overbearing enemy."

In weak moments the dichotomy of a nurturing Moon in the cool and collected sign of Capricorn can lead to a surrender to the appetites. Since the ruler Saturn is in Sagittarius in the 4th house, Hemingway got much emotional satisfaction not only from his home but also from his roots and background. His emotions were less austere than Capricorn might indicate when we blend it with the independent, open and idealistic Sagittarian feelings.

The **5th house** position of the **Moon** shows an additional side of Hemingway, the man. A born romantic (confirmed by the chart ruler in Leo), a searcher for pleasure, with a desire to taste life through love affairs, romance, amusements, children, vacations, hobbies, avocations, gambling, etc. His poetic imagination and creative ability are confirmed by Mercury sextile Neptune. All these areas were needs Hemingway pursued diligently throughout his life — whether it was gambling at the races in Auteuil, watching the bulls run in Pamplona, skiing in Austria, dude ranching in Wyoming, trekking in Africa or seeking action in some war arena.

The **Moon opposite Venus** can bring carelessness in how the affections are given — love comes and goes like moods. No matter what you do, you feel challenged by others, so you may as well do your own thing. This is exactly what Hemingway did. An inferiority complex is often supplanted by a strong urge to be in the spotlight and surely this was one of the driving motivations in Hemingway's life. With five angular planets it was always easier for him to take action than to contemplate the subconscious feelings of inadequacy.

The **trine** from the **Moon** to the **Ascendant** helped Hemingway show his feelings and others were drawn to him because of his charm and outgoing personality. This position again confirmed that he enjoyed fun and good times with friends and family. It also made it relatively easy for him to capitalize on his talents.

To finish the basic triad, we now look to the **Ascendant** to describe the outer personality. The Sun is where you begin your life as a human being or individual but the Ascendant shows when the day was born — your day — and as such describes your beginning in the physical sense. It is your body, the face you want to show to the world, the way you decide to package yourself. Hemingway has **Virgo rising** and the ruler **Mercury** in Leo in the 12th house. The more obvious Virgo characteristics gave him the discipline, orderliness and sense of organization to sit down day after day and write. The **Leo/Mercury** in the **12th** house added the inspiration, creativity and ability to work alone and behind the scenes. To quote Hotchner:

> Although his dedication to this writing was a side or Ernest the public never saw, it was the most important aspect of his character. Writing was an arduous ordeal for him, exhilarating, but demanding all of what he called his "juices". A book in progress totally consumed him and at the end of each day he would count the number of words he had written and enter them in a log. [Virgo]

Like many people who have a strong Virgo/Gemini combination in the chart, writing or communication of some form is the backbone of the personality. The Sun in Cancer helped, because it gave him nearly total recall and at the right time he could pick up on some past event and mold it into a living, palatable and believable story. As Hotchner states:

> He kept no notebooks or journals but his phenomenal recall kept places, names, dates, events, colors, clothes, smells and who won the 1925 six-day bicycle race at the Hippodrome, on orderly file.

Shy in public, he flourished in the company of friends and loved ones. He set very high standards for himself and in typical Virgo fashion expected others to live up to them too. If they didn't, he could and would correct them in no uncertain terms — if not to their face, then through some letters. He dismissed Mary McCarthy with:

> "She writes like the most intelligent trained flea."

He thought that James Faulkner had,

> "the most talent but he needs a sort of conscience — if no nation can exist half free and half slave, no man can write half whore and half straight."

From himself he expected total perfection:

> I've seen every sunrise of my life; I rise at first light and I start by reading and editing everything I have written to the point where I left off. That way I go through a book several hundred times, honing it until it gets an edge like the bullfighter's sword.

To his father he wrote:

> I'm trying in all my stories to get the feeling of the actual life across. Not just to depict life — or criticize it — but to actually make it alive.

To his publisher:

> The stories are written so tight and so hard that the alteration of a word can throw an entire story out of key.

To Scott Fitzgerald he wrote:

> There is no excuse for a bad book. We happen to be in a very tough business where there are no alibis. It is good or it is bad and the thousand reasons that interfere with a book being as good as possible are no excuses if it is not. . . .

No other words could better describe the Virgo need for perfection.

The **Ascendant square** to **Uranus** made Hemingway wish to be different and even rebellious from early on. The need to stand on his own two feet and free himself from his mother or father (Uranus in the 4th house), led him to leave home as soon as he finished high school. It explains his innate need for freedom and therefore his distaste for those people who might try to run his life. The originality and creativity also inherent in the square helped him utilize the flow of the Ascendant trine the Moon.

Mars is **in Virgo** in the 1st house. This not only emphasizes all the Virgo qualities but adds a love of work and great enthusiasm for everything he did. With this placement he was able to do even the most monotonous tasks well. It also confirmed his ability to work so carefully and systematically. It emphasizes what friend and foe alike said of Hemingway:

> However careless he seemed about his life, he was obsessively careful about what he wrote for publication, a tireless craftsman, conscious of the revolution he was working in American prose.

The **1st house** position of **Mars** perfectly describes the face Hemingway showed to the world — positive, self-assertive, combative, active, boisterous and accident prone. His great physical strength and dynamic energy propelled him headlong into things and the square from Mars to Saturn, Neptune and Pluto brought danger, excitement and violence into his life.

Mars square Saturn is probably the most difficult aspect in this chart. For a man Mars is the symbol of sexuality and as such his acceptance of himself as a man, lover, aggressor and leader can be seen in the aspects formed between Mars, the Sun and Saturn. In Hemingway's case Mars square Saturn meant that unconsciously he would feel inadequate as a man and therefore overcompensate in order to prove his masculinity, again and again, as if by asserting dominance he could build up his confidence. He may have observed his father, his first role model, and seen how dominated he seemed by his strong mother. As a result we have Hemingway the father, using the nickname "Papa" all his life, Hemingway the lover, the big white hunter, the boxer, the man known for pursuing danger — Hemingway proving to the world and to himself that he was a MAN.

The **square** from **Mars to Neptune** expressed quite differently. It provided his strong imagination (confirmed among other things by Mercury sextile Neptune and the Moon in the 5th house) and creative ability. The sextile to Mercury gave him the opportunity to be creative, while the square challenged him to use his talent and inspiration. But it also made him look for trouble, as if life did not offer enough. The kind of imagination manifested by this square is beautifully illustrated in a letter Hemingway wrote to John Dos Passos:

> We are in the bar dining room of the famous *21 Club*, or maybe the editorial rooms at the New Republic, or anywhere that literary hangerson hang out. Suddenly, a fat, bearded man appears, wielding a submachine gun. He is — no

doubt about it — Ernest Hemingway. Brrup-bup-bup-bup-bup-bup! The floor is strewn with editors, book reviewers and academic critics. . . .

This square (Mars/Neptune) also led to his alcohol problem and toward the end of his life was one of the contributing factors to his delusions and persecution complex.

Mars square Pluto again emphasizes the aggressiveness so often exhibited by Hemingway. It helps explain why he rode roughshod over others and became abusive when frustrated. To his need to prove his manhood, this square added a strong sex drive and a love of recklessness. Baker quotes:

> "He is said, by those who know, to have been a perfectly satisfactory lover without being a Don Juan. Yet he boasted, somewhat ambiguously, that he had had every woman he ever wanted."

He enjoyed telling yarns about his conquests, and, according to his letters, as time progressed he became increasingly profane and obscene — all attributable to this square.

Since this first house Mars, dignified by house position, has no trines or sextiles for flow and ease, Hemingway was required to use the energies and challenges to their full potential. He did, and it became the trademark of the man.

The cusp of the 1st house is considered the beginning of the person's life, hence there is a feeling of freshness, of newness and curiosity which carries over to the planet that rules it called the **chart ruler.** Wherever this planet is located by house and sign is where you feel most comfortable. In Hemingway's case we see a possible conflict. **Mercury**, ruler of the Virgo cusp is in **Leo** but in the **12th house.** Leo is dramatic, outgoing, proud and romantic and wants to shine while the 12th house asks for solitude, seclusion, restraint and behind the scenes activities. It is rather hard to shine behind the scenes. Mercury represents the intellectual urge and avenue of expression and here is where Hemingway managed to combine these divergent needs. He shone as a writer, pouring his life's blood, what he called his "juice" into every word.

Writing was his life and when he felt his mind going, his life's purpose was gone. As Hotchner recounts of one of his last visits to Hemingway at the Mayo Clinic in Rochester:

> "There won't be another spring Hotch, or another fall." His whole body had relaxed. He went over and sat on a busted fragment of stone wall. I felt I should get to it quickly now, and I did, but I said it very gently. "Papa, why do you want to kill yourself?" He hesitated only a moment, then he spoke in his old,

deliberate way. "What do you think happens to a man going on 62 when he realizes he can never write the books and stories he promised himself?" "But why can't you put writing aside for now. . . . [Hotchner cites all the books and short stories he has written.] You've fulfilled the covenant you've made with yourself, the only one that counts. For God's sake why can't you rest on that?" "Because — look, it doesn't matter that I don't write for a day or a year or 10 years as long as the knowledge that I **can** write is solid inside me. But a day without that knowledge, or not being sure of it, is eternity."

Mercury in Leo thinks dramatically and always with the heart. Hemingway knew how to put these properties on paper. He also knew how to cover up a certain lack of self-confidence (Mars square Saturn, Venus inconjunct Saturn, Saturn opposition Pluto) with much Leo bombast. Mars in the 1st is good at that. With the ruler of the 1st in the 12th house he learned to rely on his own inner strength.

The **most exact aspect** in a horoscope is always indicative of the person's basic character and often shows the career tendencies. Here we have **Mercury** at 25° Leo 30' **sextile Neptune** at 25° Gemini 46', an orb of 16 minutes. This sextile gave Hemingway his imaginative style and since it radiates from the 12th house to the 10th, it provided the opportunity to use this ability for his career. With Neptune in Gemini, communicating was an integral part of his professional interest.

The **second house,** among other things, shows financial affairs, earning power, sense of values and inner resources. With **Libra** here and the ruler **Venus in Cancer** in the **11th house**, we realize that Hemingway wanted to be surrounded by beautiful things (Libra) but with a warm and homey touch (Cancer) and he enjoyed sharing his belongings with friends and acquaintances (11th house). Relates Hotchner:

> On our first visit to the *Finca* [Hemingway's home in Cuba] my wife and I were to be quartered in the guest house, but Mary Hemingway greeted us with apologies that it was not quite ready. "Jean-Paul Sartre showed up unexpectedly with a lady friend and the sheets haven't been changed yet." Later we found out that the Duke and Duchess of Windsor had been there the week before. Dinner regulars at that time were a bald, deaf, powerful yet gentle Spaniard; a salty, roaring, boozing and fun loving Basque sea captain; another Basque, a Catholic Father called the Black Priest; a Spanish grandee, a gambler from the old Key West days, a sub rosa anti-Batista and his wife, a formerly prominent pelota player and more.

Most of his resources were based on his phenomenal memory of exploits and adventures undertaken with friends and his early years (Cancer and Venus/mother, Sun/father and the 11th house) which were retold in form of short stories or books. He made his money through writing, one of the more artistic professions befitting the Libra cusp and confirmed by Gemini on the Midheaven. The Libra/Cancer combination explains his love of collecting what he considered beautiful things.

Jupiter in the **2nd house** emphasizes all the aforementioned qualities. Instead of sharing with one or two friends, Jupiter made him share with 10 or 20; and Hemingway shared not only food and lodging but also cash. He gave his Nobel Prize money to his old and ailing friend, poet Ezra Pound. There were always half a dozen friends down on their luck who received regular remittances. Jupiter's location also increased his income.

Jupiter in Scorpio added depth and generosity of spirit, courage, and an uncompromising intensity about his beliefs and way of life. "If I can't exist on my terms, then existence is impossible" were his own words to Mary Welsh Hemingway.

Jupiter trine Neptune confirms Hemingway's enjoyment in helping others and also points to writing as one of the obvious career choices. With this aspect (and a few others in the chart), he could have gone into occult or mystical matters, but he chose not to. Maybe the strict religious demands made by his father (no recreational activity or playing with friends on the Lord's Day and compulsory church and Sunday School attendance) precluded his even looking in that direction.

The **inconjunct** (quincunx) from **Jupiter** to the **Midheaven** called for some adjustments of fun versus duty. Since Jupiter rules the 4th house, the parental influence was at work, and for much of his life he had to decide which values outweighed others. In order to earn money (2nd house) and achieve his professional goal (Midheaven), he had to curb some of his Jupiterian excesses.

The **3rd house** shows how you communicate, adapt to new learning and ideas, relate to your local environment and your sisters or brothers. With **Scorpio** on the cusp, Hemingway was a shrewd observer who used his words carefully; he was able to be sharp, terse, witty or tender. His mind was incisive and analytical with a quick grasp of knowledge (confirmed by the strong Virgo/Gemini tendencies). Scorpio on this cusp is an additional indicator of his fantastic memory.

Pluto, ruler of Hemingway's **3rd house**, is in Gemini in the 10th house, explaining his great need to be heard, to voice his thoughts and ideas. Self-expression was his way of projecting his ego needs. When he wasn't writing books or stories, he wrote letters. Baker estimates there were more than 6,000. Pluto shows where you are obsessive. The letter writing seemingly consoled him when he was between projects or when things went badly, and it kept his confidence high when all went well. Since Pluto was involved in the T-square, Hemingway also enjoyed notoriety, relishing gossip about himself and others. The Scorpio sting was often visible. He felt that T.S. Elliot was "a damned good poet, but he never hit a ball out of infield in his life and would not have existed except for dear old Ezra." That same Ezra (Pound) was "the lovely poet and stupid traitor." James Jones' *From Here to Eternity* elicited a stream of ugly comparisons, including such descriptive lines as "I do not have to swim through a river of snot to know it is snot." The Scorpio/Gemini combination is potent stuff.

Hemingway's need to communicate and express himself took over most of the energies manifested in the 3rd house, leaving little time for involvement with his sisters and one brother. According to most biographical material available, the long wished for brother arrived too late to be a companion and except for the very early childhood years, he did not spend much time with his sisters. He was a perfunctory brother and (later) uncle, extending his hospitality or giving financial assistance when needed but his heart and soul were not involved. It was probably better this way, since with Pluto's harsh aspects an intimate relationship would have led to many fights.

Sagittarius is on the cusp of Hemingway's **4th house** which describes the family he came from, his roots and the home he would fashion for himself. It also denotes one of his parents, the more nurturing one. With what we know of the parents, his father gave the religious impetus (Sagittarius). He was a doctor (ruler Jupiter in Scorpio), and loved the great outdoors. According to Baker:

> Ed taught him how to build fires and cook in the open, how to use an ax to make a woodland shelter of hemlock boughs, how to tie wet and dry flies, how to dress fish and fowl for the frying pan. He insisted on the proper handling of guns, rod and tackle and taught his son the rudiments of physical courage and endurance. [Sagittarius]

He was a great disciplinarian (Saturn in 4th house). States Baker:

> Grace was more permissive. She said repeatedly she wanted her children to enjoy life. To her this meant after all awareness of the intellect and the arts. She saw from the first that they all had music lessons. She bought them tickets for symphony concerts, operatic performances, all the better plays that came to Chicago and they were encouraged quite early to acquaint themselves with the paintings and drawings of the Chicago Art Institute. Her own deep dyed belief in creativity made her long to develop the talents of her children to the highest possible level.

The above paragraph well describes Gemini on the 10th house cusp with Neptune in that house and the ruler Mercury in Leo and makes us feel that in this case the 4th house represented the father and the 10th the mother.

With Sagittarius on the 4th, Hemingway enjoyed both mental and physical activities. He also relished the fact that he was treated as an individual, despite his being one of six children. With the ruler Jupiter in the 2nd house of income, he earned his living by working out of his home. The Sagittarian largess of spirit made Hemingway feel as much at home in Paris as in Key West or Cuba or Ketchum. Hotchner's description of the *"Finca Vigia"* (Lookout Farm) is a perfect description of Sagittarius in the 4th with Uranus and Saturn thrown in for good measure.

> The property was fence enclosed and consisted of 13 acres of flower and vegetable gardens, a cow pasture with half a dozen cows, fruit trees, a defunct tennis court, a large swimming pool and a low, once white limestone villa which was a bit crumbled but dignified. A short distance from the main house was a white frame guest house. Behind the main house, to one side, was a new white gleaming three-storied square tower with an outside winding staircase. The walls of the dining room and nearly 50 foot living room of the main house were populated with splendidly horned animal heads and there were several well-trod animal skins on the tiled floors. Inside the front door was an enormous magazine rack that held an unceasing deluge of American and foreign language periodicals. A large library off the living room was crammed with books that lined the walls from the floor to the high ceiling. There were over 5000 volumes on the premises. On the wall over his bed was one of his favorite paintings, Juan Gris' "Guitar Player". The staff for the Finca normally consisted of a houseboy, a chauffeur, a Chinese cook, 3 gardeners, a carpenter, 2 maids and the keeper of the fighting cocks. . . . There was also a complement of 30 cats who lived on the ground floor of the tower with special sleeping, eating and maternity accommodations. A few favorites like Crazy Christian, Friendless Brother and Ecstasy were allowed house privileges. . . .

Uranus in **Sagittarius** in the **4th house** not only calls for ups and downs in the home life, many changes of residence and partners and unusual circumstances in the home (30 cats and a fighting cock?!), but it also shows a need for freedom of expression, a love of travel and a wish to expand the mental and physical horizons — all Hemingway traits. It explains his fun in keeping those around him off balance, wondering what crazy thing he might come up with next. This is confirmed by **Uranus' opposition** to the **Midheaven** which often elicits outrageous behavior or disregard for convention and was another reason Hemingway had such a strong need for emotional freedom.

Saturn in Sagittarius in the **4th house** describes not only the strict yet traditional upbringing previously discussed, it also imbued Hemingway with intellectual discipline and excellent powers of concentration. It added bluntness to his expression, made him very touchy when he felt unjustly accused and more than anything else, explains his anxieties about getting old. Saturn in the 4th house often tends to feelings of insecurity or inadequacy, which are generated in childhood and are compensated for by working doubly hard to achieve. Hemingway was no exception to this: Psychologically speaking,

Saturn in the 4th can bring emotional instability, an unconscious feeling of not having been loved enough, and with Saturn involved in the T-square, he may have felt that his parents expected more than he could deliver. The square to Mars, previously discussed, could have played havoc with his misunderstanding of his own masculinity, forcing him to constantly prove his "macho" traits.

Saturn's close **opposition** to **Pluto** and the wide one to **Neptune** brought additional emotional strain and made him wish to always be in charge, in control, on top of any situation and it propelled him into the pursuit of power and authority.

Saturn inconjunct Venus involving his 4th house (roots) was a painful aspect to deal with. It indicated a fear of rejection brought about through early misunderstandings with his mother which colored all successive romantic encounters with a certain mistrust and innate sexual defensiveness. It also denotes difficulty in expressing love and a tendency to lavish his love and attention on groups (Venus in the 11th) rather than risk being emotionally involved with just one person and consequently more vulnerable to rejection.

The **North Node** in **Sagittarius** is also in this house; the **South Node** is in **the 10th** in **Gemini**. If we are supposed to grow in the area where the North Node is located rather than fall prey to the *deja vu* feeling of the South Node, then Hemingway did not live up to all his potential. His real growth was to be found in understanding his own deep roots, his soul and this should have been reached through Sagittarius by pioneering new philosophies, for example. Hemingway seems to have taken an easier way out, looking for fame and ego satisfaction (10th house) through writing (Gemini).

Love affairs, children, creativity, pleasures, risks and hazards are some domains of the **5th house.** With **Capricorn** on the **cusp** and the ruler Saturn in Sagittarius in the 4th, Hemingway felt he had to work hard for everything he got and therefore well deserved it. With the typical overcompensation of Saturn ruling this house, he threw himself into all 5th house matters. Love affairs were *de rigueur* and even when not consummated they were talked or even bragged about. Telling Hotchner about Marlene Dietrich for example, he said:

The thing about the Kraut and me is that we've been in love since 1924 when we first met on the *Ile de France*, but we've never been to bed. Amazing but true. Victims of nonsynchronous passion. Those times I was out of love, the Kraut was deep in some romantic tribulation, and on those occasions when she was on the surface and swimming about with those marvelously seeking eyes of hers, I was submerged.

Saturn in the 4th afforded Hemingway the opportunity to find creative outlets based on his own roots and expressed in his home. Many writers have the **ruler of the 5th house in the 4th** but it is not necessarily Saturn. Hemingway's own words when he accepted the Nobel Prize for literature in 1954 sum up the Saturnian need to be better than the best:

> For a true writer each book should be a new beginning, where he tries for something that is beyond attainment. He should always try for something that has never been done or that others have tried and failed. It is because we have had such great writers in the past that a writer is driven far out past where he can go, out to where no one can help him.

Hemingway's excessive need to seek fun, risk and hazard showed up in many area of the horoscope with the 5th house serving as confirmation. We have previously discussed the Moon's placement here and realize that it too added to his emotional ups and downs (Moon opposition Venus) with women. Interestingly enough, Hemingway used his 5th house intensely in all areas except with his children. Somehow they stood in his way. "Main thing with baby is having good nurse" was his terse statement on raising children. He spent relatively little time with any of them during their developing years, but he did take all three boys on vacations and had them for visits wherever he lived. All three became his good friends as adults, but they never occupied the large role that writing, loving and hobbies did.

Uranus in the 4th rules Hemingway's 6th house cusp and of course he was involved in work that could be performed from the home. The combination of **Aquarius on the 6th** and Virgo rising made Hemingway take great pride in his work, working harder than anyone else and though he was driven, he was neither particularly neat nor particularly clean, (Virgo). The Aquarius quality combined with Uranus in Sagittarius was often at odds with the needs of the Virgo Ascendant. Hotchner describes Hemingway's working conditions at the *Finca*:

> Ernest's bedroom, where he worked, was also walled with books. There was a large desk covered with stacks of letters, newspapers and magazine clippings, a small sack of carnivore's teeth, two unwound clocks, shoehorns, an unfilled pen in an onyx holder, a wood-carved zebra, wart hog, rhino and lion in single file, and a wide assortment of souvenirs, mementos and good luck charms. He never worked at the desk. Instead, he used a stand up work place he had fashioned out of the top of a bookcase near his bed. His portable typewriter was snugged in there and papers were spread along the top of the bookcase on either side of it. He used a reading board for longhand writing. There were some animal heads on the bedroom walls too and a worn, cracked skin of a lesser kudu decorated the tile floor. The white tower which had been built by Mary in an effort to get the 30 cats out of the house and to provide Ernest with a place more becoming to work in than his makeshift bedroom quarters, worked with the cats but not with Ernest. The top floor of the tower

which had a sweeping view of palm tops and green hillocks clear to the sea, had been furnished with an imposing desk befitting an "Author of High Status", bookcases and comfortable reading chairs, but Ernest rarely wrote a line there except when he occasionally corrected a set of galleys.

As Hemingway himself explained to Hotchner:

> I like to write standing up — to reduce the old belly and because you have more vitality on your feet. Whoever went 10 rounds sitting on his ass? I write description in longhand because that's the hardest for me and you're closer to the paper when you work by hand, but I use the typewriter for dialogue because people speak like a typewriter works.

The **6th** is the house of health and with **Aquarius** on the cusp, his nervous system was quite active. When his efforts were not directed into work, he put a lot of emphasis on his health, to the point of hypochondria. Both Baker and Hotchner remark on this tendency and one sentence by Hotchner tells the story fully:

> His bathroom was large and cluttered with medicines and medical paraphernalia which bulged out of the cabinets and onto all surfaces; the room was badly in need of paint but painting was impossible because the walls were covered with inked records, written in Ernest's careful hand, of dated blood pressure counts, and weights, prescription numbers and other medical and pharmaceutical intelligence.

The **7th house** describes one-to-one relationships and regardless of how many we may have, the basic attitude toward such a relationship and marriage will always be the same. The recipients of the relationships, in Hemingway's case nurse Agnes von Kurowsky (prototype of the heroine Catherine Barkley in *A Farewell to Arms*) and his four wives are described by alternate houses, starting with the 7th.

Though Hemingway did not marry Agnes, the relationship was more than a 5th house affair, it was a commitment; the couple lived together, ate together, slept together, and only the piece of paper called a marriage certificate was missing. When Agnes called it quits and the relationship broke up, the emotional stress was nearly as hard on Hemingway as were his subsequent legal divorces.

When the **ruler** of the **7th** is in the **10th** you often need a partner in order to fulfill some of your ego needs — Hemingway most certainly did with **Pisces** on the cusp and the ruler **Neptune in Gemini in the 10th**. He needed someone with whom he could communicate, who would be his intellectual sparring partner (Neptune is involved in the T-square), and who at the same time could understand and therefore further his needs as a writer. Three of his wives were writers themselves and all of them encouraged his writing. Pisces on this cusp usually indicates the search for a perfect union — the fairy princess who will nurture and love him when he needs it and leave him be and stand on her own two feet when he doesn't want loving. This is a rather difficult combination that not too many women can live up to and the fact that his Moon (his perception of women in general) is in austere and demanding Capricorn opposite Venus, did not improve his chances for long-lasting relationships.

Pisces on the 7th house describes Hemingway's first love commitment Agnes, quite well. She was a tall dark-haired girl, a Washington, D.C. trained nurse whose first foreign assignment for the Red Cross was in Italy. All the young soldiers in Agnes' station adored her and were determined to get well quickly in order to date this "angel of mercy" who had an almost mischievous sense of humor. Hemingway, though 7 years her junior, succeeded where others failed. Agnes herself ended the relationship to his great chagrin.

Hadley, 6 years older than Hemingway, was also tall with long auburn hair. (Hair was very important in Hemingway's appraisal of women.) Her father committed suicide when she was 11 and she lived with her mother and married sister. Her mother died when she was 28 and she seemed poised on the verge of spinsterhood, having graduated from a private girl's school and then attended one year of Bryn Mawr nine years previously. She thought of her life as sheltered and uneventful and of herself as inexperienced. Hemingway considered her lovely, good hearted and true and she worried about his welfare, what he ate and how he slept, even after they divorced. In fact, they remained good friends until the end. This is quite an apt description of Taurus on the cusp of the 9th with the ruler Venus in Cancer in the 11th house.

Wife number two was Pauline. "Small in stature with slender limbs like a delicate little bird and bobbed hair worn in bangs" is how Hemingway describes his first impression of her. She worked for the Paris edition of *Vogue* magazine, was chic, well dressed and articulate. A devout Catholic, she had attended the Visitation Convent in St. Louis and graduated from the University of Missouri. Mary Welsh Hemingway writes:

> Ernest had told me at length about his satisfactory marriage to Pauline Pfeiffer.... Pauline had run a shipshape gracious house in Key West and borne him two fine sons. She was educated and smart and read books. I knew something about his love and regard for her. . . .

To disturb this love relation between Hemingway and Pauline (Cancer on the 11th, Moon in Sagittarius in the 5th) came Martha Gellhorn. The affair was in full swing for quite a few years. They met in 1936 but he divorced Pauline in 1940 and married Martha in 1941. Blonde, tall, young and ambitious, she too was a writer and worked for Collier's as a journalist and traveled widely covering troubled world spots. Hemingway's description of Martha to Hotchner:

> She was the most ambitious woman who ever lived, was always off to cover a tax-free war for Collier's. She liked everything sanitary. [Martha is designated by Hemingway's 1st house, Virgo, with Mercury in Leo in the 12th.] Her father was a doctor, so she made our house look as much like a hospital as possible. No animal heads, no matter how beautiful, because they were unsanitary.

In fairness to Martha we should add that she found the *Finca*, restored it and made it into a place Hemingway loved. He also admitted that she worked very hard to make his children feel comfortable. He resented her constant absences though and sneered at her returning for "a spot of domesticity." Somehow he had hoped Martha could give him the daughter he wanted. That, in his mind, could have excused his leaving Pauline. Instead, their domestic affairs became a great battlefield.

He met Mary Welsh (3rd house, Scorpio on the cusp, Pluto in Gemini in the 10th) in London in 1944. A diminutive blonde, she was a feature writer for the *Daily Express*. She also worked for the London Bureau of *Time, Life* and *Fortune*. A quick and deep rapport ensued and after divorcing their respective partners, they married in 1946. Mary seemed to fulfill many of Hemingway's needs. They really communicated well. Though she was a writer who could understand his problems, she gave up much of her career to become Mrs. Hemingway and take care of him. They had their battles and marital ups and downs, but throughout the difficult last years of his life, he knew that Mary was there for him.

> "Mary is wonderful,"

he told Hotchner while at the Mayo Clinic,

> "always and now. Wonderful. She's all that's left to be glad for. I love her, I truly love her. She knows how I hurt and she suffers trying to help me. Listen Hotch, whatever happens, whatever — she's good and strong, but remember sometimes the strongest of women need help."

Aries is on the cusp of Hemingway's **8th house** — house of support from others, sex, taxes, inheritances, death and transformation. **Mars**, the ruler is in the **1st house**. Hemingway wanted to take death (8th house) into his own hands (1st house), and he did. Many astrologers feel that wherever you encounter Aries in the chart is where you as a person really start. Hemingway said of himself:

> "Only three things in my life I've really liked to do — hunt, write and make love."

Yet his love of doing these things was deeply involved in his attitude toward life and death. As he explained in a conversation with actress Ava Gardner:

"Tell you the truth, Daughter, analysts spook me!" "You mean" Ava asked incredulously "You've never had an analyst?" "Sure I have — Portable Corona No. 3. [His typewriter.] That's been my analyst. I'll tell you, even though I'm not a believer in analysis, I spend a hell of a lot of time killing animals and fish so I won't kill myself."

Death and suicide were Hemingway's constant companions. Most of his exploits courted danger and according to informed observers were part of a subconscious death wish. Mars, focal planet of the T-square and located in the 1st house, set the pace from childhood on. He often jotted down meditations on suicide:

When I feel low I like to think about death and the various ways of dying. Unless you could arrange to die while asleep, I think the best way would be to go off a liner at night. There would be only the moment of taking the jump and it is very easy for me to take almost any sort of jump [Mars in the 1st]. Also it would never be definitely known what happened . . . there might even be the chance that you'll be given credit for an accident.

He often talked about love and death as though they were one. In a tribute to the 67 dead men of the 22nd Infantry Regiment he wrote:

Now he sleeps with that old whore Death who yesterday denied her twice. Do you take this old whore Death for thy lawful wedded wife? Repeat after me. I do. I do. . . . Sixty-seven times.

After the two plane crashes in Africa the papers were running premature obituaries which he devoured with "immoral zest" according to his wife Mary. He particularly relished a clipping from a German paper, which in "Gotterdammerung" prose pronounced that the fatal crash was simply a fulfillment of Hemingway's well-known death wish, connected with the metaphysical leopard he had placed on the top of Mt. Kilimanjaro in his story "The Snows of Kilimanjaro."

He often referred to his father's suicide, usually blaming his mother. Her sense of tact was really not the best, since:

At Christmas time I received a package from my mother. It contained the revolver with which my father had killed himself. There was a card that said she thought I'd like to have it; I didn't know whether it was an omen or a prophecy.

With **Aries** on the **8th** and **Mars** in **Virgo**, Hemingway suffered some feelings of insecurity with alternating periods of brashness. Much of this has been previously discussed when interpreting the T-square. The description by women in the know that Hemingway was a "satisfactory" lover would probably have cut him to the core. His great imagination demanded more than that.

> Tall, coffee skin, ebony eyes and legs of paradise. A very hot night but she was wearing a coat of black fur, her breasts handling the coat like it was silk. . . . She slid off him [her dancing partner] onto me. Everything under that fur instantly communicated with me. I introduced myself and asked her name. "Josephine Baker, " she said. We danced nonstop for the rest of the night. She never took off her fur coat. Wasn't until the joint closed she told me she had nothing on underneath.

The **9th house** relates to the higher mind, your life's philosophy and ideals, long trips and religion. Hemingway had **Taurus** on the cusp and the ruler **Venus** in **Cancer** in the **11th house.** The combination of Taurus and Cancer called for philosophies or religious beliefs that made sense and could be proven (especially with Virgo rising), yet there are sensitivity and poetry inherent in the character, also adherence to high standards and principles. Since Venus has only challenging aspects, Hemingway was beset with conflicts of conscience in many areas of his life, especially in his religious attitude. To illustrate:

> The brief encounter with Don Giuseppi, the priest who had anointed him while he lay wounded in 1918, had served to reawaken his religious sensibilities. The end of his marriage to Hadley was still very much on his conscience. He stopped the car at a roadside shrine where he knelt and prayed for what seemed a long time, returning to the car with tears on his cheeks.

He was baptized in the 1st Congregational Church and both parents were traditional (Sagittarius on the 4th) Protestants, with his father being more demanding in this area than his mother. With a writer's imagination, Hemingway could switch religion and philosophy at will. In order to marry Pauline in Catholic rites, he implied that Hadley was a nonbeliever and that their marriage in the Protestant church was invalid. In a letter to a Dominican father he wrote:

> "I've been a Catholic, although I have fallen away badly from 1919-1923. But I have definitely set my house in order. I have so much faith that I hate to examine it."

On the other hand he was known to be very cynical about religion and in later years proud to admit it. During World War II while serving as a correspondent, the Division Chaplain was so fascinated by Hemingway's opinions that he kept coming back for more. Hemingway once asked him if he believed a widely quoted statement that there are no atheists in a foxhole. "No Sir, Mr. Hemingway" the chaplain said, "not since I met you and Colonel Lanham." The answer delighted Hemingway who added it to his collection of anecdotes.

Nevertheless, the conflict of religion versus atheism reinforced his innately superstitious nature. While ready to bet on the horses in Auteuil, he said: "Don't count on me. I've got a big problem. I can't find my lucky piece!" While deriding "All this shit" about premonitions during a raid in World War II, he quickly knocked on wood, as he spoke. As Baker states: "Whatever he said to the contrary, he was as superstitious as a medieval peasant."

Since the **ruler** of the **9th** is in **the 11th** and has no flowing aspects, Hemingway tended to waste time and energy in traveling and partying with friends and acquaintances. Recounts Hotchner:

> We swam in Key West, shot birds in Idaho, went on the matador circuit in Spain, played the horses in Paris, toured the windswept slopes of the Escorial and drove the lovely French roads where he had cycled with Scott Fitzgerald. . . .

His strong Mars, Saturn and Pluto always called him back to fulfill his real personal, root and ego needs.

Hemingway's professional life — his status and reputation — is shown by the **10th house**. Of course, we have touched on these areas before. A horoscope is an all encompassing subject. A human being cannot be totally compartmentalized; one area flows into the other. Each area as such has its own validity; it serves to confirm the rest of the delineation and points out the less obvious character traits easily overlooked in a less careful interpretation.

Gemini is on the cusp of the **10th house**; the **ruler Mercury** is in **Leo** in the **12th house** and both Pluto and Neptune in Gemini are in this house. Wherever we find Gemini we know that versatility is a key word. Hemingway was no exception to this rule. Though he used the Gemini literary, quickwitted and expressive traits to great advantage writing alone did not suffice, and he put his heart (Mercury in Leo) and soul into all his other endeavors. As showy and gregarious as he was social (the Gemini/Leo combination), he was totally serious and dedicated when it came to his writing. He used the Leo and 12th house traits of the ruler Mercury to their best advantage. He worked alone and he poured all of himself into his work. The exact sextile from Mercury to Neptune also played a role. As he told Hotchner:

> There are only 2 absolutes I know about in writing — one is that if you make love while you are jamming on a work, you are in danger of leaving the best parts of it in the bed; the other is that integrity in a writer is like virginity in

a women — once lost it is never recovered. I am always being asked about my "credo" — Christ, that word — well, credo is to write as well as I can about things that I know and feel deeply about.

Pluto and **Neptune** are in **Gemini in the 10th,**involved in the T-square. They are the highest in the chart, ruling the houses of communication (3rd) and partners (7th) respectively; they tell a good deal of the Hemingway saga. Pluto here added even more assertiveness and self-determination to his already strong character. It made him very courageous (noted before with Mars in the 1st), a leader in his own circle, with an obsessive need (Pluto) to be the best. A perfectionist, he drove himself relentlessly. As critic Charles Champlin said in a review:

> The portrait of himself Hemingway cumulatively creates in these letters is not only of the expansive drinker/lover/adventurer/warrior but — even more convincingly — of the driven writer for whom only the writing, and self judged excellence of the writing, matters at last. He was not an adventurer playing at being an author; he was an author who found respite and renewal in action.

Neptune in the 10th helped to establish the aura of glamour surrounding Hemingway and it also added to his fun in presenting an unusual image to the world. Interestingly enough, we have found that people with Neptune in the 10th seem to achieve and accomplish on their own, without parental help. So did Hemingway. Neptune's involvement in the T-square was another confirming factor to the many self doubts that plagued him.

You may have noticed that we do not delineate Pluto or Neptune in Gemini, but rather their 10th house position. Pluto transited through Gemini for 20 years (1883 to 1913) and Neptune from 1887 to 1901 for 14 years. In that length of time millions of people had the planets in the same sign, and the interpretation would be considered generational rather than personal. The house position is specific to Hemingway, so is the fact that Pluto, the ruler of the 3rd, is in Gemini in the 10th which would be the only time we add the Gemini Quality. The same procedure follows for Neptune. When interpreting Neptune we think of the 10th house position only as personally affecting Hemingway. When delineating the 7th house cusp, we discuss the possibility of multiple partnerships because the ruler Neptune is in Gemini in the 10th house.

With **Cancer** on the **11th house** and the Moon in Capricorn in the 5th (exactly opposite the cusp) and both Venus and the Sun in Cancer in the 11th, we realize that to have friends and be with them was a very integral part of Hemingway's life. Where you find Venus shows what you really enjoy and where you find the Sun is where you want to shine. The 11th house (friends, hopes and wishes) Cancer cusp indicated a willingness to help (nurture) others and a wish to play "Papa," as Hemingway loved to do.

Since the ruler was in the 5th house, he loved his friends and they loved him — while all went well. Since the Moon opposes Venus in the 11th, he fell in and out of friendships as easily as he fell in and out of love. Yet he required unquestioning loyalty from others, as Hotchner cites:

> This was one trait common to all those with whom he had long and lasting relationships. By now they were very few. The mortality rate was as high as Ernest's standards, and if you inquired about someone who had fallen by the way, Ernest would simply tell you that he or she "didn't measure up." To be true to your own identity was what Ernest demanded and it was a virtue he prized above all others.

Venus in Cancer contributed to Hemingway's enjoyment of nice things and also to his self-indulgence. He was very sensitive and easily hurt, but hid those feelings from all but his most intimate contacts. His basic reactions to life were always instinctive and emotional which made him such an interesting writer and such a fun person to be with. His desk and room piled with mementos describe not only the pack rat quality of the Sun in Cancer but also the innate sentimentality of Venus there. Though Hemingway was known as a man's man (Sun in the 11th), he had many female friends — Marlene "the Kraut," Ava Gardner, etc. This is rather typical of Venus in the 11th house. According to Baker:

> "Ernest gloried in the role of friend. While serving overseas during World War II, he sometimes called himself 'Old Ernie Hemorrhoid, the Poor Man's Pyle.'"

While still living in Paris in the twenties, Scott Fitzgerald came to visit with his daughter Scotty.

> At some point she announced she had to make pee-pee. My W.C. was on the floor below, which Scott considered too far and instructed his daughter to do it in the hallway. When the concierge objected vociferously, Scott got so mad that he started tearing down the already frayed wallpaper in my room. The landlord made me pay for repapering the entire room. But Scott was my friend and you put up with a lot in the name of friendship. After all, it was Scott who insisted that Max Perkins [editor at Scribners] read my story and since he was already well known, his word carried a lot of weight.

For a true friend Hemingway would put up with almost anything. He also loved people who made him laugh, and he especially liked risque stories or jokes that left him looking good. He roared at a letter received in 1955 from Herman Levin:

> . . . that you were tentatively interested in having one of your properties brought to the Broadway stage. I think the idea is an excellent one and I speak from

the experience of several years as producer. [Among other things he produced *Gentlemen Prefer Blondes*]. After giving the matter some careful consideration, I came up with an idea that I think is fairly bursting with potential. Considering the enormous current popularity of *The Old Man and the Sea*, can you imagine how a full-scale musical comedy production of the story would grab the public? I've already discussed the concept with a pair of songwriters. Al Lerner & Fred Loewe, both of whom were so enthusiastic they got right to work and roughed out a few numbers that might be worked into such a show: "With a Little Bit of Bait", "Get Me to the Beach on Time" and "Just You Wait, Izaak Walton, Just You Wait". All three of us are very excited about this. I feel that with a few minor changes (such as making the skiff into a boat large enough to accommodate a chorus line), the choice of a proper star (I see Rex Harrison as the Old Man), and a snappy new title (something like "Hook, Line and Sinker") a real hit could be produced. . . .

Now we have reached the hardest house to interpret, the 12th. This house describes the subconscious, the hidden personality, hidden strengths and fears, the behind the scenes activities. It is the hidden side where we not only try to fool the world, but often end up fooling ourselves. How much of this innermost self we wish to face and acknowledge is left to our free will, but certain charts have an easier time than others or a greater need to become aware or tune in.

Hemingway has **Leo** on the cusp of his **12th house** and the Sun that rules it in Cancer in the 11th. Leo does not really like to be relegated to "behind the scenes" efforts, it likes to be ensconced on the throne rather than be the power behind it. But Hemingway used the practical side of Leo on the 12th house cusp quite well; he let his books shine (Leo/Sun) for him. He could keep as much or as little of himself hidden as he wished, never having to reveal what was truth and what was fiction, what was autobiographical and what was invented. Also with Mercury in that house sextile to Neptune, he could utilize his great imagination without anyone accusing him of exaggerating or forcing him to separate dreams from reality.

With all the material we have on Hemingway the author and Hemingway the man, we still don't really know how deeply he looked within, how many of his shortcomings he really faced up to or tried to change, because proud Leo would never publicly admit to half of the findings if he did not think them flattering. Once in a while some of the softness of the man would come through, but rarely. In a conversation with Hotchner, discussing his early writing in Paris, he said:

"But every day the rejected manuscripts would come back. In the bare room they'd fall through the slot on the wood floor and clipped to them was the most savage of all reprimands — the printed rejection slip. I'd sit at that old wooden table and read one of those cold slips that had been attached to a story I had loved and worked on very hard and I couldn't help crying." "I never think of you crying", says Hotchner. "I cry, boy," Ernest said "When the hurt is bad enough, I cry."

The 11th house position of the ruler of the 12th not only confirms his need for friends and constant involvement with them but also adds a strange twist to the fact that Hemingway's paranoia shortly before his death involved being pursued by secret organizations such as the FBI and CIA. Instead of his being a manipulator for such groups, as is often the case when the ruler of the 12th is in the 11th, he felt himself being manipulated by them.

The depressions often encountered with Leo on the cusp of the 12th house also took their toll. Starting in 1960 he showed symptoms of extreme nervous depression, fear, loneliness, ennui, suspicion of the motives of others, insomnia, guilt, remorse and failure of memory. The stories of his delusions grew daily.

The 4th house describes the end of the physical body; the 8th house shows the liberation of the soul or death and the 12th indicates the philosophical death — the results of the course of life we choose to take. Hemingway chose to take his own life (ruler of the 8th in the 1st). His physical death (4th house) was fast (Uranus in the 4th) and was brought about by lifelong beliefs and a long-standing wish to commit suicide (Saturn in the 4th), while his philosophical death (12th house) started a good year before he actually shot himself. Hotchner wrote:

"The innumerable injuries from his reckless desire to live to the fullest extracted their toll."

Baker sums it all up:

Sunday morning dawned bright and cloudless. Ernest awoke early as always. He put on the red "Emperor's Robe" and padded softly down the carpeted stairway. He tiptoed down the basement stairs and unlocked the storage room. He chose a double-barreled Boss shotgun with a tight choke. He took some shells from one of the boxes in the storage room, closed and locked the door and climbed the basement stairs. He crossed the living room to the front foyer, a shrine like entryway 5 feet by 7, with oak-paneled walls. He slipped in 2 shells, lowered the gun butt carefully to the floor, leaned forward, pressed the twin barrels against his forehead just above the eye brows, and tripped both triggers.

Lesson 15
DIANA OF WALES:
A Fairy Tale Come True

This chart interpretation is probably close to what most astrologers face on a day to day basis. A client, friend or relative calls and wants a natal chart delineated; you the astrologer, already know or ask some pertinent questions to establish the present reality of the person. Now it is up to you to find all the available potential and talent, the reason for existing problems and not only their possible solutions but also avoidance of new ones.

Here are the facts: "'Shy Di' Turns Sly" scream the headlines under a picture of then Lady Diana Spencer, now Princess of Wales, as she half covers her face and coyly peeks out through two fingers.

Who is "Shy Di" as the press nicknamed her — a name that is "wide of the mark" according to people who know her. "My name is Diana" she quietly says when someone addresses her by the diminutive; she is gracious despite the pressures surrounding her and is impressively mature for a girl of 19.

The royal wedding was considered to be "the wedding of the century" and its pomp and ceremony brought the former glories of England back to life for a brief glimpse of Camelot on July 29, 1981. Diana Spencer had just turned 20 and has a full life ahead of her.

According to information received from Buckingham Palace courtesy of Charles Harvey of the Astrological Association of London, Diana was born on July 1, 1961 at 7:45 PM British Standard Time (6:45 PM GMT) at Park House, part of the 20,000 acre royal estate at Sandringham, in

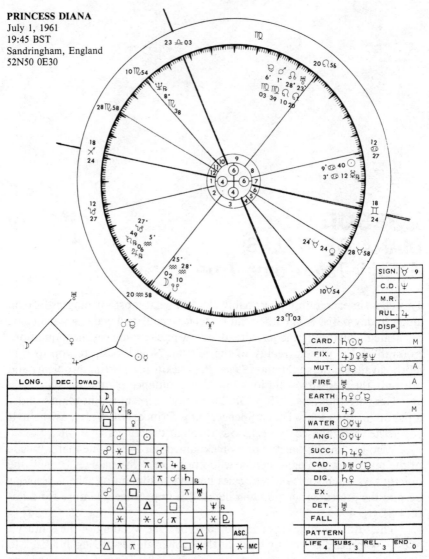

PRINCESS DIANA
July 1, 1961
19:45 BST
Sandringham, England
52N50 0E30

	SIGN.	♉ 9
	C.D.	♆
	M.R.	
	RUL.	♃
	DISP.	

CARD.	♄ ☉ ☿	M
FIX.	♃ ☽ ♀ ♅ ♆	
MUT.	♂ ♇	A
FIRE	♅	A
EARTH	♄ ♀ ♂ ♇	
AIR	♃ ☽	M
WATER	☉ ☿ ♆	
ANG.	☉ ☿ ♆	
SUCC.	♄ ♃ ♀	
CAD.	☽ ♅ ♂ ♇	
DIG.	♄ ♀	
EX.		
DET.	♅	
FALL		
PATTERN		
LIFE 4	SUBS. 3	REL. 3	END 0

LONG.	DEC.	DWAD										
			☽									
			(△)	☿ ℞								
			□	♀								
				♂	☉							
			☍	✳	□	♂						
				⊼	⊼	⊼	♃ ℞					
					△	⊼	♂	♄ ℞				
			☍		□		⊼	♅				
				△	△	□		♆ ℞			
				✳	✳	♂	⊼		✳	♇	
								△			ASC.
			△	⊼			□	✳		✳	MC

Norfolk, which the Spencer family rented from the crown. The Spencers themselves were part of royalty for hundreds of years. Diana's father, the 8th Earl Spencer served as an equerry (officer in the royal household) to both King George VI and Queen Elizabeth II. The illustrious lineage stretches all the way back to the rule of Charles I. Born with an automatic title, Diana was a "Lady" at birth. In fact, according to a *Time* article of April 20, 1981:

> She has more royal blood in her than Prince Charles, her 16th cousin once removed. Four of her ancestors were mistresses to English kings. Three dallied with Charles II (1633-85), a compulsive philanderer whose amorous activities produced more than a quarter of the 26 dukedoms in Great Britain and Ireland. The 4th royal paramour, Arabella, daughter of the 1st Sir Winston Churchill, was the favorite of James II (1633-1701) and bore him a daughter. In short, while Diana's blood may run blue, even purple, scarlet women and black sheep have added to its color.
>
> Also of note were two daughters of the 1st Earl Spencer: Georgiana, the beautiful Duchess of Devonshire, better known as the Duchess of Dimples, who achieved unwedded bliss with the eventual George IV and her comely sister Henrietta who boasted "In my 51st year I am court'd, follow'd, flatter'd and made love to, *en toutes formes*, by four men."

Not all the Spencers were so sportive. George, brother of the 3rd Earl Spencer, converted to Roman Catholicism and as Father Ignatius of the Passionist Order, had a reputation as a saint. There is a proposal afoot to consider him for beatification. One of Princess Diana's great-aunts was Queen Victoria's goddaughter. Her grandmother, Lady Fermoy, is lady-in-waiting to the Queen Mother who considers her one of her closest friends. When Diana moved into Clarence House, the Queen Mother's residence, for a crash course in "queening," her grandmother's presence proved helpful and reassuring.

Diana's brother is Queen Elizabeth's godson and she grew up calling the Queen of England "Aunt Lillibet." Diana is the youngest of three sisters — Sarah and Jane and has a younger brother, Charles. A second brother died shortly after birth in 1960. She grew up at Park House in Norfolk, only a short distance from the royal estate at Sandringham. There was only a low stone wall separating the two estates, and the three princes with their princess sister would regularly climb over it to share the small, open-air swimming pool at the Spencers.

After the difficult (*Newsweek* calls it "messy") divorce of her parents when Diana was eight years old, the Earl Spencer and the children moved to their ancestral home, Althorp in Northamptonshire, a 15,000 acre estate with a 100 room mansion. For a while, Diana and her brother and sisters shuttled back and forth between parental households.

Diana attended Westheath, an expensive boarding school, where she excelled in sports and dancing and recorded fair to middling results on standard exams. She and Charles, according to the *London Observer* "share a deficiency in mathematics." At 16 Diana left school and went to a finishing school in Switzerland, but to everyone's surprise, she left after less than three months.

When she decided to settle in London and accept a part-time job as a kindergarten teacher her father bought her a $200,000 flat that she shared with three friends. Both her parents have remarried. In 1976 her father married a countess who is the daughter of romantic novelist Barbara Cartland. Her mother married the wallpaper heir with whom she was accused of adultery; they now live in Australia.

Though Charles and Diana grew up next door to each other, the nearly 13 years which separate them caused both to move in totally different circles. Only in July of 1980 did the romance blossom when they discovered a mutual passion for salmon fishing and when Charles realized that the funny little girl from next door had blossomed into a beautiful young woman. Though the press got wind of the story and hounded Diana mercilessly, the couple managed to throw newsmen off and had many secret rendezvous'. The final announcement of the engagement and subsequent wedding is now history.

These are the facts known to date. But **who is Diana**?

The astrological picture shows a sensitive **Cancer Sun** in the **7th house**, a cool and collected Aquarius Moon in the 3rd and free and breezy Sagittarius rising. The six planets above and four below the horizon, four east and six west of the meridian, is nearly even; Diana is obviously well balanced in her need of others and ability to stand on her own feet, outgoingness and need to be somebody versus subjectivity and a wish to work behind the scenes.

Diana has three planets and the Midheaven in cardinal, five planets in fixed and two planets plus the Ascendant in mutable signs. With the predominance of 4 planets in the earth element, her final signature is Taurus (fixed earth) which adds a great deal of determination and makes her quite set in her ways — more so than the Cancer Sun or Sagittarius Ascendant indicate at first glance. This is confirmed by the strong T-square involving the Moon, Venus, Uranus and Mars, which we will discuss later.

The sub-signature (predominance by house position) reveals four planets in cadent houses and four in the houses of life, equating to mutable fire or a Sagittarian/9th house inner emphasis. This innately enthusiastic, fun loving and idealistic inner nature is confirmed by her Sagittarius Ascendant and large (over 62°) 9th house.

When we look at Diana's house placements, we note that she has no planets in the houses of endings. This is mitigated by the Sun, Mercury and Neptune in water signs, but the lack may indicate a certain difficulty or even reluctance for looking within. Interestingly enough, her mother-in-law Queen

Elizabeth, has the same lack. Worth noting is the enormous variety in the size of the houses. The 3rd and 9th houses measure over 62° while the 4th, 5th, 10th and 11th are only approximately 18° each. This spacing may lead to a rather confining private (4th and 5th) and public (10th and 11th) life, but it also would indicate that communicating in all its forms (3rd house) and public relations, her ideals, life philosophies and travel (9th) will always assume great importance for her.

There is no set pattern to this chart, which in a way leaves her free to shape her own future rather than being forced into a definitive mold. Neptune is nearly 9° of a fixed sign, called a critical degree. This adds even more emphasis to Neptune which is already strong as the most elevated planet in the chart and the only one not involved in a configuration, giving Diana a certain mysterious charisma and making the world see her as glamorous.

Most important is the fact that Diana has two strong configurations: a **T-square** involving the Moon at 25° Aquarius opposite Uranus at 23° Leo and both square Venus at 24° Taurus. This tight T-square also involves Mars at nearly 2° Virgo. Thus the following are all intermingled and challenging each other: the Moon (emotions) in the 3rd and ruling the 8th house; Uranus (freedom urge) from the 9th house ruling the 3rd; Mars (action planet) in the 9th ruling her 4th house and Venus (affectionate nature and social values) in the 5th house and ruling the 5th and Midheaven. We will discuss each aspect of the T-square as we get to it, but at a quick glance it is obvious that this genteel young lady has guts, a mind of her own and the ability to know what she wants and how to get it.

The second configuration is a **yod** involving six planets. The finger is Jupiter at 5° Aquarius, inconjunct Mercury and the Sun in Cancer in the 7th house and inconjunct Mars and Pluto in Virgo in the 9th house. Saturn at nearly 28° Capricorn is also drawn into the configuration since it inconjuncts Mars at nearly 2° of Virgo and is within a rather wide orb (5° 23') of an inconjunct to Mercury. Again we have many areas of the life involved. Jupiter is the chart ruler ruling the Ascendant, and as such expresses much of Diana's personality; yet as she is establishing her own values (Jupiter in the 2nd) in a very individualistic way (Aquarius), the four inconjuncts (also called quincunxes) say adjustments, compromises and reorganization are necessary in her public life and one-to-one relationships (Sun and Mercury in the 7th), in her beliefs and philosophies (Mars and Pluto in the 9th). Being born with a title and becoming royalty brings with it restrictions, strain and many adjustments.

Diana's **Sun** is in **Cancer** in the **7th house**. She is instinctively home loving, patriotic and maternal. Because the Sun's ruler, the Moon, is in Aquarius in the 3rd house, her need to nurture extends to a genuine concern for humanity. Since the Sun is in Cancer she will care what others say or think of her; but with the Aquarius overlay Diana will know how to rise above this when necessary. (Remember her first appearance with Charles when she wore a strapless gown which caused a minor sensation.) What she does need is to achieve emotional security (confirmed by the Moon's involvement in the T-square) and a quiet place to retreat to.

There is a dichotomy between the Sun in Cancer which likes to be dependent and the ruler in Aquarius which wants to be independent. This is reinforced by the 7th house placement of the Sun where partnerships and relying on another person assumes enormous importance. Marriage has great meaning for Diana and with the right partner she can learn and grow through it. (She and Prince Charles have highly interesting chart contacts which we will discuss in a future book on comparisons and composites.) Diana's desire to relate is matched by her tenacity and need to hold on to a partner. Her great sensitivity (Cancer) is helped by an ability to detach (Aquarius) when things get really rough; but the moodiness always present in a Cancer Sun will be even more pronounced with the ruler in often erratic Aquarius. When she's happy she's very, very happy — but when she is sad, she's very, very sad!

With the **Sun conjunct Mercury**, Diana's need to express herself (Sagittarius rising, chart ruler in Aquarius, a very large 3rd house) is enhanced and with her reasoning ability and inner individuality in the same house and sign (Cancer), she will be quite subjective in her opinions and general approach to life.

The **Sun quincunx Jupiter** confirms the previously noted pull between dependence and independence; add to this an inborn feeling of inadequacy (supported by the T-square) which causes her a need to prove something to somebody. As a result she will try doubly hard to be considerate and kind; her friends say she never forgets to send birthday cards or call when someone is sick. If she uses this inconjunct negatively, she may take on more than she should or she may indulge herself. Used positively, she can learn to adjust her values (Jupiter in the 2nd) to existing needs and use restraint, not easy with any Jupiter/Sun contact.

Diana's **Sun** very closely **trines Neptune**, indicating innate creativity and a great imagination. It also makes her a born romantic and confirms her tender nature, her love of home, mate and family already seen her in Cancer Sun. Since the Sun is in the public 7th house and Neptune is in the even more public 10th, this aspect makes her very charismatic to her people; to them she is the "Fairy Princess." In her private life she could use her creative talent for writing (Neptune rules the intercepted 3rd), painting or any other form of communication. Negatively used, this aspect can lead to daydreaming or other forms of escapism.

There is a pleasant **sextile** between **the Sun and Pluto**, indicating good recuperative powers, resourcefulness and confirming her strong will, already established with the Taurus signature. It may also give her the opportunity (sextile) to share some of her philosophies (Pluto in the 9th) with the public

(Sun in the 7th) and to do some long distance traveling (9th) with her husband (7th).

Diana's sensitive and feeling Sun is in direct contrast to her emotional nature, seen through the **Moon** at 25° **Aquarius in the 3rd house**. This Moon placement can detach when the chips are really down, but in Aquarius it is not totally unemotional, especially when its ruler Uranus is in Leo in the 9th house and both are involved in squares to Venus. In fact, Diana will feel up sky high and down in the dumps in easy succession and release of some kind will become very important so that she does not overload herself emotionally. Yet the airy and intellectual side of Aquarius will enable her to look at problems in a philosophical way (ruler in the 9th) or approach them through reasoning and logic (Moon in the 3rd house). A cause or project can always help her release tensions and as future queen she should be able to find plenty of good causes to keep her busy, especially since she will instinctively be drawn to humanitarian or religious ones.

Diana is a charming friend and companion and a fun conversationalist. Original at times, her imagination is fertile and she has lots of energy at her disposal — so much so that we would again urge her to indulge in some hobbies or projects, lest the nervous system becomes overtaxed. Diana is broadminded and an idealist and in her own way she enjoys being unconventional. The Sun in Cancer may wish to go unnoticed, but the Moon in Aquarius with its ruler in Leo loves a bit of theatricality. Despite the brouhaha created by her strapless gown, Diana picked the same designers, a virtually unknown couple, to make her wedding dress, in preference to the established royal dress designers. This dichotomy between the inner individuality (Sun) and emotional personality (Moon) is stressed not only through her wish to be dependent on one hand and independent on the other as we mentioned before, but also by the warm Cancerian involvement on a one-to-one basis versus the impersonal and always unpredictable Aquarian behavior which loves all humanity rather than only one person.

The 3rd house position of the Moon often indicates a lack of ability to concentrate, especially when it comes to studying. This may be the reason she left school at 16. She probably learns best by listening. Ever restless, she loves to be on the go and with Uranus in the 9th house, long trips will be right up her alley. Of course as heirs to the British throne, she and her husband will do an inordinate amount of traveling. This may be a good outlet for some of her energies. When the Moon is in the 3rd house we often find a close and emotional involvement with siblings. In Diana's case she was quite close to her brother and two sisters since children of divorced parents do so often form a closely knit bond.

Since the **Moon** is at 25° Aquarius and **Mercury** is at 3° Cancer, there is only a very wide (8° orb) **trine** between the two planets, too wide to have great impact on Diana's basic personality, but we must remember that the

Moon is approaching the aspect and that by approximately age 8 this trine was exact, which may have helped her overcome some deep resentments at the time of her parent's divorce. It also helps her to be a sympathetic listener and mitigates some of the bluntness found in a 3rd house Moon and Sagittarius Ascendant.

A totally different personality profile ensues from the strong **T-square** involving Diana's **Moon** opposing its own ruler **Uranus** and **Mars** and squaring **Venus**. The Moon not only describes your emotions and feelings but also how you react to yourself as a woman and how you see your mother. With the square to Venus and opposition to Mars, the male/female role model was not the best and already early in life Diana must have felt the stress between her parents, culminating in the eventual divorce. She may now see her mother as a friend rather than as the archetypal mother image (Moon in Aquarius in the 3rd). Her mother undoubtedly tried to raise Diana with enough independence to stand on her own feet, but with the square to Venus (the other planet describing the mother), we see that Diana harbored resentment toward her mother. As a result she may not be really secure in her own femininity and may be reluctant to establish close emotional ties. (The Sun in Cancer also likes to protect its vulnerability.) This reluctance may be the reason she never had a steady boyfriend and only went out on occasional dates. In fact, her uncle, Lord Fermoy, very bluntly said, "She's had no lovers!"

The **Moon's opposition to Mars** indicates that Diana's feelings are very intense and that when aroused, she can really strike back. Her temper is quick and she can be amazingly sarcastic and biting. She probably finds it hard to accept criticism of any kind, easily feeling attacked. For her sake we hope she can overcome this, since as a public person she undoubtedly will be attacked by both the public and press many times. Of course, the challenge manifested in the opposition can be channeled and properly used it can give Diana enough energy to move mountains. Just as Venus is another symbol to describe the mother, Mars is a secondary male symbol describing the father — Sun and Saturn being the principal ones. Diana may have thought of her father as caring (Sun in Cancer) and authoritarian (Saturn in Capricorn), but emotionally (Moon) she felt that he did not understand her needs or those of her mother. In later years the Martian energy will most likely be used to become aware (opposition) of her own female needs, especially in sexual matters since the Moon rules the 8th house.

The **opposition from the Moon to Uranus** is every bit as difficult. This is the ruler opposing its own planet and until Diana is aware of the polarity between Leo and Aquarius, the divergent factors of the two signs will pull her in many directions. As a result she will often be tense and restless (we know that she is a nail biter), often touchy and always impulsive. The Sagittarius Ascendant corroborates this. She may have felt that her mother let her down and was rarely there when she needed her. This feeling probably started before the divorce and the separation only reinforced her sentiment of not being truly loved. In a more positive vein, this opposition endows Diana with a good mind and unique imagination which she could creatively express through her 5th house where Venus, the focal point of the T-square, is located. In a way she already started using the positive energy when she became a kindergarten teacher (a 5th house matter).

An easy outlet for the **Moon** comes through the **trine to the Midheaven**, signifying that as she becomes a more public person, people will react well to her which in turn will help to reassure her, imbuing her with confidence and a feeling of accomplishment.

To describe Diana's outer personality, her physical appearance and how she presents herself to the world, we note that the **Ascendant** is 18° Sagittarius and the ruler Jupiter is in Aquarius in the 2nd house. Both Sagittarius and Aquarius need freedom, lots of it. Freedom to think for themselves and to express these thoughts; freedom to roam and to act. "She's got her own ideas and she's not easily swayed," say her friends. This will be one of the big hurdles and the many adjustments she'll have to make show vividly in the four inconjuncts to the chart ruler Jupiter. Sagittarius rising always denotes an open and frank person, in fact, if Diana were a client we would counsel her to be careful how and when she says something lest she offend without really meaning to.

The **Ascendant trine Uranus** indicates that she enjoys saying or doing some *outre* or unique things, making it even harder for her to hold back her inherently impulsive nature. On the other hand her breezy and friendly attitude endears her to people who will forgive her many harmless trespasses. Generous and optimistic, talkative and excitable, with a delightfully naive quality, she will rarely go unnoticed in a crowd, not only because she is tall, as Sagittarius ascending often is, but also because she has a unique style about her that attracts attention. Diana's love of the great outdoors and her enjoyment of fishing and sports in general can be partly attributed to Sagittarius rising. On a less positive note, as is true with many people who have this Ascendant, Diana may have to watch her weight in later years.

Where the ruler of the Ascendant is by house placement is where we really want to be. With **Jupiter in the 2nd house**, Diana is presented with another pull in a different direction. The 2nd house represents her earning ability, her inner and outer resources and as such, her security urges. So on one hand Diana needs to feel secure and has to earn her own money in order to feel self-reliant and independent. Aquarius however, also loves to be a rebel and to occasionally rock the boat and the Leo quality of the ruler Uranus adds an element of theatricality. In other words, Diana enjoys being the center of attention, but then just as quickly she will want to retreat into her secure little world. Since Jupiter's ruler Uranus is in the 9th house emphasizing that her ideas, ideals and philosophies are the backbone of her personality, we feel that one way out of the dilemma would be for her to become involved in social and humanitarian causes and an inspiration to her people. This way she could combine the Jupiterian largess with the Aquarian ability to find new and interesting ways to handle routine matters and thus assuage her social consciousness.

Jupiter in the 2nd house often promises material possessions, in fact often beyond practical needs and unless the entire monetary system collapses, Charles and the Royal Family will always be very rich in land and personal income. Most likely Diana will live in high style with more servants than she can count, a London residence, a 347-acre estate in the beautiful Cotswolds and a bungalow in the Scilly Isles. This is just for starters. Diana will also benefit from Charles' income of $1.25 million per year.

Jupiter, as previously mentioned, is the finger of a strong yod and points to a need to reorganize much of her life (she has eight inconjuncts all told) if she expects to function as a princess is supposed to. With **Jupiter quincunx Mercury** she must learn not to blurt things out but to think before she speaks (not easy for Sagittarius rising). **Jupiter inconjunct Mars** signifies that she can't afford to be as impulsive as her innate nature dictates. The **inconjunct** from **Jupiter to Pluto** indicates that she is expected to give up control and let others take charge. This is particularly difficult for her, since in her mind lack of control is synonymous with vulnerability. In her developing years these inconjuncts worked on a different level. With Jupiter quincunx Mercury she probably tended to be a bit sloppy in her work and had to learn to discipline herself and improve her habits. With the inconjunct to Mars she may have taken excessive risks and fearlessly jumped into many situations before she was ready. She may also have overextended herself and taken on more than she should, which she may still do even as she grows older. The quincunx to Pluto manifests fully only at a certain maturity level; in early years it often shows up as a wish to dominate and Diana may have tried to manipulate her sisters, brother or schoolmates. The most satisfying adjustment in later years will be found by helping those less fortunate or by fighting for social justice.

The **square from Jupiter to Neptune** does not deny the creative potential found in the contact of these two planets, but it does require Diana to buckle down in order to channel the energies and avoid the self-indulgence common with this aspect. She may set her ideals too high and be in for many disappointments.

The **2nd house** has **Capricorn** on the cusp and Saturn is dignified in Capricorn in this house. Despite a carefree outer mask (Sagittarius rising), Diana is quite concerned with possessions (substantiated by the chart ruler in the 2nd house) and material things. Her generosity will rarely stretch to her belongings — what is hers will stay hers and she will guard it. She is really quite practical and prudent and not extravagant. Though born to money, she never went the Gucci, Pucci or *haute couture* route, followed by most of her peers. Sensible pants, skirts and sweaters were much more to her liking. With the ruler of the cusp in the same sign and house, her feet are solidly planted on the ground and she will soon learn that her real inner security can be found by relying on her own talents and resources. Regardless of how scattered or idealistic she may be in other areas of her life, the Capricornian need to succeed will help her many times when royal demands seem nearly overwhelming.

Saturn in Capricorn makes Diana practical and careful when it really counts and she has the ability to surround herself with an aura of dignity surprising in one so young, but which is helpful considering the public person she is expected to become. This Saturn placement enables her to work hard at whatever she does and enjoy it while she's doing it. She values her family heritage and will do much to uphold tradition (confirmed by the Sun and Mercury in Cancer).

Though Diana comes from a rich family and consequently started life with a silver spoon in her mouth (Jupiter in the 2nd), wherever we find Saturn is where we feel insecure and tend to overcompensate; so despite money and a titled background, it seems that Diana is not sure of her values or self worth, and will work very hard to establish herself as a person or identity in her own right. Since Saturn is partly involved in the yod with Jupiter, she will have to make adjustment after adjustment, often to the point of compromise.

Particularly difficult is the **inconjunct from Saturn to Mars**, because it will tear Diana between responsibility to her family (Mars rules the 4th), herself and her vision of how she wants to be perceived by the public (Mars is in the 9th). In order to do the "right" thing, she may overdo, hoping to win applause.

The **quincunx from Saturn to Uranus** shows that she needs and wants approval, yet is often pulled between old traditions versus new concepts, her basic need to be free versus her knowledge that in her position she never will be able to do what she really wants to. This can be quite frustrating, but Sagittarius rising and Saturn in Capricorn can have a wonderfully dry sense of humor and when she learns to relax and roll with the punches, she will soon start laughing at some of the situations she finds herself in. Since both Mars and Uranus inconjuncts emanate from the 9th house, we must assume that her lack of higher education adds to her feeling of inadequacy and that she has to learn to find new ways of expressing her higher mind.

Saturn trine Venus is considered the classical aspect for a woman who is looking for a mate who is older or more mature so she can look up to him, often in order to compensate for a not totally harmonious relationship with her father. This seems to be the case with Diana and Prince Charles should ably fulfill the role. With Venus in the 5th house, Diana will undoubtedly be a good mother. We have already seen the artistic leaning (Sun trine Neptune) and the Saturn/Venus trine validates this. It also shows her appreciation for the arts which can enrich her life. Diana plays the piano and Charles plays the cello; surely, they can make beautiful music together. With Venus in Taurus in the 5th painting and ceramics could be other artistic outlets.

The **square from Saturn to the Midheaven** may be indicative of the resentment she felt toward her father as a child, especially when the parents did not get along and then divorced. It also shows the tenseness she feels when she is supposed to present a picture to the world as Lady Diana or Princess of Wales.

The **3rd house** is very large (nearly 63°) and with **Aquarius** on the cusp and the Moon in this house, she is highly motivated to communicate; in fact, she puts much of her emotionality into expressing herself. She is happy when she can find unique ways of presenting her ideas (Aquarius on the cusp, Uranus in the 9th) and she is most vocal about causes she espouses. With Pisces intercepted in the 3rd house, she may tend to scatter her mental or intellectual energies in quite a few directions, but this interception adds depth to her thinking and again emphasizes her sensitivity, especially with Neptune in Scorpio. Since the rulers of the 3rd are in the 9th and 10th houses, she will travel long distances for her career (being a princess and future queen), but she will also be able to communicate some of her ideas and ideals (9th) to her people (10th).

The **4th house** represents one of the parents. Classically, **Mars** — ruler of Aries on her 4th house — is a male principal, while Venus — ruler of the Libran 10th house — represents the female figure. Yet we know that as a child she regarded her father as nurturing (Sun in Cancer) and her mother as intellectual and detached (Moon in Aquarius). We also know that it was her mother who broke up the household and that Diana and her siblings stayed with the father; therefore we could say that her mother disrupted the home (Mars ruling the 4th), whereas her father tried to keep harmony and a semblance of family life (Libra on the Midheaven). Both Mars and Venus are involved in the T-square, showing challenges and tensions in Diana's attitude toward both parents. To be honest, we do not know the answer and even Diana may not be sure. Many people with a similar 4th/10th house axis state that they can make a good case for either house representing either parent and that they — as well as Diana — saw the mother and father as "parents," interchangeably nurturing (4th) and authoritarian (10th).

Diana's foundation and roots as seen through the 4th house show a restless and often difficult adolescence, with a feeling of not being offered enough love and tenderness (Mars in Virgo). Because the ruler is in the 9th house, we can surmise that Diana got a solid religious upbringing and that both parents tried to instill high ideals and moral standards. With Aries on the 4th cusp, Diana wants to be in charge of her own home. This may not be possible in the position she has chosen for herself and Mars' involvement in the T-square and yod confirms that she may have to face quite a few challenges (royal battles!) until she can solve the dilemma. The **conjunction of Mars to Pluto** will serve to intensify the problem, but it will also give her inner strength and outer stamina.

The **5th house** of children, love and romance, fun and recreation, has **Taurus** on the cusp and the ruler Venus in Taurus in the house. Taurus is stable, loyal, artistic and very sensual. Since Diana's chart signature is also Taurus, we realize that much of her real personality can be expressed through 5th house matters. She has already shown her inclination toward some artistic (dancing), recreational (sports) and child involved (kindergarten teacher) aspects of the house. Taurus here shows that she is a very loving and romantic person and we can assume that she will bear children and love them. Her tactile senses are well developed and for full enjoyment she needs to touch things. Taurus is the most sensual sign of the zodiac and with Venus (what you really enjoy) in the 5th, she may surprise Charles and herself by her strong desire nature. Venus in Taurus is dignified and describes her charming mannerisms and good looks. It confirms her rapport with nature and an inborn artistic inclination, but also attests to a certain pleasure-seeking sociability that could become excessive, since Venus is the focal point of the T-square.

The squares do not deny the 5th house matters, but she may have to apply herself to achieve some of them. **Venus square Mars** is particularly difficult, since Mars rules the 4th house and therefore points not only to the parental fights previously discussed, but also to the fact that Diana may be quite volatile in her own home and show intense anger when she and her loved ones have a difference of opinion. Swings between love and hate seem to be part of her nature.

The **square from Venus to Uranus** is just as stressful and since Uranus rules the 3rd house, her verbal outbursts will surprise people who do not know her intimately; but both Uranus and Mars are quick to forgive and forget and it is healthier for her to get her frustrations out into the open. (Charles may not quite agree!) On the positive side this square to Uranus makes Diana an exciting person to be with and it also imbues her with an outrageous sense of humor.

The **inconjunct of Venus to the Midheaven** proves her strong need to be loved and accepted by her father, which in adulthood may be transferred to her husband. She will have to learn how much of herself she can give to her people without depleting herself. Since Venus, ruler of the 5th is in the 5th square the Moon, she may have some problems in childbirth.

Taurus is also on the cusp of the **6th house**, reemphasizing the importance of Venus in this chart. Taurus the Bull usually attests to good physical stamina and despite the T-square, Diana should bounce back fully and easily from any illness. We presume she suffered from occasional sore throats as a youngster, as so many people with Taurus on the 6th house cusp do. Diana would be well advised to watch her figure as she gets older, since the combination of a Venusian 6th house and Jupiterian Ascendant often leads to weight problems. Since the ruler of the 6th house is located in the 5th, work and service are two areas she loves and if work involves some artistic endeavor, it would be even more fulfilling. Another interpretation could be that one of her duties (6th) will be to bear children (ruler in the 5th).

In the **7th house** we find more contradictions. Airy, communicative and independent **Gemini** is on the cusp; but Mercury the ruler, is in sensitive, shy and dependent Cancer in the 7th house and of course the Sun is there too. The Gemini facet wants intellectual companionship, whereas Mercury in Cancer wants emotional support, protection and praise. Gemini needs freedom of thought and speech — Cancer needs a cautious and publicly acceptable type of expression. Since the 7th house describes Diana's attitude toward marriage and partnerships, it looks as though Charles has quite a few roles to fill. With Mercury in the 7th there is often an early marriage and Diana fits this role. Since Mercury has few challenging aspects, marriage and the ability to relate to the public should be easy for her.

Mercury sextile Mars makes her very curious and she can express herself most imaginatively. Since she is always friendly, people will like her and let her get away with her outspokenness. The **trine of Mercury to Neptune** has both good and bad effects. It usually makes studying of abstract subjects like mathematics and science difficult, but it gives a fresh and different approach to what could be dull or banal routine. As she matures, this trine together with the **sextile to Pluto** can give her great depth of understanding, keen perception and sincerity in her relations with others.

Mercury in Cancer reemphasizes that Diana's reasoning is deeply intertwined with her emotions and that though not a great intellectual, she is a bright and imaginative young lady. With the ruler of the 7th in the 7th Diana will strongly identify with her partner, and she can have an enduring relationship with him. Since Mercury is involved in the yod, she needs to adjust to her married life in order to grow and mature (Jupiter).

In the **8th house** we look for support from the partner and to a lesser extent, the public, and for attitudes toward sex. Since the **Moon** which rules the 8th house is in the 3rd, Diana should get much verbal and intellectual support from the public (Moon trine the Midheaven) and also from Charles, though the Moon's square to Neptune and opposition to Mars and Uranus may mean occasional clashes of philosophical outlook. Sexually, these same squares can serve positively as wonderful challenges and exciting tensions. Diana's attitude toward love is very sensual (Venus in Taurus) and sex to her is an emotional experience (Cancer on the cusp); but she should not shy away from experimentation (Moon in Aquarius). With the Moon's squares and oppositions she may at times have doubts and need reassurance. In the public eye she and Charles should appear as the ideal couple (Moon trine Midheaven), but in private life she may not get quite as much recognition.

With **Leo** on the cusp of the **9th house** and Sagittarius ascending, truth and idealism form an important backbone for her philosophy and her basically optimistic approach to life. Since the ruler the Sun, is in Cancer in the 7th house she will want a partner who shares in her ideological opinions and understands her background. Charles seems to meet those criteria. This placement also indicates a great love of travel, preferably with a husband or partner. In her job as future queen Diana will get more than she bargained for, since the Royal Family is still expected to travel to the ends of the earth, and more than once!

The 9th is also the house of higher education, which in Diana's case was not an intellectual or college-oriented one. She studied cooking and French at the Swiss finishing school and obviously got bored rather quickly and opted for work instead. Leo on the 9th is nearly always a good teacher; Diana taught little tots, bringing in the 5th house. The 9th and 3rd are the largest houses in the chart and since Uranus, Mars and Pluto are placed here, the 9th assumes much importance in Diana's life. The vision of her role and the inspiration she can bring to others all mean more to her than the actual rites she will perform in public. After all, her husband is the crown prince, she is just his wife, acting (Neptune in the 10th) the role of princess.

Uranus in Leo in the 9th house enables Diana to be somewhat different in her approach to life than the prevailing fashion among her peers. She rejected debutante society and had no intention of "coming out." She was never seen in night clubs or discotheques. She does not take tea at Fortnum and Mason, an exclusive London shop for delicacies. She rarely drinks, except for an occasional glass of wine and she never smoked. In fact, according to the *London Observer*, it was hard to see exactly where she fits into London's social life. A free thinker — they eliminated the word "obey" from the marriage ceremony — she could become an excellent social reformer, and the **sextile to the Midheaven** makes many of her ideas acceptable to her people.

Mars adds plenty of activity to the 9th house. Since it is **in Virgo**, Diana loves to work and to give service and she is enthusiastic when she can contribute to a good cause. She probably has little patience with the social butterflies of her circle; if anything, she may need to curb a tendency to be too critical of others. **Mars in the 9th** often indicates in-law problems and with Mars and Uranus as part of the T-square and Pluto also in this house, this does seem a distinct possibility. Mars in the 9th also confirms Diana's rather stubborn adherence to what she believes to be right, her restlessness and love of travel.

Restless, eager and adventurous, **Pluto in Virgo in the 9th** house enables Diana to try new experiences, to dream many impossible dreams (9th) and even to bring them into reality (Virgo). Travel and foreign lands beckon her and with her innate curiosity she will ask many questions and dig deeply for the answers on all subjects that interest her. This position of Pluto again substantiates her good intuition and gives her an inborn understanding of human nature.

Because the **sextile from Pluto to Neptune** is a generational one (in effect for nearly 13 years) it will not shed any new light on Diana's basic character. All people born during that time were looking for more open government and leadership, for human justice and acceptance of sex on a less puritanical level. In Diana's case, since the sextile takes place from the 9th to the 10th house, we could add that Pluto's mass appeal may help her in receiving easy public recognition.

The **10th house** holds the key to the honors Diana can receive, her reputation, her status, her career and her ego needs. With **Libra** on the cusp and Venus in Taurus in the 5th house she has a great eye for beauty and is probably an incurable romantic who will sacrifice for love (5th). Diana will lend charm and creativity to her public appearances, and she may be recognized as much for her children (5th) as for herself. Since Venus is the arm of the T-square, she could provoke some controversy; but the trine to Saturn will help her carry her responsibilities well and easily.

Neptune in Scorpio in this house will add to her image as a glamour queen and she probably enjoys this rather unusual projection. With this placement she will serve humanity with ease (Neptune has many flowing aspects) and could bring much inspiration to her people. She will also need inspiration, since as the first Princess of Wales since 1910 she is automatically down in the books for about 170 official engagements a year: Royal Ascot, Trooping of the Color, Opening of Parliament, Chelsea Flower Show, Wimbledon, badminton, garden parties, regattas, factory visits, ribbon cuttings and other ceremonials and inaugurals. A daunting prospect that may overwhelm her many times, but we hope that the Venus/Saturn trine will help her cope.

Scorpio on the cusp of the **11th house** can add a touch of fatalism to Diana's nature. Since the 11th can indicate circumstances over which she has no control, she may decide to take the easy way out and "ride the waves." With the ruler Pluto in Virgo in the 9th house, the religious and philosophical part of her nature will accept that which she has to, including humanitarian and group involvement.

On a more private level she has an intense need for her friends. According to her own statement, what she hated most to give up were "the cozy evenings with my friends left behind at 60 Coleherne Court," frequenting with them the late supermarket near their apartment, buying grapefruit and milk for breakfast, going on shopping trips with them to Harrods or skiing with them in Europe. Her last words to them, as she was leaving the flat for the last time, were: "For God's sake ring me up, I'm going to need you!"

One interesting facet between Charles and Diana (there are many and we will discuss them in a future book) is that Charles' Sun falls in Diana's 11th house and we can assume that he will become her true friend.

Much of Diana's sustenance and strength can be found in her beliefs and ideals with Pluto, ruler of the **12th** in the 9th house. With Pluto in Virgo she is quite self-critical. With **Scorpio** on this house Diana longs for some privacy and time by herself. She is a very sensitive person, easily moved to tears as we saw when the press pursued her mercilessly and when Charles' favorite horse got hurt. Yet she hates public display of emotion. Sagittarius rising with its ruler Jupiter in Aquarius wants to come across like the rock of Gibraltar and act unperturbed; with Scorpio on the 12th she wants to keep sorrow and personal feelings strictly to herself.

The very private Diana will never be completely alone again; an armed detective discreetly accompanies her wherever she goes. Such is the price of royalty. What about Diana's subconscious and her future role in finding inner fulfillment? Scorpio on the 12th with the ruler in the 9th can eventually become a powerhouse which lights the way to the unconscious mind. Pluto's many sextiles will give her the opportunity to recharge her batteries when she is by herself and she will have to learn to steal, if necessary, a few minutes each day to achieve this inner equilibrium.

With the **North Node in Leo in the 9th** house and the **South Node in Aquarius in the 3rd**, Diana benefits from devotion to an ideal and faith in God and country (the Sun, ruler of Leo is in Cancer). Her philosophies will help her expand and gain self-respect. She may find it easier to live in her own little neighborhood (3rd) and retreat into some abstract reasoning (Aquarius), but the growth potential lies in tuning in to her higher mind.

Lesson 16
BARBRA STREISAND:
The Entertainer's Entertainer

There is another way to delineate a horoscope. Sometimes there are charts with factors that seem to jump out at you, and then we use a process which we refer to as "zooming." With this method we zoom in on the noticeable factors and then draw the rest of the chart in to substantiate and confirm our findings. To give you some other insights, we also include some seldom used tools, such as Arabic Parts, fixed stars, etc.

We will use Barbra Streisand's chart to illustrate this method. She was born in Brooklyn, New York on April 24, 1942 at 5:04 AM EWT according to the August 1967 *Predictions* magazine.

The first thing noticeable in her chart is the **bowl pattern** with all but one planet below the horizon. That planet, Venus, is in the 12th house. This pattern often gives a very subjective and private person which Barbra is, in spite of her very public profession. We say in Volume II that a bowl person is very self contained and often self satisfied. The self containment is very true of Streisand but the self satisfaction is not.

With **Aries rising** she is a go-getter, constantly striving for more recognition and attainment. In the bowl pattern, the unoccupied portion of the chart becomes the challenge — the place where the person needs to understand the self in order to function properly. Streisand feels the need to fulfill herself through the 7th to the 11th houses, the public half of the chart.

Another noticeable factor is her **lack of cardinal planets**. If this quality

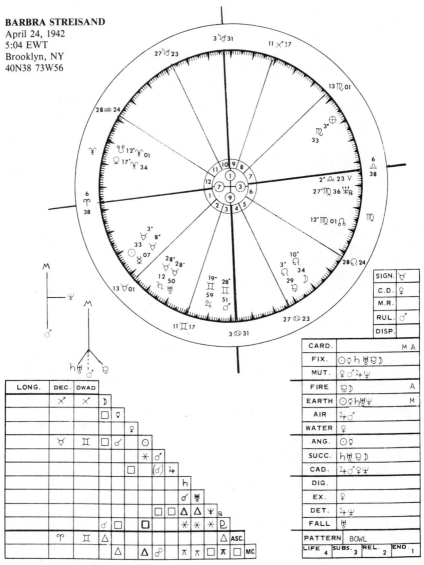

BARBRA STREISAND
April 24, 1942
5:04 EWT
Brooklyn, NY
40N38 73W56

SIGN.	♉		
C.D.	♀		
M.R.			
RUL.	♂		
DISP.			

CARD.				M A
FIX.	☉ ☿ ♄ ♅ ♀ ☽			
MUT.	♀ ♂ ♃ ♆			
FIRE	♀ ☽			A
EARTH	☉ ☿ ♄ ♅ ♇			M
AIR	♃ ♂			
WATER	♀			
ANG.	☉ ☿			
SUCC.	♄ ♅ ♀ ☽			
CAD.	♃ ♂ ♀ ♆			
DIG.				
EX.	♀			
DET.	♃ ♆			
FALL	♅			
PATTERN	BOWL			
LIFE 4	SUBS. 3	REL. 2	END. 1	

LONG.	DEC.	DWAD								
	✕	✕	☽							
			□	☿						
					♀					
	♉	♊	□	♂		☉				
					⚹	♂				
				□	(♂)	♃				
							♄			
						♂	♅			
				□	□	△	△	♆ ℞		
		♂	□		□		⚹	⚹	⚹	♇
	♈	♊	△						△	ASC.
				△		△	⚷	𝄐	𝄐	□	𝄐	□	MC

were totally lacking in the horoscope, the cardinal initiative, action, quickness and pioneering spirit would not be evident. In Barbra's case, this lack is compensated for by the Aries Ascendant and the Sun and Mercury in the 1st house. In fact, she overcompensates for this lack of cardinality with aggressiveness, opportunistic attitudes and a compulsion to excel which borders on obsession. The Sun exactly square Pluto verifies this.

Also outstanding is her **Taurus stellium** comprised of Sun, Mercury, Saturn and Uranus across the cusp of the 2nd or Taurus house. This contributes to her compulsion to be best at everything she does and it makes her very materialistic and quite unbending. The energy manifested in this stellium plus her Aries Ascendant are nearly overpowering and she rubs people the wrong way with her honesty and direct approach to life. A workaholic, she's also a perfectionist, a strongly Taurean trait.

Her **Sun** (the inner core of her being) and her **chart signature** (found by counting how many planets are in each quality and element) are both Taurus which indicates that she is very sensual and has a practical approach to life; but it can also make her possessive, argumentative and self-indulgent. Very set in her ways, she frequently displays an overconfident temperament, accompanied by so much self-esteem that others are put off. In part this is due to the intensity of the Moon conjunct Pluto in Leo and in part to the Sun in the 1st house. Wherever the Sun is, is where you want to shine and Barbra shines by being her strong self. Often quiet, reserved (in spite of the Aries Ascendant) and sometimes even sad, her true personality comes through only to close contacts.

Al Coombes, in an article in the *Ladies Home Journal*, describes Barbra as a complex and conflicting personality who triggers distinct responses in other people. Some regard her with deep respect and admiration, others with intense hostility and resentment. Her sister, Rosalind Kind, claims that her abrasiveness is a tool to stop people from getting too close to her. She's a workaholic and "she's got to get that gold." An apt description of a Taurus Sun and signature with the Sun that rules the 6th house of work square Pluto and the Moon in the creative 5th house.

The side of her that the public sees is belied by the concentration of **planets below the horizon**. This describes a subjective and instinctual person who is not truly the extrovert she acts in public. Lately she has become almost paranoid and has developed a fear of performing in public which is easily understood when one looks at the shyness and need for privacy inherent in her horoscope.

The **Nodes of the Moon** are in Virgo and Pisces with the North Node in the 6th house and the South Node in the 12th. This placement indicates that it is easier for her to fall back on the familiar pattern of the South Node and withdraw into the privacy of the 12th house, and make decisions based on feelings and past action (12th house), than it is for her to come out of her shell to analyze her actions and work. Isolation can be her self undoing, obviously, as her career demands that she come before the public; it is necessary for her to be seen and heard. With the North Node in the 6th house, fulfillment comes through service to others. As Isabel Hickey puts is, "Humility, the last virtue to be attained, can be the keynote of this life if the individual is willing to serve others with no concern about the self," (from *Astrology, A Cosmic Science.*)

Whenever a chart has an **intercepted** pair of **houses** (in this case, the 6th and 12th), a tremendous focus of attention is put on this area of the person's life. Because of the interception in the 6th house, the Sun (ruler of the cusp), Mercury (ruler of the intercepted sign), Venus (ruler of Libra) and Neptune are all involved in the affairs of that house. With Pisces intercepted in the 12th house, we have to consider Uranus (ruler of the cusp), Neptune (ruler of the intercepted sign), Mars (ruler of Aries) and Venus when we look at the 12th house. In analyzing the pair of intercepted houses, it is necessary to bring into your reading all these various factors.

In Barbra's case, the **Sun** (ruler of the 6th house cusp) **and Mercury** (ruler of the intercepted sign, Virgo) are both placed in the **1st house** of self-expression in Taurus, the sign of voice. Since we are speaking of the 6th house, we see that it is easy for her to project herself in her work through her glorious voice. Neptune, the planet of illusion, is intercepted in the 6th house, indicating the potential for her to work behind the scenes with imagination and inspiration. Neptune rules the intercepted sign in the 12th house (Pisces), reinforcing the possibility that she would be interested in acting, which is a 12th house activity. She is hiding her true self behind a role.

When a **planet** is **intercepted** it expresses somewhat differently than when it is free. In this case, her imagination and inspiration work on an inward level since the interception emphasizes the power of the planet, her expression of it comes across with much conviction. She will not "take a back seat," because the Sun is in the 1st house and Aries is rising. But Barbra does on occasion act like a hermit and become quite introspective (verified by nine planets below the horizon).

The **trine from Neptune** to Saturn and Uranus in the **2nd house** indicates her great earning potential if and when she got into the proper field to use Neptune's creativity well. Neptune is retrograde and strongly aspected (two squares, two trines and a sextile); the inward action indicated by the retrograde motion produces tremendous personal insight and her natural talent can be easily utilized through her work (Neptune in the 6th house).

Venus, which also has some influence in the 6th house because it rules 6° and 41' of it, is in the 12th house in the actor's sign Pisces. Its square to Jupiter in the communicative 3rd provides the amplification of that magnificent voice. In analyzing the 12th house, we must view it as providing a great deal of inner strength. Uranus, ruler of the cusp is trine Neptune, ruler of the intercepted sign, suggesting that the proper application of the imagination and inspiration (both Neptunian attributes) can prove financially rewarding in a unique fashion (Uranus in Taurus in the financial 2nd house). Uranus is conjunct Saturn and the **fixed star** Pleiades, showing that money was not always available to her. Mars rules 6° and 41' of the 12th house and is in the 3rd, again giving her the ability to communicate with force and energy from behind the scenes in motion pictures. Lately she is acting as producer on the film *Yentl*. She purchased the story and is trying to get the production off the ground against great odds. With her strong Taurus stellium and the indomitable will of Mars widely conjunct Jupiter, she'll probably pull it off.

The Gemini **decanate** is **on the 12th house** cusp and with Mercury (ruler of Gemini) in the 1st house, it is obvious why she feels a need to direct and produce to promote her 12th house ideas in a 1st house fashion. With Aquarius on the cusp, the native feels an inner turmoil and unrest which in Barbra's case is satisfied on a practical level by earning the money that Uranus in the 2nd house shows she is capable of. But on a more spiritual level, this placement indicates a need to have a firm sense of her own self worth which she has attained by succeeding in her work (Uranus trine Neptune in the 6th).

The **Part of Honor** (a list of the most important Arabian Parts can be found in Volume II of *The Only Way To . . . Learn Astrology*) is 22° Pisces 07' in the 12th house, indicating that any honor she might attain would come through 12th house activity, which we can relate to performing and relying on her own inner resources. The **Part of Vocation** is also here at 10° Aries 35'. It reinforces her need for a career that relates to the 12th house, but one through which she can project herself since it is in Aries.

Venus in the 12th is the planet in **Oriental Appearance** (also found in Volume II). It rises ahead of the Sun which strengthens and enlightens its action. Since the planet is Venus, Barbra's prime motivation is artistic self-expression. The **Eclipse Point** (also explained in Volume II) is in the 12th house at 25° Pisces 45'. Anyone with an Eclipse Point in the 12th needs a certain amount of privacy — time away from others to recharge his or her batteries. In Barbra's case this is doubly true since it is not only in the 12th house but also in Pisces, the natural 12th house sign.

Configurations are very important in assessing how a person is going to act out the energy in the natal chart. The horoscope only shows your potential for good or bad and the choice is yours — how you use it and even if you use it. When there are configurations, (grand trines, T-squares, grand crosses, yods, etc.) the energy seems to be focused and the native is forced to use the aspects, because as one planet acts, the others are automatically drawn in.

Barbra has two configurations, both of which involve the Midheaven or Ego point. There is a **T-square**. The **Midheaven opposes Mars and both square Neptune** in the 6th ruling the intercepted 12th, again emphasizing the importance of the intercepted axis. This T-square challenges her to work (6th house) before the public (Midheaven) in a brash (Mars in Gemini) communicating (3rd house) way. With Neptune as the active arm of the T-square, her great imagination has helped her to succeed in her work, but it has also caused confusion and prevented her from seeing her work situation clearly. The empty arm of the T-square falls in the 12th house indicating that after giving her all in a performance she seeks solitude and a reclusive atmosphere.

Her other configuration is a **boomerang**, again bringing in Mars and the Midheaven. This time the **Midheaven inconjuncts both Saturn and Uranus** in Taurus in the 2nd house and **Pluto** in Leo in the 5th, and shows that she has an opportunity (sextile) to gain fame and recognition (Midheaven) through creative efforts (Pluto in the 5th) and earn money (Saturn and Uranus in the 2nd), if she can make the adjustments required. In every boomerang there is a yod, and the focal point (in this case the Midheaven) is called the finger of God. Usually the need to act arises through this focal point, but when the yod becomes a boomerang (because of the planet in opposition to the finger) the need to act is focused on the opposition point — in Barbra's case Mars. So her need to act is motivated by a need to be heard (Mars in the 3rd in Gemini) rather than the need for recognition (10th house).

Some astrologers feel that the Ascendant and Midheaven do not work in configurations but we find them to be valid and to work quite well, if you are sure of the birth time.

In any chart the parents are shown by the Sun and Moon, Saturn and Venus and the 4th and 10th houses. As a child, Barbra felt estranged from her family (Moon ruler of the 4th square the Sun). Her relationship with her mother was strained. Her father, a psychology teacher, died when she was fifteen months old. Saturn, ruler of the 10th house (father) conjunct Uranus shows the potential for the sudden loss of a parent. This is confirmed by the square between the Sun and Pluto and the Moon. Pluto is in the 8th house from the 10th (the 5th), denoting that the parent lost would probably be the father. Barbra idealized her lost father.

Saturn, his significator, trines Neptune the planet of idealism and she felt cheated that he died when she was a baby. She has contributed thousands of dollars to the Pacific Jewish Center's day school, and was honored when they planned to name the new wing in memory of her father, Emmanuel Streisand.

Saturn, ruler of the 10th house, does trine Neptune the planet of adoption and foster parents. Her mother married a used car salesman, Louis Kind. Barbra, who was often left in the care of relatives and who agonized that her mother would forget to pick her up, felt very threatened by her mother's new partner and could not accept him. Neptune squares Jupiter and Mars in the early environment 3rd house. Just having Mars in the 3rd house gives tremendous ups and downs in the early years and the square adds even more upheaval.

Her mother did not approve of Barbra's aspirations to act. She would not allow her to sing and put on skits at home, admonishing her to, "Get a job. You don't have enough talent to act." The **Moon**, ruler of the 4th house which describes her mother is in **Leo** in the **5th**. The challenging aspects (conjunct Pluto and square Sun and Mercury) show the lack of harmony with her mother and the dissension in her home. This feeling of insecurity (verified by Saturn in the 2nd) has carried over into her adult life and she is very reclusive and unwilling to share details about her personal feelings and outlook.

She has always felt she was different from her peers — always an outsider who didn't fully understand why she was unpopular. In elementary school classmates nicknamed her "Big Beak." A solitary child, as is so often the case with a 1st house Sun, Mars in the 3rd and Saturn ruling the 11th house of friends, she spent much time playing alone on the sidewalk in front of her home. She never owned a doll but invented one by filling a hot water bottle and dressing it up.

She carried a 93 grade point average. (Mercury, ruler of the 3rd house of early education conjuncts the Sun; Jupiter, planet of growth, is in the 3rd house, so is the energy planet Mars which also sextiles the Sun.) She spent much time studying and she did not date a lot in high school. Upon graduation in 1959, she headed for Manhattan and lived from day to day out of a suitcase, taking odd jobs and accepting handouts from friends. Saturn, ruler of the 11th house is in the 2nd and the **Part of Friends** is in the 3rd at 18° Gemini 25'; her relationship with her friends is unique to say the least, since Saturn conjuncts Uranus. With the ruler of the Part of Friends in the 1st house, it is easy to see why she likes to boss them around.

As she became successful, the friends who had provided for her in time of need felt snubbed and to them she seemed unappreciative and arrogant. She has the Virgo **decanate on** the **cusp of the 11th** house of friends and the ruler Mercury square Pluto. Even though the Part of Friends is in the 3rd house and she found it easy to communicate with them and attract them to her (it conjuncts Jupiter), it squares her Venus so that she was uncomfortable when she felt beholden to them.

Alan Miller, her first drama coach views her as a loner, but an opportunistic one who does anything and everything she can to escape and obliterate her painful past including snubbing those who have helped her along the way to success. He relates that when she was having trouble with *Funny Girl*, she asked him for help after she had ignored him for more than a year and a half. She introduced him as her cousin and didn't want anyone to know he was coaching her. When he started charging her for his services, she said she felt "funny" paying someone who was like a father to her. Again we see the Sun square Pluto operating as "other people think they know you but they never do". Moon conjunct Pluto "feelings are intense to the point of brusqueness and tyranny," and Mercury square Pluto prompting her to "tell it like it is" as she sees it, without regard for the feelings of others.

To her public she seems strong, unabashed, even brazen — all traits that have been contributing factors to her success, but because of her disorganized childhood and the lack of parenting, she had a hard time attaining a firm understanding of her inner needs. Perhaps through her child and her concern that he be brought up in a different atmosphere than the one she experienced, she will come to a better understanding of herself. Pluto in the 5th house of children sextiles Uranus, ruler of the 12th and also Saturn and Neptune which should provide opportunity for a rewarding relationship with her children.

The 4th and 5th houses are linked together. Both have Cancer on the cusp and the Moon in the 5th house provides a deep and abiding love for her child Jason. With the Moon conjunct Pluto, she must be careful not to become obsessive toward him. Since the Moon is in the Sagittarian decanate and dwad, religion is a very important factor in her relationship with him and because of Jason she has returned to her Jewish faith. Her interest in religion is strongly motivated by intellectual curiosity because Jupiter, ruler of the 9th house of religion is in the 3rd in ever questioning Gemini.

Jupiter square Neptune caused her some apprehension that she would have difficulty relating to the orthodoxy of Judaism, but after studying with her son while he prepared for his bar mitzvah, she became very knowledgeable and comfortable with that knowledge.

Streisand is a communicator; this is amply illustrated by Mercury, the ruler of the 3rd house conjunct the Sun in the 1st and **Mars**, the action planet, **in the 3rd**. People with this house placement of Mars often have attention-getting voices. Jupiter here expands her ability to sell herself. With the Libra **decanate** and **dwad** on the **3rd house cusp** and Venus, the ruler, exalted in Pisces in the 12th, we can see why movies were her ultimate goal for self-expression. Art and writing are also possible choices with these placements; but with so much emphasis on Taurus which rules the voice, it's easy to see why she chose to sing.

Saturn, ruler of the Midheaven, the career potential, is in the 2nd house of income and trines Neptune, the ruler of show business and movies in the 6th house of work. This indicates her huge success but since Mercury, the co-ruler of the 6th house squares the Moon and Pluto, you can see that it was an uphill battle. The squares do not deny success. In fact, because of the energy they provide they almost guarantee achievement, but they do cause her to work hard. The biography by Frank Brady relates that as an aspiring actress she took odd jobs, collected unemployment insurance and got by for months without a permanent home, carrying a small bundle of clothing with her because she never knew where she would spend the night. She slept in offices, on stairways, on the floors of friends' studio apartments and even carried a cot around with her. But always the drive to succeed was stronger than anything else as is so often the case with Capricorn on the Midheaven.

Saturn in the 2nd house is sometimes depicted as a sign of poverty and difficulty in attaining money and this was true of Barbra in her early years. Saturn here is insatiable in its desire to achieve some form of self worth, and this is also true in her case. Wherever Saturn is, there is a tendency to overcompensate and because of her driving personality and the strong aspects in her chart, Barbra was bound to achieve all the things money can buy. This is verified by the Taurus stellium and signature. Taurus will only settle for the very best. Because Saturn is conjunct Uranus, she can get away with the wacky wardrobe that she is known for. The **Part of Increase** is at 23° Taurus 07' in the 2nd house and verifies her great earning power and need for money to buy the material possessions which represents security to her.

When we examine Barbra's chart in connection with her love life and the kind of people she attracts to her, the intercepted Venus in Pisces in the 12th house plays a very important part. Venus rules her 7th house and because there are no planets there, Venus becomes very influential in describing this area of her life. With Libra on the 7th house cusp, harmony and balance are necessary for her to feel comfortable in any close relationship. Learning to reach out and be with others is a principle need, but since Venus (the ruler of others) and Mars (her Ascendant ruler) make no aspect, she does not exert herself much in partnership relations. She needs someone who will accept her as she is — demanding and arbitrary (Venus squares Jupiter). Since Venus is in the 12th house, she tries to keep her intimate relationships just that — intimate — and she resents anyone who pries into her private life.

Married to Elliott Gould, the actor, for eight years and then divorced in 1971, they remain good friends as suggested by Libra on the 7th. Her longstanding affair with ex-hairdresser Jon Peters is a very private relationship as typified by the ruler of the 7th in the 12th. They live at the end of a winding, private road on a 20-acre ranch nestled at the foot of the Santa Monica mountains in Malibu, California. This five million dollar estate with its own film studio, tennis court, stables, swimming pool and bird aviary is a self-contained retreat, well befitting a Leo Moon, the ruler of the 4th house. High electronic fences and trained attack dogs guard the property and these trappings suggest a privileged solitude that only wealth can bring, but this same paradise may well be indistinguishable from a self made prison.

Peters is represented by the 9th as well as the 7th house, since he is in essence her second spouse. The 7th house shows the attitude toward marriage, what we seek from it and how it affects us. It specifically describes the first partner. The 9th house must be added to give more information about the second partner, the 11th indicates the connection with the 3rd partner and so on around the chart skipping a house as we go. Since Jupiter rules the 9th house and squares Venus, the ruler of the 7th, Barbra's and Jon's relationship is stormy, and they are often at each other's throats; but they manage to patch up the rifts and stay together. Mars which rules both the **decanate** and **dwad** on the **9th house cusp** is sextile the Sun, indicating some harmony. Mars (her Ascendant ruler) and Jupiter (describing Jon) have a wide conjunction in the 3rd house, which helps them to communicate with each other.

The **Vertex Point**, which is considered people oriented and reactive, is in Libra in the 6th house just below the cusp of the 7th and it shows her working relationship with Peters. The **Earth** is in the 7th house, and we say that the Earth shows our mission in life. Barbra's need of others is verified by this placement of the Earth (which is always exactly opposite the Sun by degree and sign). If we consider it as the ruler of Taurus, it has a connection with the 2nd house, and we might assume that her self worth is tied up with her relationships to a partner and the public. If we take it a step further and say that the Earth represents the Shadow referred to by Carl Gustav Jung, then we might say that to truly develop her personality she needs a partner — someone she can relate to on an intimate and private basis (Venus in the 12th and nine planets below the horizon).

Venus in Pisces needs love and tenderness and without this Barbra feels lost. In spite of the brassy exterior she presents, partly due to the Aries Ascendant, this placement of **Venus** in the **12th house** shows her deep need for privacy and a nurturing and sustaining love. In spite of the emotional ups and downs and the fights, so far, she and Jon have an enduring affiliation and he provides the nurturing and taking care of which Barbra so obviously needs.

With Scorpio on the 8th house cusp, her sex drive is strong and healthy. Mars, the co-ruler of the 8th sextiles the Sun and Pluto squares the Sun. The help and support she receives from her partner are indicated by the same aspects. It is forthcoming, but she finds it difficult to accept it graciously (Sun square Pluto) and her emotions often get in the way (Pluto conjunct the Moon). With these aspects, sex is a healthy escape valve for her intense emotional feelings.

Mercury in Taurus has definite likes and dislikes, is acquisitive, fond of money and what it can buy and is interested in the arts and the opposite sex. With Mars in Gemini making her argumentative, excitable and very active, the Taurus stellium gives focus to her energy and helps her develop the discipline of concentration. The Moon in Leo contributes to her resentment of interference and criticism and to her fiery temperament and dramatic ability. This Moon placement, plus Jupiter and Mars in Gemini in the 3rd house add to her abilities as a comedienne.

The people she works with view Barbra as a genius who is driven by a need to create. Friends claim she is a giving, kind person with insecurities and inconsistencies, and her horoscope proves all of this. Compulsive about excelling, sometimes blind toward others, sometimes considerate — a mix of toughness and vulnerability — she is a very private, public person.

PART III

Delineating for a Purpose

There are many areas of chart interpretation that do not necessitate a complete and thorough delineation like we have shown you in Part II of this book. Specific questions can elicit specific areas to be considered. Since astrologers are asked many kinds of questions, we have chosen the ones that seem to be most prevalent: physical well-being or health; physical appearance; the types of relationships you seek with your parents, your children, your relatives, your mate, your friends; and the most frequently asked about subject — vocational aptitude.

We will show you the techniques of finding the areas that relate to the questions asked, of scanning important factors and remembering basic trends. As we have stated many times in all our teachings, we can only give you the tools; to put them into workable use requires time and lots of practice. In this section we give you pertinent examples by using horoscopes of clients and students, but we urge you to make use of the many other charts provided.

As you learn about marital attitudes it might be fun to look at Mickey Rooney's chart and see what he is looking for in a one-to-one relationship and seems to have so much trouble finding. Search George Gershwin's horoscope for his musical talents or Wilma Rudolph's for her athletic ones. See if you can find Elizabeth Barrett-Browning's physical weaknesses after studying health aspects in our delineation. Look at Marlene Dietrich's or Eleanor Roosevelt's 5th houses to see how they feel toward their children. Since Elisabeth Kubler-Ross is one of triplets, check the chart to determine her attitude toward her two sisters. Perhaps gangster Mickey Cohen's relationship to his parents helps explain some unfulfilled primal needs he never understood or worked out. Whatever the case, this can be fun, so enjoy it.

Lesson 17
Looking for:
Physical Well-Being or Health

Since originally most physicians had an understanding of astrology, astrology and medicine went hand in hand and as you learned in Volume I of *The Only Way to . . . Learn Astrology*, each sign and planet has an affinity for a part of the body. But, although you can tell much about a person's physical makeup and health and even the areas of weakness from the chart, it is necessary for you to understand and to make others aware of the fact that you are not a physician (unless you have a degree in medicine), therefore you cannot actually diagnose or prescribe. At best, you can tell someone to consult a doctor if you see obvious signs of illness. THIS IS VERY IMPORTANT.

When looking for a health problem, the areas of the horoscope that must be considered are the Ascendant, Ascendant ruler, planets in the 1st house, the 6th house, its ruler, sign on the cusp, planets in the house and the Sun, its ruler, sign and house placement.

There are also some general rules to take into consideration:

All cardinal sign people — and that means those who have a preponderance of planets in cardinal signs, angular houses, a cardinal signature, a cardinal sign rising or on the 6th house cusp — will generally be susceptible to the cardinal sign problems such as: **Aries** headaches, **Cancer** stomach problems, **Libra** kidney difficulties, **Capricorn** bone or skin diseases.

All fixed sign people — those who have many planets in fixed signs, in succedent houses, a fixed signature, a fixed sign on the Ascendant or 6th house cusp — may suffer from fixed signed difficulties, such as: **Taurus**, throat problems, **Leo** heart or back problems, **Scorpio** genital disorders and **Aquarius** blood or nerve afflictions.

All mutable sign people — those who have many planets in mutable signs or cadent houses, a mutable signature, or a mutable sign on the 6th house cusp or the Ascendant — may have to deal with maladies relating to the mutable signs, namely: **Gemini** bronchial or lung problems, **Virgo** bowel and digestive difficulties, **Sagittarius** liver or hip diseases, and **Pisces** ailments of the feet and sensitivity to anesthetics.

All Aries do not have headaches but they may be susceptible to the other cardinal sign problems.

All Taurus people do not have nose and throat problems but could have symptoms of other fixed sign difficulties.

All Geminis do not have tuberculosis or emphysema but could have other mutable sign troubles such as digestive upsets or severe foot disorders.

Usually the sign on the Ascendant and the sign on the cusp of the 6th house are the sensitive areas, unless their rulers are well placed and well aspected. Naturally, the severity of any illness or health problem depends upon how the planets involved are aspected. With challenging aspects the disease will be more acute and harder to deal with.

It is important to realize that house placement is just as important (maybe more so) as sign position. A person with a very challengingly aspected Sun in the 1st house may be more likely to suffer from severe headaches than the person with a difficult Aries Sun.

Attitudes have a lot to do with disease. The native who has a very challenged Jupiter or Venus may have problems dealing with feelings of bitterness which could result in diabetes or hypoglycemia. The person with a lot of fixity and a very difficultly placed Saturn may have never learned to bend or concede to the wishes of others and therefore may have to deal with the physical handicaps of arthritis or rheumatism.

Natives with strong Scorpio and Cancer tendencies who keep their emotions bottled up or their resentment and hostility tightly locked in, may let these feelings eat away at their insides and thus leave themselves open to cancer cells that eat from within. People with a strongly activated Pluto, Mars or Moon are often victims of this kind of behavior.

Anyone with a very active 6th, 9th or 12th house needs to find a way to make productive use of their time or the tendency is to enjoy poor health.

Following are charts that illustrate some health problems. Chart #1 is a woman with a severe case of rheumatoid arthritis, a very crippling disease. It was especially difficult for her because she was a very active person who did a lot of handwork (Sun in Gemini), enjoyed taking care of her home and children and was the family chauffeur. Her husband had been in a serious accident during the war and couldn't drive a car so she had to be an extremely mobile person.

The potential for such a crippling disease is clearly seen in her chart. There is a grand cross in mutable signs but in succedent houses, suggesting that there may be a slowdown of her mobility at sometime in her life. The Sun, ruler of the Ascendant, is in the grand cross and squares Uranus in the 8th house of surgery. The doctors have removed veins from her ankles (Uranus) and wrists (Gemini) in the hope of alleviating some of her pain, but to date, these operations have been unsuccessful.

Saturn, ruler of her 6th house of health is in the 3rd of local travel and

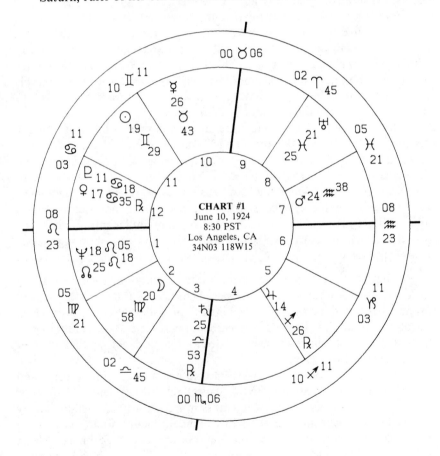

inconjuncts Mercury and Uranus — both challenging aspects when it comes to health. Neptune in the 1st house opposing the action planet Mars shows the sapping of her physical energy. Interestingly, with Neptune in the 1st house opposing Mars in the 7th, when she first started experiencing the symptoms, the doctors (7th house) did not immediately diagnose her case as rheumatoid arthritis. They thought she had injured her hand in some way.

In Volume I the chart of Franklin D. Roosevelt illustrates the problem of infantile paralysis or polio. "This is a virus disease marked by inflammation of the nerve cells in the spinal cord accompanied by fever and often paralysis and atrophy of muscles." (Webster's New Ideal Dictionary)

Both Virgo and Aquarius relate to the nervous system and he had Virgo rising and Aquarius on the cusp of the 6th house. Mercury, ruler of the Ascendant is in the 6th house of health in Aquarius and squares Pluto exactly, which is a very challenging aspect. The Sun is also in Aquarius and squares Saturn which indicates that his mobility may be limited at sometime in his life. The Sun squares Jupiter and Neptune and these squares may relate to the fever accompanying the poliomyelitis.

The following chart (#2) illustrates another case of polio. This time the disease was contracted when the little girl was six and a half years old. Mercury, ruler of the 6th house is in the 12th opposing Neptune in the 6th and this suggests a health problem that could hospitalize her (12th house). Neptune also opposes the Sun in the 12th house. Uranus, ruler of the higher nervous system, is in the mutable sign Gemini and exactly opposes the Moon and conjuncts Saturn. The Ascendant (physical body) inconjuncts both the Moon and Neptune in the two health houses (6th and 8th), show ing the adjustments that were necessary for her to live with the crippling affliction.

Cancer victims suppress resentment and hostility; the signs most likely to restrict their emotions and feelings are Scorpio and Cancer. Many cancer prone people are quite rigid and fixed in outlook and also very intense, which astrologically suggests fixed signs, succedent houses and Mars and Pluto prominent. However, our research as limited as it is, does not say that all fixed sign natives are cancer prone.

Chart #3 is a woman cancer victim who had a radical mastectomy and hysterectomy and eventually died of cancer related problems.

Venus, the ruler of her Ascendant is in Leo in a fixed stellium widely square Mars in Scorpio in the 1st house and conjunct Neptune, ruler of the 6th house of health. Both Venus and Neptune conjunct the Sun. The Moon ruler of female problems, is exactly inconjunct the Sun, which with the other difficult health indications is a very challenging aspect to deal with on the physical level. The Moon opposes Saturn exactly, indicating a perception of parental lack of love and tenderness. She was never able to overcome or express a deep feeling of resentment toward her mother.

If we consider the Earth as a co-ruler of Taurus which is the sign on

Chart #2
March 26, 1943
7:45 AM CDT
Milwaukee, WI
87W55 43N02

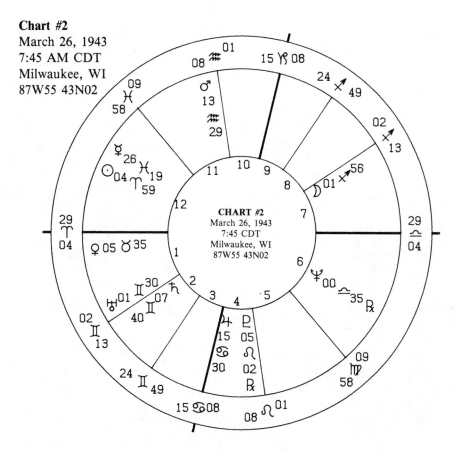

CHART #2
March 26, 1943
7:45 CDT
Milwaukee, WI
87W55 43N02

the cusp of the surgery 8th house we see that it also inconjuncts Saturn and this health aspect (along with the Mars/Venus square) indicates possible surgery at some time in her life.

We are including in this lesson two charts that you might find interesting for research purposes. They are the horoscopes of a brother and sister, both of whom contracted cancer of the kidneys which spread to the brain and killed each of them within a year of the discovery.

Chart #4 is the man, who died after unsuccessful surgery in April 1974. Chart #5 is his sister. Her cancer was discovered in the summer of 1980 and she died in January 1981.

In Chart #4 his Ascendant ruler Mercury squares Uranus, ruler of the 6th house, as does the Sun. Mars, Neptune and Venus are conjunct in the 1st house; Mars rules the 8th and they all square Saturn. The Sun in the 12th house conjuncts Jupiter — in this case, a not so beneficial aspect because it enhanced the growth of the cancer. The disease started in the kidneys (Libra on the 1st) and progressed to the brain (the polarity sign, Aries).

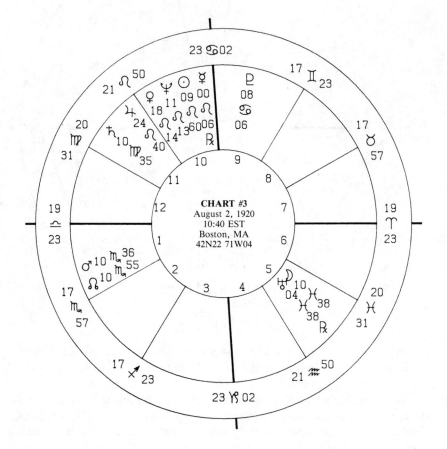

CHART #3
August 2, 1920
10:40 EST
Boston, MA
42N22 71W04

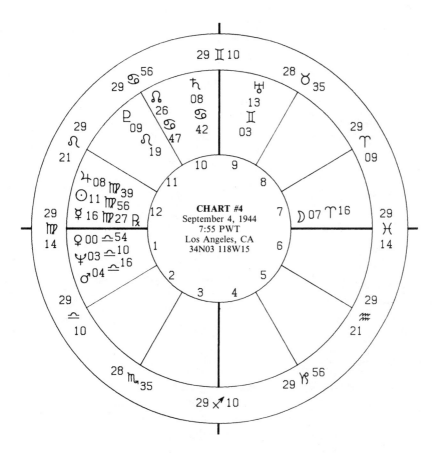

29 ♊ 10

29 ♋ 56

29

♃08 ♍39
☉11 ♍56
☿16 ♍27 ℞

29
♍
14

♀00 ♎54
♆03 ♎10
♂04 ♎16

29
♎
10

28 ♏ 35

29 ♐ 10

♇09 ♌
26
♌
19 47

28 ♉ 35

♄08 ♋42

13 ♊03
♅

10 9

11

12

1

2   3   4   5

8

7 ☽07 ♈16

6

29 ♑ 56

29 ♒ 21

29 ♈ 09

29 ♓ 14

29

CHART #4
September 4, 1944
7:55 PWT
Los Angeles, CA
34N03 118W15

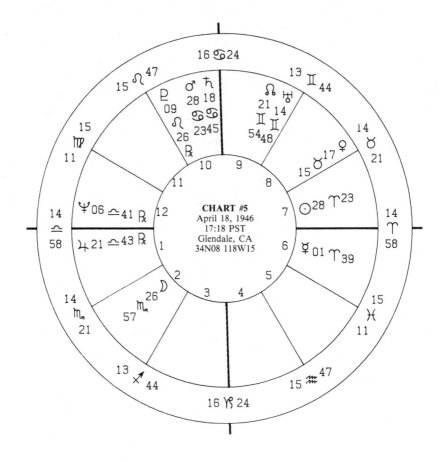

CHART #5
April 18, 1946
17:18 PST
Glendale, CA
34N08 118W15

In Chart #5 Venus, the ruler of the Ascendant is in the 8th inconjunct Jupiter in the 1st house which is an indication of possible surgery. This is verified by Neptune, the ruler of the 6th in the 12th and opposing Mercury, the ruler of the 12th in the 6th, showing confinement connected with the health. The Sun squares its ruler Mars and opposes Jupiter, a formidable T-square indicating potential health problems. Saturn, the ruler of the end of life 4th house squares the Ascendant.

Since many types of cancer are still a mystery to medical science, it is likely that the planet Neptune is involved and this may be one area for astrological research. In all three charts we have used, Neptune is prominent. Saturn is also involved; but Saturn has bearing on ill health in general and its prominent presence in these charts may indicate that the poor attitude toward the self and the stored resentment against parents helped to bring on illness.

Lesson 18
Looking for:
Physical Appearance

When you run into people who have a rudimentary understanding of astrology, they will frequently confront you with: "Tell me what I am." They are of course referring to their Sun sign. but the more you study astrology, the quicker you realize that the Sun is just one of the important factors that make you uniquely YOU. The same principle applies to appearance. In fact the physical body is more often described by the Ascendant than by the Sun, or at least a blend of the two.

But party games aside, there is an important reason to learn what some of the physical characteristics of each sign are and how to judge a possible Ascendant: If there is any doubt about the time of birth your astrological knowledge of appearance can make the difference. We will give you some of the most important rules.

In judging appearance, the principal factors are the ascending sign, planets in the 1st house and in the 12th conjuncting the Ascendant (within 8° or 9°), the signs these planets are in, the sign and house the ruler of the Ascendant (chart ruler) is in and of course, the Sun sign. Often a planet in aspect to the Ascendant from the 10th house (especially close to the Midheaven) has a bearing on the looks.

You must always blend the Sun sign, Ascendant and Ascendant ruler, as these three seem to have the most effect upon the actual appearance. Rulers and/or the Sun in the upper part of the chart usually add height. People who have many planets above the horizon may also be taller than expected.

These same indicators below the horizon tend to shorten the physical stature. Racial, ethnic and hereditary factors must be taken into consideration.

A student of astrology who was just a beginner had read that Capricorn was a tall sign. She commented to her hairdresser that he was rather short for a Capricorn. He replied that for a Japanese, 5'8" was considered quite tall. In other words, the descriptions apply relative to the standards of each race or ethnic group.

The decanate and even the dwad of the Ascendant or Sun are other helpful factors in describing a person's features. A stellium of four or more planets can have a distinctive effect on the appearance by emphasizing that particular sign, regardless of where the Sun or Ascendant may be. The chart signature, if there is one, also helps to sketch the overall picture you present and should be given consideration.

We would love to be able to give you some general guidelines and say that the tall, thin signs are such and such and the short, fat signs are so and so — but unfortunately we have not found this to be true. Some signs tend to height, some to girth, some to beauty and some to prominent bones, but none of them do so at all times and as we have shown you in other forms of delineation, many factors have to be weighed and blended. There are no absolutes in astrology!

Libra has always been described as one of the tall signs, and indeed it can be; but we have several charts of people with Libra Ascendants or Suns who are quite short, due to other factors in the chart. Basically that is what appearance is all about, just as you learned in Volume I of *The Only Way to . . . Learn Astrology* when we looked at Franklin Roosevelt's horoscope and pulled all the parts into a complete picture.

We often compare the delineation of a chart to putting together a jigsaw puzzle. You start with the edge pieces and assemble the frame. This compares to the astrological "overview" of the chart. Then you examine the rest of the pieces and see which ones go next to each other and start to build your puzzle, just as you examine the planets in the signs and houses and by aspect in order to put the person together. It is the same way with analyzing the physical image. You gather the pieces of information and then put them all together to see what the person looks like.

Here are a few helpful hints:

The Moon near the Ascendant adds weight and gives a round "moony" type face.

Mercury in the 1st house or within 8° or 9° of the Ascendant in the 12th house adds to the height and may give a pointed chin.

Venus rising makes a person attractive or appealing, gives a beautiful complexion and even features; sometimes there can be dimples or a cleft chin.

The Sun in the 1st house gives somewhat of an Aries or Leo appearance, adds both height and weight and usually these natives have a big, broad smile.

Mars near the Ascendant may give red hair, pimples or a scar on the face and often the person tends to have a ruddy complexion. In Oriental or black races this may appear as a reddened (or rosier than normal) cast to the skin.

Jupiter adds height and girth when found near the Ascendant. It also enlarges the part of the body depending on the sign. For example, Jupiter in Gemini may give large hands.

Some people feel that retrograde planets in the 1st house have an effect on the appearance. We have not found this to be consistently so, but there is a personality difference which influences the behavior rather than the looks. For instance, people who have Mars retrograde move at deliberate speed rather than falling headlong into the door, and Mercury retrograde slows down their speech pattern.

Saturn rising makes the native shorter, thinner and bonier and therefore the native is often photogenic because of the good bone structure. It may shrink the part of the body described by the sign, such as in Pisces giving smaller feet. We have a client who has Libra rising and the ruler Venus is in Pisces conjunct Saturn — he wears a size 6½ shoe.

Uranus in the 1st house or near the Ascendant in the 12th can make the person look totally unlike what you may expect. If all the other indicators say short, Uranus here can make the person taller than average. If the other indicators suggest very heavy, Uranus rising may contradict that and the person may be very thin.

With Neptune rising the person takes on an aura of glamour or mystery. Usually the eyes are large, liquid and beautiful. In some cases Neptune as well as the Moon adds weight because of fluid retention. With Neptune in the 1st or conjunct the Ascendant in the 12th, you never quite know what to expect, because the person can change like a chameleon, be gorgeous and glamorous one minute, homely and nondescript the next.

Pluto in the 1st house or aspecting the Ascendant intensifies and accentuates everything about the rising sign. Often the eyes are green or some other improbable color. If Pluto is in Cancer, there may be a weight problem; if it is in Leo, there may be flowing hair, a beard or mustache.

The Nodes near the Ascendant seem to be important. We observe that the North Node tends to increase the height or weight, while the South Node works the opposite, making the person shorter or thinner than normal. With the South Node conjunct the Ascendant within 2°, there may be a physical denial of some kind. We have several charts that support this, such as a boy with undescended testicles, a woman born without a finger and a thalidomide baby who was born without an arm.

Following are some basic descriptions of the 12 signs of the zodiac as they rise, represent the Sun, Sun or Ascendant ruler or a stellium in the chart.

Aries: Basically, with Aries prominent you are active and on the go, so you do not tend to gain weight unless other factors in your chart suggest it, such as Venus or Jupiter in the 1st house or conjunct the Sun. You usually have a high, sloping forehead, a prominent, pointed nose — not always long, just pointed — and if you are a male, you may have a noticeable adam's apple. Unless there are opposite indications, you are tall, lean, wiry and muscular. Muscularity is also apparent when Mars aspects the Sun or Ascendant. Frequently you have a triangular-shaped face, reminiscent of a ram, with a narrow chin, two vertical lines between the eyes and very prominent brows. Your eyebrows may grow together, giving the impression of one solid eyebrow. Naturally this is more noticeable in men, since many women pluck their brows into more acceptable shapes.

With Aries strong in the chart, you ordinarily have small eyes and they may be green or hazel; frequently farsighted, you often seem to be peering into the distance. Sometimes you have a droopy upper lid. Your hair is plentiful, coarse and unruly. In men there is a tendency to a receding hairline,

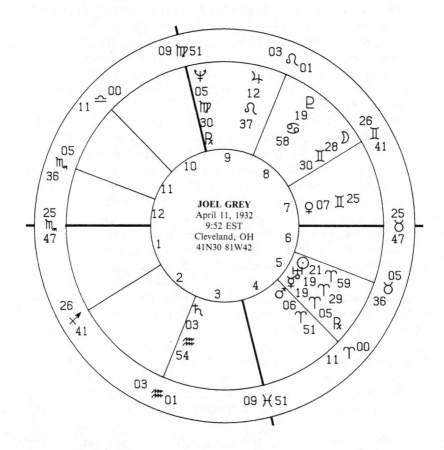

Source: *Gauquelin Book of American Charts.* A

the forehead seems to become higher and higher. Your head juts forward as does your whole body when you walk. You always seem to be in a hurry to get where you are going. If the Sun or Ascendant is in the Sagittarian decanate, Aries has long legs. The perfect example of an Aries profile is Barbra Streisand, who has an Aries Ascendant. (Her chart is on page 188.) Please note that her Ascendant ruler, Mars is in Gemini and that she has a 1st house Sun in Taurus.

Entertainer Joel Grey is an Aries and his Sun is part of a four planet stellium which really seems to personify most of the Aries characteristics. His small stature is due to a predominance of planets, including the Aries stellium, below the horizon. Since Mars the ruler of the stellium, is also in Aries, all Aries traits become even more pronounced, such as the nose, the forehead, the lean and wiry look, the triangular shape of the face and many of the other distinctions just described. (See his chart on page 214.)

Taurus: Taurus is considered one of the square signs, as are the other three fixed signs — Leo, Scorpio and Aquarius. Taurus is a sign of great beauty because it is ruled by Venus. This does not mean that if your Sun or Ascendant are in Taurus you are a raging beauty, but you are definitely attractive and have a pleasing physiognomy.

Your brow and compact nose, mouth and chin all run straight up and down. Your ears are small and close to your head, your chin is round and your jaw heavy. You have prominent round eyes that are often blue, heavy lidded and languid. Naturally the blue eyes do not apply to races who have mostly dark eyes, theirs would be a lighter brown; the Caucasian round eyes become the Oriental's less slanted or more almond-shaped eyes.

If Taurus is predominant in your chart, you may have a no-neck look or a bull-like appearance. Since Taurus is considered a short sign, you may be stocky with a long trunk and relatively shorter arms and legs and wide shoulders. Your hands are rather short and fleshy; so are your feet and your legs are often heavily calved. When walking you tend to put the heel down first and it looks as though you toddle.

Your flesh is solid and you get wrinkles late in life. You are also very late in greying. Dimples or a cleft chin are often a giveaway with Taurus rising or a Taurus Sun, but this can also be true when Venus is close to the Ascendant or conjuncts the Sun. You usually have luxurious hair and rarely become bald, unless other factors in the chart, such as a lot of fire, indicate it.

Taurus as well as Leo often has a separation between the two front teeth. This is not always noticeable since you may have had your teeth fixed. Pancho Gonzales of tennis fame has the typical Taurus look. His Ascendant, Sun and Venus, ruler of both, are in Taurus; so is Mercury. He has the square build, the separation between the teeth, the thick, wavy hair and the natural venusian good looks. (See his chart on next page.)

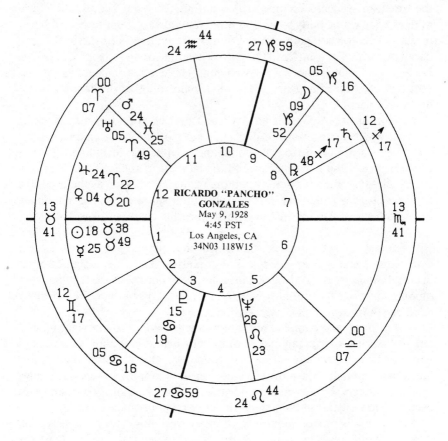

Source: *Contemporary Sidereal Horoscopes.* A

Gemini: Usually slender and lanky even when you aren't tall, you have long arms and legs. Your hands are always active and as a typical Gemini you have long, slender fingers, and you wave your hands around when you talk. Your forehead is high and you may have a large bump on each temple, almost like the beginning of horns. Any mother of an impish Gemini child will insist that is what they are! But people who have these prefer to call them "intelligence bumps".

Your eyes are wide set, very alert, quick and restless and are generally brown or hazel. Your nose is a lot like the Aries nose — long, straight and pointed. (Again, please keep ethnic and racial characteristics in mind.) Pinocchio was probably a Gemini native! You have a nervous, active walk and are fidgety and restive, never able to sit still for any great length of time.

Since you are so mobile, you are quite capable of doing two or more things at the same time. You also will burn off your calories and not gain weight unless many other factors contradict this.

If you are a typical Gemini, your shoulders tend to slope and you are narrow chested and at times pigeon breasted. You have a pointed chin, a wide mouth, thin lips and — like all the air signs — a pronounced overbite. You are one of the most youthful signs; but as you age, the jowls droop and the flesh under your chin sags, kind of like a curtain.

A classic example of a Gemini Ascendant is Gregory Peck. (See his chart on page 218.) With the Sun and Ascendant ruler (Mercury) above the horizon in Aries, he is tall. Venus conjunct the Ascendant makes him handsome and gives him his beautifully resonant voice, while Mars, ruler of his Aries stellium is in Leo, draws attention to his full head of hair. As a typical Gemini Ascendant, Peck uses his hands to express himself. While young, he was very slender and lanky; now as he ages, his jowls are beginning to droop and the flesh under the chin is sagging.

Cancer: You are generally short, with short arms and legs. Unless the Moon is in Gemini, Sagittarius or Capricorn, you always have the pleasing roundness that is present in all the water signs; we don't mean you are fat — just round. Since you enjoy eating and drinking, you do have a tendency to put on weight, especially around the stomach area. Men of this sign may develop a beer belly.

You have relatively small hands and feet and a well-developed breast, even if you are a male. You often seem top heavy because of your well-developed chest and small undercarriage, and frequently you have no hips.

Your face is rather large, round and moon-like, very wide between the ears, while the ears themselves are small. Your brows are bulging and your nose is short and may turn up at the tip with wide, flaring nostrils. Your dreamy, round, protruding eyes have a soft, anxious expression and they are often green with full, heavy upper lids. Again we remind you that Blacks, Browns and Orientals rarely have green or in some cases round eyes, just bigger or lighter than usual.

You have a kindly and sympathetic smile and a pale complexion that is very sensitive to the sun. A full and somewhat sensuous mouth often is a Cancer trademark. You have a tendency to grey early and often the young-looking person with white hair turns out to be a Cancer Sun or Ascendant. Cancers commonly have a sidewise, heavy walk, much like their namesake the crab.

Burl Ives looks very Cancerian even though his Sun is in Gemini, but he has Cancer rising and his Moon is in Taurus, a sign with similar traits to Cancer. Since his Sun and three other planets are in the 12th house, it adds to the "watery" look found in Cancer and Pisces. (See his chart on page 219.) Another typical Cancer is Judy Garland. She had the top heavy appearance we referred to.

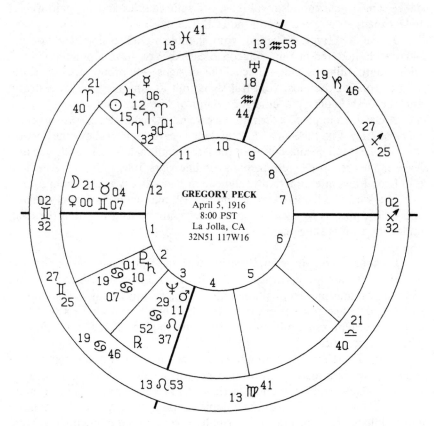

Source: AFA from birth certificate. A

Leo: Leo is considered the shortest sign in the zodiac, yet we do know some very tall Leos. If for example the Sun is above the horizon and a reasonably tall sign like Sagittarius or Libra rises, this must be taken into consideration and you would not expect the person to be short. A good example of what to watch out for is Chart #6 on page 232. He is a Leo with Libra rising and his Ascendant ruler is in Gemini. He also has eight planets above the horizon. He is 6'3'' tall.

As a typical Leo, you have a large body, the largest head in the zodiac and are often big boned, deep chested, muscular and well put together. Your hips are narrow and you have a slender waist, broad shoulders and a straight carriage. People are in some way aware of your hair; it may be like a lion's mane or you may be totally bald or have very little hair, very fine hair or

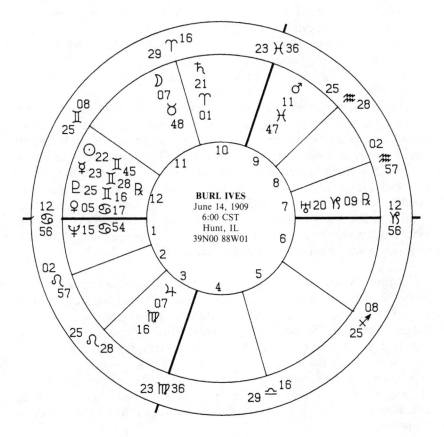

Source: Autobiography—*Wayfaring Stranger*. B.

a full beard and luxurious moustache. Or, like Lucille Ball who is a Leo with Cancer rising, your hair may be some wild color. You also seem to throw your head back and let your hair fall into place as though you were tossing a mane.

You have lively, sparkling, laughing eyes which are sometimes green, luminous and even catlike. You can have a loud, cheerful voice like a lion's roar, but at other times the men have high pitched voices while the women have low, sultry "whiskey tenor" type voices. If you see someone whose hands remind you of paws — wide and relatively short — you are looking at a Leo Sun or Ascendant person.

Your ears are large and the lobes are attached to the side of your head, making it hard to wear earrings. Your chin is prominent but rounded and you have full lips and the lower one may protrude. Leos tend to have little brown moles or birthmarks and sometimes a rather lumpy appearance.

Your nose is broad and rather full at the tip and as you get older the tissues sag away from your nostrils and the corners of your mouth in curtain like folds. If you are a woman with a Leo Sun or Ascendant, you may tend to get heavy at the top and bottom while you age, yet maintain your trim waistline. Some Leos have large, round eyes and you can see the white all around the iris.

Robert Redford serves as a good example of a Leo Sun native. He has only the Sun and Mars in Leo, but because the Sun is dignified here, it carries a lot of weight as far as appearance goes; though the Pisces Ascendant adds glamour and charisma, the dignified Sun is more obvious here than anything else. Redford is short of stature, thin-waisted and broad-shouldered. His head is large with lots of hair and he has the lively, sparkling eyes mentioned, as well as the moles and birthmarks. (His chart is on page 221.)

Pablo Picasso is another good example of a person with Leo rising; he looks much more like a Leo than a Scorpio, his Sun sign, except for the piercing eyes which are a typical Scorpio trademark.

Virgo:　Virgo is the most photogenic of all the signs and some beautiful people have Virgo Suns or Ascendants, including such glamorous stars as Raquel Welsh, Sophia Loren, Lauren Bacall, Sean Connery and Rossano Brazzi. Like all of the mutable signs except Pisces, Virgo tends to elongation. It gives you a long head, neck, body, arms, legs, fingers or feet — even when you are not tall.

If Mercury is in Gemini, Sagittarius or Libra or if it is above the horizon, you may in fact be quite tall. Your forehead is high and full, your cheek bones are high, your chin is pointed and your face is usually thin with an aquiline nose.

Sometimes your features are small and bird-like and your eyes are close together. When Virgo is rising you may be flat-chested and the women sometimes have a little boy or Peter Pan look. Your lips are thin and the upper lip is often quite long. You may have hooded eyes and frequently there is a widow's peak. Your hair is fine, plentiful and often wavy or curly.

Your walk is rapid and active and — much like Gemini — you are fidgety restless and quick moving. You more than any other sign like everything to be neat, with a fresh and clean look and so you want your hair to be just right to frame your face. You also are quite aware of the clothes you wear and you always look a lot younger than you are.

Your voice is soft and melodious, unless there is strong Leo, Aquarius or Aries in the chart. Like all of the mutable signs, you tend to have large hips, but you can also have the wide shoulders to balance them out.

Sissy Spacek is a good example of a Virgo Ascendant. (See chart on page 222.) She has the flat-chested little boy look, the elongated features and the fine hair with a widow's peak. Because Saturn, ruler of her Sun, is also in Virgo, the Virgo appearance is strengthened.

Libra: Because Libra is often referred to as the sign of great beauty, you will always have a pleasing appearance even if you are not outrageously beautiful. There is an innate refinement that gives you a gracious expression. You have a well-shaped head and an oval face with symmetrical features. Your nose is mostly short but straight and your mouth is like a cupid's bow with a short upper lip.

Others are aware of your teeth in some way; they may be pearly or a trifle protruding and sometimes they overlap. Remember President Carter and his toothy smile? He has a Libra Sun and Ascendant.

You are tall and slender when young but get heavier with age. Your curves tend to develop into plumpness around the middle as you get older but because you are a Libra, it seems quite pleasing. Like other Venus ruled or Venus in the first house descriptions, Librans may have dimples or a cleft chin.

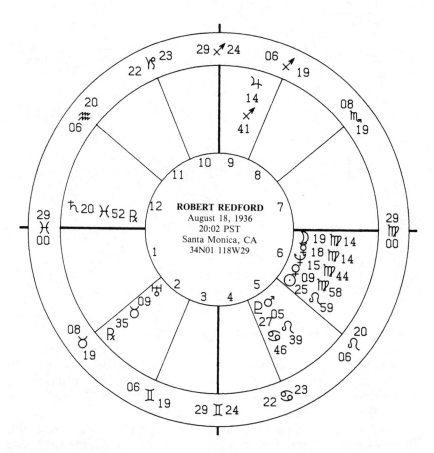

Source: Rodden—*American Book of Charts. A*

You have a soft look, the tendency to wavy or curly hair, a clear skin and a beautiful complexion. You keep your exquisitely shaped nails well tended. Your ankles and wrists are slender and more often than not you will wear a triple A shoe. Your voice is melodious; perhaps you have worked on it since loud noises, including those produced by yourself, seem to bother you. Dark circles under the eyes, the "racoon" look, are often a Libra signature.

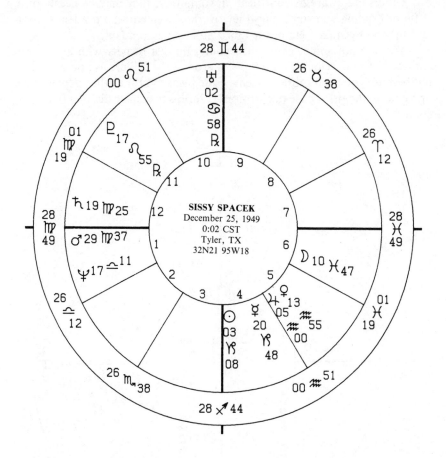

Source: From her to Lois Rodden. A

You have well-shaped ears, a rounded chin and a slender, graceful neck. Actresses Julie Andrews and Deborah Kerr have Libra Ascendants which helps to account for their great beauty and soft charm. So do Elizabeth Taylor and former sex and beauty symbol Jean Harlow.

Another typical Libran is Barbara Walters, who has the Sun, Ascendant, Sun and Ascendant ruler Venus all in Libra. As mentioned, she has innate refinement and always comes across as gracious — if she didn't, she could not get away with many of her sharp questions. Her head is well shaped and oval, she has a lovely smile and as she matures, so does her figure. Because she has Mars in the first house, her complexion seems a bit ruddier than is otherwise associated with the typical Libra. (See her chart below.)

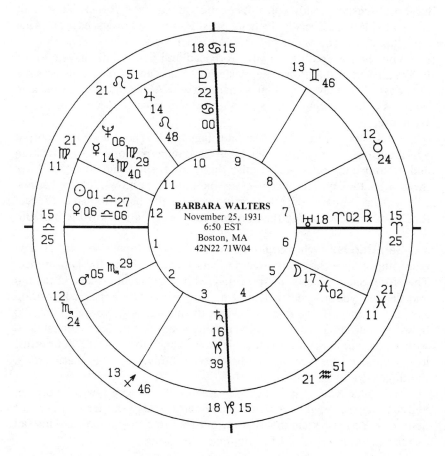

18 ♋15

13 ♊ 46

21 ♌ 51

♃ 14

♄ 48

♇ 22 ♋ 00

21 ♍

♀ 06 ♍ 14 ♍ 29 ♍ 40

12 ♉ 24

21 ♍ 11

⊙01 ♎27

10   9

11

8

15 ♎ 25

♀ 06 ♎ 06

12

BARBARA WALTERS
November 25, 1931
6:50 EST
Boston, MA
42N22 71W04

7

♅ 18 ♈ 02 ℞

15 ♈ 25

1

6

♂ 05 ♏ 29

2

5 ☽ 17 ♓ 02

21 ♓ 11

12 ♏ 24

3   4

♄ 16 ♑ 39

13 ♐ 46

21 ♒ 51

18 ♑ 15

Source: Lois Rodden says birth certificate, but cannot trace source. C

Scorpio: This fixed sign is another of the square, big boned, deep-chested ones, and in apperance is often hard to tell from its polar opposite, Taurus. Scorpio is generally one of the short signs unless Mars is elevated or in a tall sign. For appearance purposes it is better to use Mars as the ruler of Scorpio than Pluto, because Pluto moves so slowly (over 20 years in some signs). For instance, Pluto was in Leo from 1937 to 1959, and certainly not all Scorpios born then looked alike.

With Scorpio prominent, you are frequently thick set, stocky and like

Taurus, you have a short, thick neck. Your nose is significant and may have a bump or high, bony bridge. Your eyes are piercing with a deep intent look — this is especially noticeable when Scorpio rises. Your face is usually square with a great deal of width just beneath the eyes and a heavy, square jaw.

Your ears are small and close to your head and you have a full-lipped, large and sensual mouth which may droop at the outer corner. Your teeth seem fairly large, especially the front ones. Somewhat bowlegged, you swing your hips when you walk, in fact, you often enter a room pelvis first.

Your hair grows low on your forehead and you usually have a lot of body hair and also a protruding posterior. A student of ours calls hers her "tea wagon" and says it is a family characteristic. Almost all of her immediate family is either Scorpio Sun sign or Ascendant, or has Pluto or Mars in the 1st house.

Television star Ed Asner (see chart on page 225) has the typical Scorpio appearance with both the Sun and the Ascendant as part of a Scorpio stellium and of course the ruler Mars is also there. He is short and stocky and has the no-neck look plus the piercing eyes and prominent brows, the low hairline and the heavy square jaw. His short stature can also be attributed to the fact that six planets, including the Sun and chart ruler, are below the horizon.

Sagittarius: When Sagittarius rises, the ruler Jupiter seems to assume more importance than other chart rulers in determining the appearance. Therefore, Sagittarians seem to be divided into different groups. Often tall and slender, you get your height at an early age and are inclined to stoop as you get older. If you don't grow out of this habit, you develop a hump between your shoulder blades. Everything again seems to be elongated as with Virgo, but in Sagittarius there is a raw-boned look added. Your arms, legs, hands and feet are long and somewhat bony; when Sagittarius rises, the thighs are often elongated.

If Jupiter is in Taurus, Scorpio, Leo or Pisces or below the horizon, you may have a weight problem and be considerably shorter than we just described. You also seem to lose some of that stretched out look and instead assume the well fed look of an indulgent Sagittarius.

It is often easy to spot you if you are a Sagittarius, because your toes turn inward when you sit down, you shuffle or stamp your feet when you walk and your eyebrows and eyelashes are darker than your hair. Your hips are frequently wide and there is a definite separation between your legs at the top of your thighs.

You may have a long oval face with a lot of length from the nose to the chin which is often protruding and you may have a pronounced horsey look. Your nose is noticeable and may have a high bridge or bump like Scorpio, but it is usually shorter. In Caucasian races this is known as the blue-eyed sign, but in all groups the eyes seem alert and farsighted.

You have prominent front teeth and often laugh with a horse's whinny.

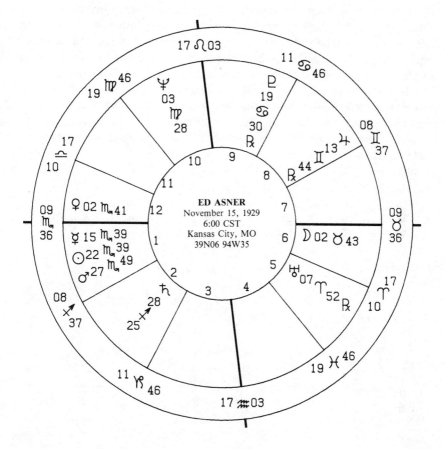

Source: Penfield quotes baby book. A

Your ears frequently stand away from your head and point upward. Remember Clark Gable's large flapping ears? He had Sagittarius rising. You have abundant wavy hair but the male's thins early and turns bald in long streaks on top which he usually combs over to the side in order to cover the bald spot. Sagittarius rising women often have red hair — either naturally or with a little help from their hairdresser. For our example we use Bette Midler, who has a Sagittarius Sun and an Aries Ascendant. (See her chart on page 226.)

Capricorn: There are two distinctly different looks to Capricorn. One is short, slender and narrow chested with a small, thin neck, a bony frame and a pointed nose which often has a downward turn. If you are this type you may be knock-kneed and have very narrow hips. The facial structure is very prominent. Your skin is tautly stretched and you are quite photogenic. Your hair may be a bit thin and wispy and your eyes rather small and close set; you are thin lipped and have a strong but narrow chin and your features often seem pinched together in the center of your face. You have a high square forehead, broad planed cheeks and a tendency to frown or squint.

If you are the second type, you are large boned and have a big frame. You have a lantern jaw which looks somewhat underslung and there is great breadth to your face beneath the eyes — much like your opposite sign, Cancer. Your cheekbones are very prominent and you sometimes have an underbite.

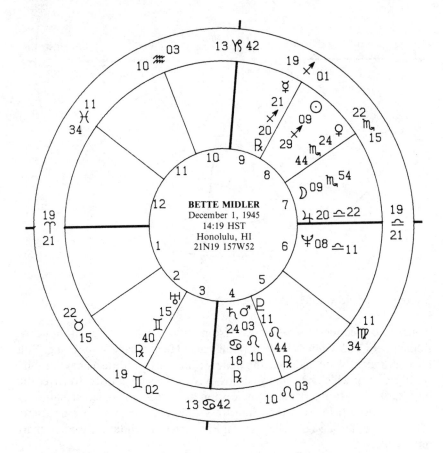

Source: *Contemporary Sidereal Horoscopes.* A

Both types have an erect carriage and you tend to strut when you walk. This can be a sign of great beauty, especially since the bone structure can be exquisite. Marlene Dietrich, Ava Gardner and Faye Dunaway are three

Capricorn Suns while Jayne Mansfield and Goldie Hawn have Capricorn Ascendants. All five are known as much for their looks as for their acting abilities. Queen Elizabeth II is another good example, in fact, she more or less incorporates a mixture of the two types. (Her chart is below.)

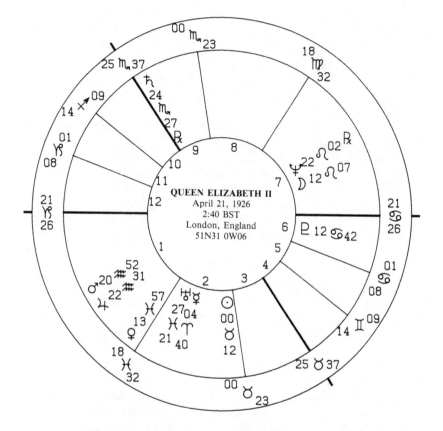

QUEEN ELIZABETH II
April 21, 1926
2:40 BST
London, England
51N31 0W06

Source: Fagan in *American Astrology* states "recorded".

Aquarius: The last of the fixed signs, Aquarius has a lot in common with the other signs of the fixed quality. Large boned and square built, this is considered the tallest of the fixed signs, unless of course other things in the horoscope give indications of short stature. Of all the signs this is the most easily spotted because of the squareness that is so obvious. Aquarians look square from the front or the side and even the head has a square look. The comic strip character Dick Tracy was undoubtedly an Aquarian.

Your features are chiseled and the back of your head is flat as your derriere. Your jaw has a jutting spade-like look and you have a compressed, thin-lipped mouth but a brilliant smile. Aquarius, like Gemini and Libra, the other air signs, has somewhat protruding teeth. Your eyes are relatively large with a direct look. Most air signs have clear eyes, but Aquarius eyes more than the others seem to reflect the sky. There is a broad delta between your eyes and you generally have large upper lids and the corners of your eyes tilt up.

Your hands are square with long fingers and spatulate nails which you often bite. Because of your inherent nervousness, you tend to little quirks like cuticle chewing and hair twisting. You have thin, sometimes weak ankles and high-calved legs, a springy walk, a loud voice and a large head. As an Aquarian woman you wear your hair in an unusual way — not the current style — perhaps in a French twist or coronet braid.

Aquarians can be very attractive and there are many movie stars who have this Sun and Ascendant, including some known beauties like Merle Oberon and Farrah Fawcett. But Leos and Aquarians, more than natives of any other sign, are often ugly.

As an example of a typical (and good-looking) Aquarius, we chose Burt Reynolds. (See his chart on page 229.) Though Gemini rises, both the Sun and the Ascendant ruler Mercury are in Aquarius. He has that square look jutting jaw, the brilliant smile and the clear eyes. With Gemini rising and the Sun and chart ruler elevated, he is above average height.

Pisces: Pisces is one of the small, rounded signs. You are not really fat, but you do have a curvy look that prevents you from being skinny or bony. Your flesh is soft and somewhat formless, your hips are wide and your hands and feet are small but broad and drop shaped with narrow wrists and ankles. Your skin is pale and your face fleshy. Pisces rising tends to wrinkle prematurely.

Your eyes protrude and you have sleepy lids; though you never seem very alert, you seldom miss anything that is going on. Some of you have large, liquid, beautiful eyes, as has Elizabeth Taylor who has a Pisces Sun. They are also well defined with long lashes and arched brows. There may be a drooping line at the corner of your eyes and also at the corners of your full-lipped mouth.

Your nose is short, small and flat; and many times it looks like there is no bridge. Your chin is round and can be double or triple, even though you may not be fat.

You have the shortest legs in the zodiac and a slow, dreamy, sauntering walk. Your shoulders are round unless there is a lot of fixity in your horoscope. You have plentiful but rather untidy hair, flabby ears, a deep voice and you usually love to dance. There is a plastic look to Pisces, as though you can mold yourself into any shape you choose.

Sidney Poitier well represents the rather typical Pisces look, including the light or pale skin, the beautiful but sleepy looking eyes and the full-lipped

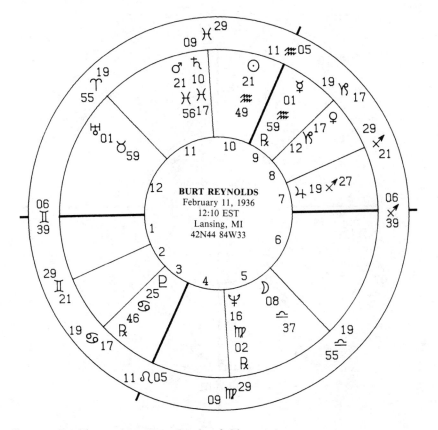

Source: Rodden—*American Book of Charts.* A

mouth. He has a stellium in Pisces including the Sun and four other planets. (See chart on page 230.)

We hope this gives you an idea or at least a starting point. Remember, there are plenty of other charts in the book you can practice delineating appearance with. Good luck.

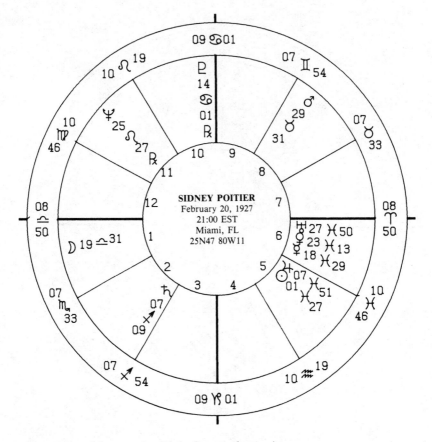

Source: From him on the Dick Cavett show. A

Lesson 19
Looking for:
Relationships

One-to-One or Conjugal Relationships

We believe the most prevalent questions any astrologer hears are, "What kind of person should I marry?" "I'm a Cancer. Is a Capricorn right for me or should I look for a Scorpio or Pisces?"

Unfortunately, as we are sure you have discovered by now, there are no hard and fast or easy answers to questions like these. This is not the place for us to go into a profound discussion of comparison and compatibility between two charts; that will be in a future volume of *The Only Way To . . . Learn Astrology.* But we want to give you a few pointers on how to deal with these types of questions.

The attitude toward marriage or partnership and the basic characteristics sought from a partner are described by the cusp of the 7th house, its ruler and the planets, if any, in this house. For amplification, we recommend that you go back to Part I (Rulerships) in this book and review the ruler of the 7th house in the various houses. Also in Volume II, Lesson 14 on "Delineating the House Cusps" read the material referring to the 7th house.

In a woman's chart you must also look to the first applying aspect made by the Sun. Sun and Mars placements give more information about the male image she seeks. In a man's chart the first applying aspect the Moon makes will give an indication of what he needs from a partner and will help describe her. The Moon and Venus give some additional input on the type of lady he's looking for, but the whole chart must be taken into consideration.

In the following chart, this man has Aries on the cusp of the 7th house,

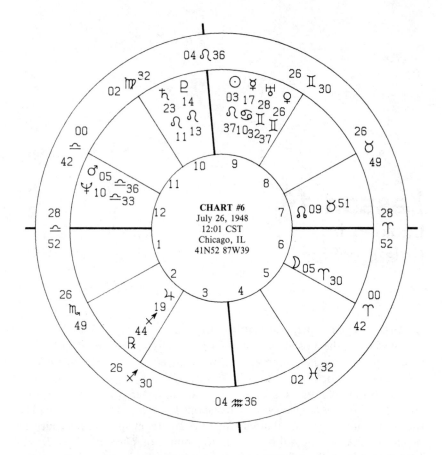

so he seeks a strong and active partner; but with Mars, the ruler of Aries in his Ascendant sign, Libra, he wants her to be cooperative, social and charming — all Libran qualities. Mars, the 7th house ruler is in the 12th house and conjuncts Neptune, so he needs his partner to have some chameleon qualities and to present a different picture in public than in the privacy of their home. With no planets in the 7th house, the Moon and Venus become very important in describing his partnership needs. The Moon in Aries backs up what we've determined from the cusp. Venus in Gemini indicates the desire for a partner to communicate with on a philosophical level (Venus in the 9th). The Moon's first applying aspect is to Mars, further showing that he would prefer someone who is assertive rather than clinging. When you examine the chart carefully, you see that he has no earth planets. Both of his wives and all of his serious commitments, besides fulfilling the needs we outlined, have been strongly earth sign people. He is satisfying an innate lack through his partners.

The word marriage has to be defined for today's society. When we speak of a 7th house commitment, we mean a long-standing relationship that is considered a marriage whether there is a marriage certificate or not. In other words, a couple live together, share a home and their resources (including a bank account) and are totally committed to each other.

To describe a possible second marriage partner, look to the 9th house; for the third, look at the 11th house and so on around the wheel, skipping a house each time. Remember the basic needs and attitude toward marriage or partnership commitment are shown by the 7th house. The other houses only give additional factors about succeeding mates.

To see if a person is likely to have more than one marriage, you must consider the sign on the cusp of the 7th, its ruler and any planets in the 7th house. If any of these are in a dual sign (Gemini, Sagittarius or Pisces) more than one marriage is a possibility. If Uranus, Mars or Pluto is in the 7th, or if the ruler of the 7th house squares or opposes the Sun, Moon, Mars, Venus or Uranus, it is possible the person will marry more than once. However, we have found that there should be at least three of the above indications. Even then, free will and the rest of the chart must be taken into consideration. A strongly placed Saturn can change many of the previous dispositions.

People who have Scorpio/Taurus or Cancer/Capricorn across the horizon tend to cling to a relationship long after it is salvageable. Perhaps religious commitments prohibit divorce; all these things must be judged.

Saturn in or ruling the 7th house is, according to ancient astrology, an indication that the native will marry an older person or become a widow or widower. We have not found this to be true. We feel it indicates that you seek security and loyalty from a partner and that just as often (all other factors considered) may marry someone quite a bit younger. Uranus in the 7th house also has a bad reputation. Some astrologers immediately presume divorce. We do not. It may mean that the person you choose for a partner has been divorced or is of a totally different background from yours. Quite often it indicates a sudden or hasty marriage and it always signifies the need for independence — yours or your mate's.

Let us also put to rest the old maxim that if you don't have a planet in the 7th house, you will never marry. We are surprised at how many times people believe this outrageous statement. Mickey Rooney, who has been married eight times, doesn't have any planets in his 7th house; but he has a dual sign (Gemini) on the cusp and Mercury, the ruler, squares Pluto. His Moon opposes Neptune, so he has some difficulty seeing just what it is he needs from a partner. (His chart is in Volume II.)

Children or Filial Relationships

The 5th house cusp, its ruler and planets in it describe your attitude toward all of your children, whether you want any, and it specifically depicts your first born. If you will have any children depends on many factors, and the whole chart must be carefully examined. Water signs on the cusp of the 5th house or the ruler in a water sign was considered fruitful by the ancients and still seems to be true, unless the ruler is very challenged or there are other factors in the chart that deny children. For example, the wish for a career or self expression may be stronger than the urge to be a parent. The partly fruitful signs are the earth signs. The fire signs are considered barren and the air signs partly barren.

In our research we have not always found this to be true. We also cannot say that dual signs involved with the 5th house give multiple births. Naturally, the foregoing refers mostly to female charts. A man's chart may show many children, but if he marries a woman who is unable to have offspring or does not want any, that certainly has to be taken into consideration.

When Saturn is involved with the 5th house, the person usually takes the responsibility of a family very seriously. We frequently find this in the charts of those who adopt children, take in foster children, or who even teach. Of course, there have to be some other contributing factors, such as Neptune in or ruling the 5th or the 11th, the house that relates to other people's children. Neptune is considered the planet of adoption; quite often when it is in the 5th house or ruling it and challengingly aspected, a parent may give up a child for adoption. Despite what you may read in some textbooks, we do not find that Saturn in or ruling the 5th house denies children. It may bring some problems in raising them or difficulty in pregnancy but we have many clients and students who have a 5th house Saturn and a home full of children.

When Uranus and Mars are involved with the 5th house, your children may not always get along well with each other. Jupiter, the Moon and Sun there all seem to indicate a large family and the aspects will tell whether or not they are compatible. Many times Pluto in the 5th house seems to indicate a small family and sometimes shows the parent who has trouble letting go of the child.

Just as with marriage partners, each succeeding child is shown by skipping a house; consequently, the 7th house shows the second child, the 9th the third and so on. Again, this only amplifies the child's personality and the native's relationship with the child. It does not necessarily indicate that the child's Sun sign will be that on the cusp of the house. The chart on page 236 shows how one woman relates to her children. She gave birth to ten.

Her children are ruled by Mercury in Aries in her 12th house. Virgo is on the cusp of the 5th house so her attitude toward her children is one of service (Virgo) but in a compassionate and emotional way. Mercury is in the 12th and conjuncts the Moon. It is in Aries which indicates that she would be quite dominant, but loving and the opposition to Saturn shows that she might experience sorrow through them.

Her first child is a boy with the Sun in Scorpio and Pisces rising. (Her 5th house ruler is in the 12th.) He has Mars conjunct his Sun (confirming her Aries attitude with Mercury ruler of the 5th in Aries) and he has a very strong, yet compassionate nature and a personality similar to his mother's. Her second child — represented by the 7th house with Scorpio on the cusp, Mars in Capricorn in the 9th and Jupiter in the 7th house — is a boy with the Sun in Virgo, Sagittarius rising and the Sun in the 9th house (her 7th house ruler is there). Her husband is a Virgo, and this son is very much like him (the 7th is the partner's house). Both of these children have turned out to be successful businessmen, the first in the automotive field and the second in electronics.

The third son, described by the 9th house, was an Aries (her Mars is there). Saturn rules the 9th and opposes Mercury, ruler of the 5th. This boy was burned to death at the age of six. The fourth child is a girl. The 11th house is ruled by Neptune and the child is a Gemini with Libra rising and Neptune (the mother's 11th house ruler) exactly conjunct her Ascendant. She is fulfilling many of her mother's dreams by pursuing a show business career. Her fifth child is represented by the 1st house and this girl is a Taurus, the sign on the mother's Ascendant. We will not go on and describe the other children but we are sure you can see how this works. Try it with charts of people you know.

Friendships or Congenial Relationships

The friends you seek are shown by the 11th house. Whatever sign is on the cusp describes your attitude toward them as well as theirs to you. The planets in and ruling the 11th add more information about how you get along with them. Saturn here may indicate that you seek stability and maturity through your friends and thus relate well to older people. On the other hand, Mercury may show you that you get along best with those younger than you are. Mars here often signifies that you are a leader among your acquaintances and in groups. The Sun in the 11th may give a person a large following of friends, but it can just as well depict a person who has no need of others. If the ruler of the 11th is in the 6th, you may meet most of your friends at work.

With Jupiter in the 11th house, you may be quite sociable and enjoy a large circle of acquaintances. With Venus there you love your friends and are very popular with them. Uranus in or ruling the 11th can attract many different and unique types of friends and you may belong to several circles or groups who do not associate with each other. Neptune involved here can mean artistic or glamorous friends; but it may also mean "beware of false friends." Those with the Moon here tend to mother their companions and Pluto intensifies the feelings toward others and may give a need to dominate.

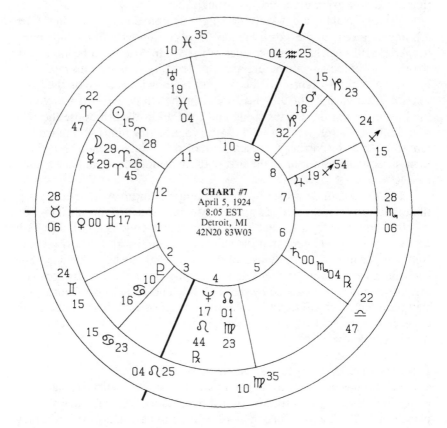

CHART #7
April 5, 1924
8:05 EST
Detroit, MI
42N20 83W03

Siblings or Consanguine Relationships

The 3rd is the house of brothers and sisters and there have been theories advanced that it represents the sibling immediately older than the native. That theory then goes on to say that the 5th house is the next younger sister or brother, the 7th is the next younger and so on. The 1st house becomes the next older sibling, the 11th the next older and so on. We have not necessarily found that this works, but we haven't done enough research to really judge and you may want to try it for yourself.

The 3rd house does tell about your relationship with your siblings and your attitude toward them. Some texts insist that you can tell astrologically if there are sisters and brothers. We have found none of the existing theories to be consistent with fact and prefer to ask our clients. Mars in the 3rd, if it has some challenging aspects may deny siblings; or it may just indicate some healthy fights with your brothers or sisters if you have any. Neptune or Pluto here may bring half or stepsisters and brothers. Pluto here often deepens your feeling toward your siblings, sometimes to the point of obsession.

When Uranus is in the 3rd, you could feel like the black sheep in the family, especially if it has some difficult aspects. The Sun, Moon, Mercury or Venus in the 3rd may make you the champion of the family and very much engrossed with your relatives. Saturn here or Capricorn on the cusp could represent the child who has to take care of or be responsible for brothers and sisters. Jupiter does not necessarily imply many siblings; it often signifies your wish to be good to them, share with them and show your generosity to them.

Father and Mother or Parental Relationships

Astrologically, our parents are represented by the 4th and 10th houses. This goes hand in hand with today's psychological approach to the parental influence on the root system of a child. The 4th house represents the archetype of the female or mothering principle of nurturing, of beginnings, of roots; the 10th house indicates the male or father principle of authority, of limitations, of reality and the highest you can reach. Neither of these houses necessarily describe your actual father or mother; they indicate your perception of your father and mother. If in your eyes your father gave you nurturing and caring and your mother set limitations and was the disciplinarian in the family, then the 4th house may represent your father and the 10th your mother. Maybe they both interchangeably performed both functions; then you will see them as a unit and both will be found in both houses. The same principle applies if only one parent was around to perform both duties.

When we say 4th and 10th houses, we refer to the sign on the cusp, the ruler's placement and aspects and any planets in the house in the natal horoscope. For additional information you should also look to Saturn for the father and the Moon for the mother. These two planets are the natural rulers of the 4th and 10th houses and therefore represent your prototypal concept of your parents and the role models you are seeking. For further understanding of the parental image each of us carries, you look to the Sun for the father perception and to Venus for the mother. In some instances for an even deeper awareness of the relationship and your expectations from it, look to Mars for the father and Pluto for the mother.

To illustrate, on page 238 is the chart of a young woman: She has Aries on the 4th house cusp; the ruler Mars is in Aries in the 3rd house, conjunct Venus, ruler of the 10th house. Both parents are of equal importance to her since the rulers are together in the 3rd house. In her eyes both are quick, eager, impulsive, combative, competitive and dynamic (both rulers and the 4th house cusp in Aries). She found it easier to respond to limitations and discipline (Libra on the 10th) than to the ever-active atmosphere of her home. Both parents seem to represent the 4th/10th house axis.

Though she idealized her father (Sun in Pisces) and he played a large role in establishing her values (Sun in the 2nd), she had many disagreements with him (Mars and Saturn involved in a strong T-square, or grand cross if you count the Ascendant). She also had to learn to see him realistically which required many adjustments (the Sun inconjuncts its ruler Neptune and Pluto, forming a yod).

The mother, too, played a large role in cementing her inner resources, since the Moon is also in the 2nd house. With the Moon in Aquarius, she regarded her mother as a bit eccentric but appreciated the freedom and mental stimulation received though her (Moon trine its ruler Uranus). She felt that her father and mother did not get along (Moon inconjunct Saturn).

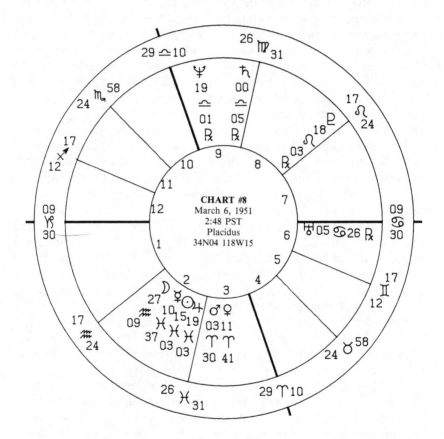

CHART #8
March 6, 1951
2:48 PST
Placidus
34N04 118W15

To further explain parental relationships but also to illustrate that how you perceive your parents is just that — your perception — on page 240 is the chart of a young man who happens to be the brother of the girl in the previous horoscope. Look at how differently they each see the parents.

In his chart the ruler of the 4th house, Pluto is in Leo in the 1st house, close to the Ascendant; Venus, ruler of the 10th is in Libra in the 2nd. This young man has some complex reactions. Though he sees his mother as nurturing and caring (Moon in Cancer), she does not give him the same feeling through the 4th house. Its ruler Pluto is in Leo which demands drama and needs to dominate and the co-ruler Mars is in Virgo which demands perfection and likes to criticize. The Sun and Saturn representing the father principle are both in Scorpio, the sign of the 4th house cusp; therefore both parents seem to be incorporated in the 4th house and play a large role in his early stages of development.

Saturn conjunct the Sun usually implies a feeling of inadequacy toward the father, a fear of not being able to live up to what you believe the father demands of you. The 10th house stands quite alone. The ruler Venus makes no major aspects, is dignified in Libra and accidentally dignified in the 2nd house, all strengthening factors. Once he matures and sets some of his priorities, he should have no major problems in accepting discipline, in realizing his own limitations and in working hard to achieve ego satisfaction — a must for a Leo Ascendant and Sun conjunct Saturn.

Both parents were instrumental in establishing his value system (Venus and Mars in the 2nd) and he has fashioned his personality after both of them (Pluto/mother conjunct the Ascendant, the Sun/father, ruling the Ascendant). Though he feels close to his mother and considers her a friend (Moon in the 11th house) he also sees her as a bit eccentric (Moon conjunct Uranus).

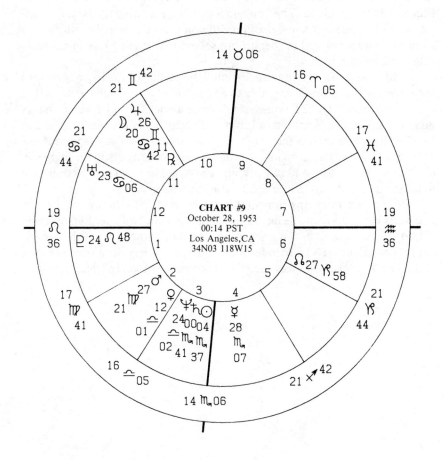

14 ♉ 06

21 ♊ 42

16 ♈ 05

21 ♋ 44

♃ 26
☽ 20 ♊ 11
42 ♋ R

17 ♓ 41

♅ 23 ♋ 06

10   9

11

8

19 ♌ 36

12

7

19 ♒ 36

♇ 24 ♌ 48

CHART #9
October 28, 1953
00:14 PST
Los Angeles,CA
34N03 118W15

1

6

2

3   4   5

☊ 27 ♑ 58

17 ♍ 41

♂
♍ 27
♀ 12
♎ 01
24 ♓ ☉ 04
♎ 02 ♏ ♏ 41 37

☿
28 ♏ 07

21 ♑ 44

16 ♎ 05

21 ♐ 42

14 ♏ 06

Lesson 20
Looking for:
Vocational Aptitudes

Next to "Whom should I marry?" the most often asked question is: "What's my vocational aptitude?" or "I want to be an actor but I also want to be rich; what should I do?" or "Is there help for me? I love to write but I hate sitting still for such a long time?" Does astrology really have the answer to such questions? Yes and no. We do see vocational aptitudes and talents that can help a person find a direction, and in this section we will explain some of the ways you can find those abilities. But no, we cannot choose for you if you prefer to be a poor actor or a rich industrialist, nor can we predict if you will be a rich actor. All we can establish is whether you have acting talent, the ability to make money, or the will to succeed. We do not know where the free will may lead you at a given moment, nor what the priorities of that moment may be. The answer to the third question is yes, we can see the literary talent as well as the restlessness or scattering of energies, but we do not know when or if the questioner ever really wants to buckle down.

There are three specific areas of the chart that must be considered when we discuss vocational potential. The 10th house is the highest you can reach for; it has to do with career, business and recognition. The 6th house outlines the kind of work you do and how you do it. The 2nd house, besides showing how much you can earn, also depicts the self-satisfaction you get from your efforts.

The element on the cusps of these houses will often indicate the general field of endeavor. Fire signs signify work that allows action, enthusiasm and leadership. Earth signs need a field that is stable and productive and that allows achievement of practical goals. Air signs prefer a career through which you can communicate your ideas and use your intellectual resources. Water signs like an area where you can productively use your caring and nurturing feelings.

If there are interceptions in the chart, you may find it necessary to combine these general suggestions. For instance, with a fire sign on the Midheaven and water signs on the 2nd and 6th house cusps, you need a vocation in which you use your caring ability (water) in a leadership capacity (fire). With an earth sign on the 2nd and air signs on the 6th and 10th, you will have to communicate (air) your ideas in a practical way (earth).

As was true in our other discussions on specific delineation, the rulers of the key houses (2nd, 6th and 10th) and the planets in them must be taken into consideration, as well as Venus, the natural ruler of the 2nd house, Mercury, the natural ruler of the 6th house and Saturn, the natural ruler of the 10th.

You cannot lose sight of the whole chart. If there is a stellium in one specific sign or house, it must be carefully considered and blended in. Another important factor is opportunity. You would not suggest that a person become a surgeon if the chart or life circumstances did not indicate that there was financial assistance available to see the person through all the training it takes to reach that goal. The same indications that show an ability for surgery also show the potential to become a good butcher.

Lawyers, salesmen and politicians have similar charts. They are all capable of putting a point across and they all need charm and persuasiveness.

Other important considerations besides the vocational houses are the most exact aspects in the chart, especially the squares, and any planet that aspects the 10th house. Many times people go no further than their 6th house in their pursuit of work. They are happy to be in a job that affords them some sort of financial success and the ability to serve (6th house).

The important planets, signs and houses for different types of career selection follow. Remember that this is very general. We will give you some specific charts to support these indications.

Career in the Arts: Strong Venus, Neptune and Mercury placements (elevated, angular, many aspects). Prominent Gemini, Libra, Aquarius (Sun, Ascendant, vocational houses). No particular house needs emphasis but it helps to have the creative 5th well aspected.

Athletic Career: Active Mars, Sun, Jupiter, Neptune or Mercury. Sagittarius, Virgo and Aries prominent. The 1st, 5th and 6th houses activated.

Business Management: (This includes stocks and bonds and any corporate activities.) Saturn, Sun or Moon prominent. The signs involved are usually Aries, Leo, Cancer, Capricorn and Sagittarius. The 1st, 5th and 10th houses should be well fortified. To be a top level executive usually demands three astrological signatures: Mercury in some aspect to Uranus, preferably a challenging one. Aries, Leo or Scorpio on the Ascendant, Sun or Moon (two of the three). Jupiter aspecting Saturn or the 10th house.

Communications and Advertising: The Moon, Mercury, Jupiter or Venus should be in good astrological position. Gemini, Sagittarius, Libra and Aquarius significant and the 3rd, 9th, 7th and 1st houses activated.

Farming: (This category includes all earth related career fields such as geology, mining, archeology and anthropology.) Saturn, Pluto and the Moon are usually prominent as well as Cancer, Capricorn, Aries and Virgo. The houses involved are the 4th, 9th and 10th.

Financial Field: (This includes banking, bookkeeping, accounting and money management of any kind.) Venus, Mercury, Pluto and Jupiter are usually in the foreground. The signs that are activated are Taurus, Scorpio and Cancer as well as the 2nd house and particularly the 8th. Bookkeeping also needs some Gemini or 3rd house influence.

Food Service: (Restaurants and markets) The planets most often found to be important are the Moon, Mercury, Uranus. The signs are Cancer, Aquarius, Libra and Virgo. The houses are the 6th, 11th and 2nd.

Law Enforcement: Mars, Sun, Pluto and Saturn angular, ruling the Sun or Ascendant or receiving a lot of aspects. Aries, Libra, Sagittarius and Capricorn well represented as well as the 6th, 7th, 10th and 12th houses.

Legal Careers: Mercury, Saturn, Sun, Jupiter and Venus significant. Gemini, Leo, Libra and Sagittarius prominent and a strong 7th or 9th house. Politicians and salespeople generally have a similar signature, but the politician needs a strong 8th and Aquarius and/or the 11th house come into prominence. Salespeople need Pisces or Neptune and a strong 3rd or 10th.

Medical Field: Mars, Jupiter, Mercury, Moon and Saturn play an important role here. The signs that are usually significant are Virgo, Pisces, Scorpio, Sagittarius and Capricorn. The 6th, 8th and 12th houses come into prominence. Naturally, if the person wants to go into administration, it is important to have a strong 10th house. The more technical side of the medical field such as X-ray, or computer medicine needs Uranus importantly placed in the vocational houses.

Musicians: Neptune, Saturn, Sun, Moon and Venus show up meaningfully here as well as Cancer, Leo, Pisces and Virgo and the 5th, 12th and 10th houses.

Performers: Moon, Neptune and Venus. Leo, Pisces and Aquarius. The 5th, 12th, 7th and 10th houses.

Religion and Theology: Saturn, Jupiter and Mercury are the planets most often involved. Sagittarius, Libra, Scorpio and Capricorn are the signs. The houses usually occupied are the 9th, 10th and 3rd.

Scientists and Technicians: Pluto, Uranus, Mars, Mercury prominent and Scorpio, Pisces, Capricorn, Gemini and Aries significant. The houses involved are the 8th, 6th and 12th.

Social Services: The Moon, Jupiter, Mercury and the Sun are usually angular, elevated or prominently aspected. Aquarius, Cancer, Pisces and Virgo are the signs most often involved. The important houses are the 11th, 6th and 12th.

Transportation: Here we usually find Jupiter, Mercury, Uranus and the Moon significant as well as Sagittarius, Gemini and Aquarius. The houses are the 3rd and 9th.

White Collar Workers: Mercury, Moon and Saturn. Virgo, Capricorn, Cancer and Gemini. The 3rd, 6th and 10th houses.

Here are a few more thoughts on the subject:

Always analyze what the profession or work entails.

The arts need artistic talent plus in most cases, the ability to work alone. Strong Taurus traits indicate a wish to touch and therefore these people would prefer ceramics or sculpture to painting. Clay or marble feel heavenly, wet paint does not. A conductor needs musical talent plus the ability to lead (strong Aries or angular planets.)

Aside from action and therefore a strong Mars, certain athletes need good timing and discipline so there should be a prominent Saturn in the chart.

When you manage or work in some executive capacity, it helps to be well organized. That means earth, Saturn or Mercury involved in the vocational houses. You must also be able to relate to those people you manage, which again needs a strong Mercury or Venus or Moon.

In vocational astrology the 8th house is always considered other people's money or support. It has to be prominent if you are a stockbroker, banker or financial advisor. But politicians also need other people's support as shown by the 8th house, in their case, however, it may mean votes instead of money. Frequently we find that political charts have the ruler of the 8th in the 12th house; this indicates that some of the support they receive may come from behind the scenes or out of smoke-filled rooms.

Legal careers need to be well analyzed. There are many types of law and the corporate lawyer obviously will have different needs from the criminal lawyer, who has to stand in front of a jury and emote in passionate terms (strong Leo). He also seems to have a combative 7th house strongly connected to the 4th and 12th houses. Judges need less fire but more earth and usually have Jupiter importantly placed.

The real actor needs less Leo but lots of Neptune to become whatever the role demands and also to give that certain charisma and mysterious quality that makes the public pay attention. Rather than being out front like the criminal lawyer, many actors are very shy and private and love to hide their true personality behind a role; this is why the 12th house is so often important in performers' charts.

Religion has a strong Sagittarius/9th house emphasis. The higher vibrations of spirituality have Neptune/Pisces overtones, and the real saints and seers have strong earth emphasis because they seem to have reached the stage of seeing reality (earth) in its most evolved terms. Neptune/Pisces is prominent in the arts for talent and imagination; in certain sports that need agile feet; in the psychological and related fields for intuition and in religion to provide illumination or spirituality.

Aside from monetary considerations, the difference between a tailor/dressmaker or *haute couture* designer, the piano tuner or composer and the billing clerk or mathematician is often found in the 9th house of vision and ideals. The scope of vision can make the difference between a pedestrian or exalted occupation.

The foregoing is not complete by any means, but it does give you a starting place. A whole book could be written on this subject and several have been. A tool that you will find invaluable in research on careers is *The Rulership Book* by Rex Bills. It is an encyclopedia of astrological terms and has sections on the signs, houses and planets as well as an alphabetical listing where you can look up any word and find its astrological counterpart.

In the chart on page 244 we will delineate the career area.

This man has Cancer on the 10th house cusp and the Moon that rules it is in the 3rd house in Capricorn. Pluto rules his 2nd house and is in the 10th. Mars the co-ruler of Scorpio, is on the cusp of the 2nd house. Neptune rules his 6th house and is in the 11th. Now what does all this mean as far as career is concerned? With Cancer on the 10th and the Moon in the 3rd, we may think sales (3rd house) to the public of some domestic commodity (Cancer). Certainly he has a need to communicate in some way with the Moon in the 3rd house. This is verified by Mercury in Gemini, the natural 3rd house sign. His Ascendant ruler Venus is in the 7th and trines the Moon, another indication of the need to work with people rather than alone.

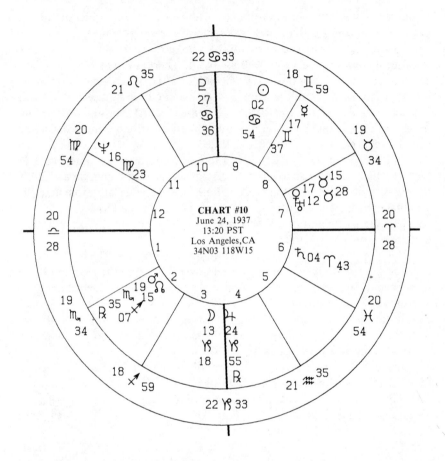

CHART #10
June 24, 1937
13:20 PST
Los Angeles,CA
34N03 118W15

Neptune, the 6th house ruler, is in Virgo, the natural 6th house sign. We again see his need to serve others, probably in a job where he works for a large corporation (11th house). With Pluto in the 10th and Saturn, the natural ruler of the 10th, in Aries, the indication is that he would want to lead rather than follow in any type job he would hold. Saturn in the 6th house is often referred to as a workaholic. His Sun is in the 9th house which can be an indication of a person who aspires to a college education. He did not go to college. Jupiter, ruler of his 3rd house of education is opposed to Pluto, ruler of the 2nd; and Mercury, ruler of his 9th, squares Neptune and inconjuncts Mars in the 2nd. He was the middle child of five; his parents did not have the money to send him to college, and he had to make the adjustment demanded of the inconjunct.

He worked as a box boy for a local market chain from the time he was sixteen; after a two-year stint in the Army (Saturn in Aries in the 6th house of service), he came back to that job and worked his way up to store manager.

His friendly and charming manner (Libra rising) was very apparent and he was offered a sales job by one of the market's suppliers.

In the ensuing fifteen years he has worked his way up to be general manager in charge of sales for a large food supply corporation. He travels a lot (Sun in the 9th) and deals with people on both the executive and management level, and is considered a great financial success (ruler of the 2nd is in the 10th conjunct the Midheaven). He is the perfect example of a Sun in Cancer in the 9th house and a Cancer Midheaven. At one time he was flying to the East Coast for a business meeting. The board of directors of the company he was calling on had never eaten Mexican food. He is an excellent gourmet cook. So he packed one suitcase with all the ingredients for a gourmet Mexican dinner and when he arrived, he turned out a masterpiece that still has those businessmen talking.

The two charts on page 248 and 249 are of two nurses. Chart #11 is an ICCU nurse who deals with terminally ill patients and she has a lot of responsibility on her job. Venus, the ruler of her Ascendant, is in the 8th of death conjunct Mars, the co-ruler of the 2nd house of income. Neptune, ruler of the 6th house of work is in the 12th (hospitals). Nurturing Cancer is the sign on the Midheaven and the Moon is in Taurus, another nurturing sign, in the 7th house of other people. With Pluto in the 10th house, you know that she would like to be a take-charge person. With Jupiter conjunct the Sun and so much 7th house emphasis in her chart, she started out to be a lawyer; after two years of law school, she changed her major to nursing. We said that the 6th and 12th houses play an important part in charts involving the medical field. She has Mercury, the ruler of the 12th, in the 6th in Pisces, the natural 12th house sign; Mercury and Neptune (in the 12th) are opposed to each other which provides a lot of energy in service fields. They are also in mutual reception and accidentally dignified by house position which suggests that she will feel comfortable in the role of nursing and caring for others.

Chart #12 also shows definite signs of the nursing profession. Mercury, ruler of the 10th house is in the serving sign Virgo, in the hospital connected 12th house. Neptune, the natural planetary ruler of the 12th, is in the 1st house. Her Sun and Mars (the energy planet) are both in the 12th house in Leo adding a lot of emphasis to that house. She is a cardiac, surgical nurse. This is shown in her chart by Venus, the ruler of the 2nd house conjunct Pluto, the natural ruler of the 8th house of surgery. She is in a position of authority and does some nursing teaching as shown by Uranus, ruler of the 6th house of work, conjunct Saturn in Gemini in the 9th.

In analyzing these two charts for personality, character and events, you would not find many similarities; but when you consider them from a vocational viewpoint, you can see the likenesses.

By the way, the difference between a surgical nurse and a surgeon is not so much one of innate talent but rather of mental and financial ability as well as dedication and opportunity — all attributes to be found in other areas of the horoscope.

Earlier we said that in law enforcement charts it was necessary to have Mars, the Sun, Saturn and Pluto prominent; plus Aries, Libra, Sagittarius and Capricorn involved as well as the 6th, 7th, 10th and 12th houses.

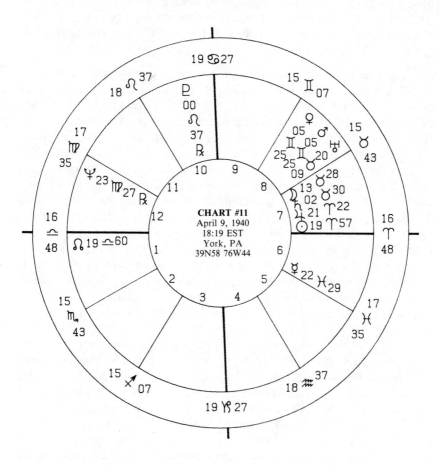

CHART #11
April 9, 1940
18:19 EST
York, PA
39N58 76W44

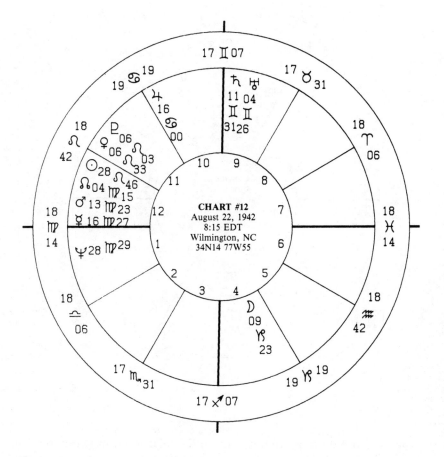

Below is the chart of a crime prevention control officer who works for the sheriff's department.

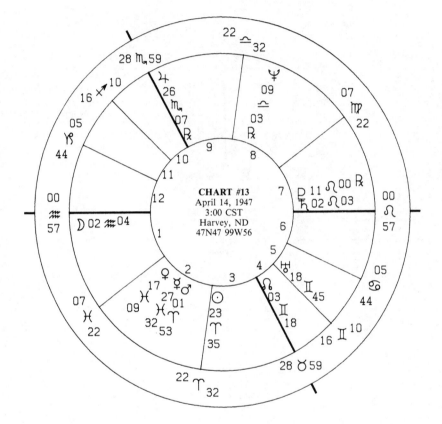

CHART #13
April 14, 1947
3:00 CST
Harvey, ND
47N47 99W56

With Scorpio on the 10th house and the ruler Pluto in Leo in the 7th house, in wide (but applying) conjunction to Saturn, he wants control and to be in charge in a disciplined (Saturn conjunct Pluto) way. Because the ruler of the 10th is in the 7th house, he may prefer to work with a partner; because it is in Leo he needs to be in a position of leadership and authority. The co-ruler Mars is in Aries in the 2nd house and his Sun is also in Aries, stressing the often militant attitude found in law enforcement. The 6th house of work has Cancer on the cusp and the Moon in Aquarius in the 1st house, showing his need to be personally involved with the public. The Moon sextiles Mars (co-ruler of the 10th) and opposes Saturn and widely opposes Pluto (ruler of the 10th), tying the 6th and 10th houses together.

The 2nd house of income and resources shows a natural inclination for law (the ruler Neptune is in Libra), but since the ruler is in the 8th house, it would be criminal law rather than corporate law. With his Sun in the 3rd, he needs to communicate and he and his partner go into the schools and address other large organizations to demonstrate how people can help the police by preventing crime. Pluto, ruler of the Midheaven, is in the 7th house of law and he has Jupiter dignified by house in the 9th and conjunct the Midheaven, showing the potential for working with the law. Jupiter and the Midheaven trine Saturn and Mars, indicating how comfortable he is in this position.

He probably could go into the legal field, but with his angular Pluto and Saturn and his Sun and Mars in Aries, he leans more toward law enforcement than law enactment which requires more Mercury/Gemini and Jupiter/Sagittarius prominence than his chart indicates.

ATTENTION TO ALL READERS: To get your **free** HOROSCOPE, please check the back of Volume I.

ATTENTION TEACHERS: To get your free TEACHING GUIDE which shows you how to successfully combine Volumes I and II in beginning teaching and how to use this volume for basic instruction, see the back of Volume II or write to:

ASTRO COMPUTING SERVICE
P.O. Box 16430
San Diego, CA 92116

NOTES

NOTES

NOTES

NOTES